MAKING SHABBAT

THE MANDEL-BRANDEIS SERIES IN JEWISH EDUCATION

Sharon Feiman-Nemser, Jonathan Krasner, and Jon A. Levisohn, Editors

The Mandel-Brandeis Series in Jewish Education, established by the Jack, Joseph and Morton Mandel Center for Studies in Jewish Education, publishes scholarly monographs and edited volumes of compelling research on Jewish educational settings and processes. The series is made possible through the Mandel Foundation.

For a complete list of books that are available in the series, visit brandeisuniversitypress.com.

Joseph Reimer, *Making Shabbat: Celebrating and Learning at American Jewish Summer Camps*

Alex Pomson and Jack Wertheimer, *Inside Jewish Day Schools: Leadership, Learning, and Community*

Joseph Reimer

MAKING SHABBAT

CELEBRATING AND LEARNING AT AMERICAN JEWISH SUMMER CAMPS

Brandeis University Press / Waltham, Massachusetts

Brandeis University Press

Manufactured in the United States of America
Designed by Mindy Basinger Hill
Typeset in 10.3/15 pt Minion Pro

Library of Congress Cataloging-in-Publication Data

Names Reimer, Joseph, author.
Title Making Shabbat : celebrating and learning at American Jewish summer camps / Joseph Reimer.
Description 1. | Waltham, Massachusetts : Brandeis University Press, 2022. | Series: Mandel-Brandeis Series in Jewish Education | Includes bibliographical references and index. | Summary: "Early in the 20th century, Jewish camp leaders had little interest in creating spiritual experiences for their campers. Yet Jewish camps have gradually provided primal Jewish experiences that campers could enjoy, parents appreciate, and alumni fondly recall. This book considers how Shabbat at camp became the focus for these experiences"— Provided by publisher.
Identifiers LCCN 2022012373 | ISBN 9781684580972 (paperback) | ISBN 9781684580989 (ebook)
Subjects: LCSH: Jewish camps—United States—History. | Jewish religious education. | Sabbath.
Classification LCC BM135 .R45 2022 | DDC 296.6/80973—dc23/eng/20220322

LC record available at https://lccn.loc.gov/2022012373

5 4 3 2 1

FOR GAIL AND OUR GRANDCHILDREN

AMAL, TEHILA, MOSHE, AND RINA

CONTENTS

MAKING SHABBAT

1 / INTRODUCTION

DAVID OFFIT HAS SPENT FOURTEEN SUMMERS at Camp Ramah in New England as a camper, counselor, and senior staff member. He knows this camp intimately and loves it passionately. He is a perfect informant to explain what I have come here to learn: What is distinctive about celebrating Shabbat, the Jewish Sabbath, at Jewish summer camps?

> On Friday night when our counselors stand up and scream "MI-PI-EL" [a traditional Shabbat song], the campers want to do the same thing. Whether you are doing it on Shabbat or at a Red Sox game, being with a group of people chanting and cheering on the same team is an amazing experience. That you can create these experiences and connect them to Shabbat means you've created this amazing moment that people want back. You can't get enough of it. (Offit 2016)

David focuses on a moment at the end of the Friday evening meal in the dining hall when the community begins to sing the traditional Shabbat songs. When the singing grows intense, the counselors rise from their seats and start screaming out the words and banging on the tables. Seeing this state of excitement, the campers jump to their feet and join in the screaming and banging, lending their bodies and voices to the growing sound and movement. Everyone is caught up in doing what they could never do at home: go wild for Shabbat in the company of their friends.

This reminds David of rooting for the Red Sox at Fenway Park when fans cheer as loudly and forcefully as they wish. As the fans love the excitement of being part of Red Sox Nation, so campers and staff love being on the team that celebrates Shabbat together. Once you get a taste of this excitement, David states, "you can't get enough of it." You will be back for more.

When I ask about taking Shabbat home, David describes what he and his friends have created in their neighborhood.

> When I moved to New York, my friends and I created a Shabbat dinner and a service once a month for a hundred people. We loved that. . . . When I go to a great Friday evening service, someone will say, "That really felt like a camp service." Or if we have singing after a meal and it was good, someone will say, "It felt just like being back at camp." That is the main point of reference for a really joyful Jewish experience. (Offit 2016)

Summer camp is the reference point "for a really joyous Jewish experience." David and friends gather to revive what they had experienced at camp. Jewish summer camp provides a model for an emotionally and spiritually satisfying Jewish experience.

After spending four summers as a researcher experiencing Shabbat celebrations at Jewish residential camps, I am trying to understand why so many campers, staff, and alumni feel this vital attachment to Shabbat at camp. As David suggested, you have to grasp the group energy that camps create, and then figure out how that energy is generated, what is being celebrated, and how the bond between staff and campers operates. For camps have fashioned a powerful model of satisfying Jewish experiences that David intuits but few have articulated.

I am writing this book to tell the story of how Jewish camps have emerged as creators of positive spiritual experiences for Jewish youth in North America. When Jewish camps began at the dawn of the twentieth century, their leaders had little interest in creating Jewish spiritual experiences for their campers. Yet over the course of the past century, Jewish camps have gradually moved into providing primal Jewish experiences that diverse campers enjoy, parents appreciate, and alumni fondly recall. How Shabbat at camp became the focal point for these primal Jewish experiences is the subject of this book.

FOCUS ON SHABBAT AT CAMP

To tell this story, I focus on how these camps celebrate Shabbat, the Jewish Sabbath. These camps pull out all the stops for celebrating Shabbat on Friday night and Saturday. They marshal all their Jewish resources to make Shabbat vital for their campers and staff. By focusing on Shabbat, I want to capture their engagement of camper and staff interest and energy.

A paradox stands at the heart of this book. Multiple studies of American

Jews tell us that the more Americanized this population becomes, the fewer are inclined toward Jewish practices that are more regular in time and demanding in observance. Thus we find far more Jews celebrating the annual seder on Passover than celebrating Shabbat on a weekly basis. We find more Jews attending Jewish film festivals than speaking Hebrew or reading Torah. In our busy world, people tend to the quicker expressions of Jewishness than to the activities that require particular preparation and effort (Cohen and Kotler-Berkowitz 2004; Cohen and Veinstein 2011; Pew Research Center 2013).

In this contemporary scene, we should be surprised to find that Jewish camps are investing heavily in celebrating Shabbat. There are many easier ways to mark Jewishness at camp: sing Jewish songs, stage *Fiddler on the Roof*, or celebrate Jewish heroes like David Ben-Gurion and Ruth Bader Ginsburg. Why would camp leaders choose to invest in celebrating Shabbat? Why do parents who foot the bill and campers who attend these celebrations agree to this practice? They may want a Jewish environment for the summer, but must that come with the religious trappings like Hebrew prayers, Torah readings, and Havdalah candles? Must Shabbat consume time on both Friday evening and Saturday when there is so much else to fit into a camp season? What is going on with this Shabbat celebration?

While Shabbat celebration and observance varies from camp to camp, it is all the more striking how nearly universal to Jewish residential camps some form of Shabbat celebration is (Sales and Saxe 2004). Even some highly secular Jewish camps celebrate Shabbat in their own ways (Fox 2019). What is the attraction of celebrating Shabbat for Jewish camps, staff, and campers?

It was not always so. In *Nemesis*, his last novel, Philip Roth (2010) depicts a Jewish camp during the summer of 1944. Roth describes in detail the weekly ritual event that took place there. It was not Shabbat, but Indian Night. Each week the camp director, Mr. Blomback, convened the Grand Council.

> Mr. Blomback emerged from the oval doorway in a feather headdress, white feathers with brown tips all round his head and trailing behind in a tail down below his waist. His tunic, his leggings, even his moccasins were elaborately decorated with leather fringe and bands of beadwork and long tufts of what looked like human hair . . . All the campers stood until Mr. Blombeck stolidly made his way from the tepee to the center of Council Ring. The drumming and the rattling stopped, and the campers took their seats. (2010, 207–208)

Seventy years later, no Jewish camp director would convene a Grand Council or dress up in Native American costume. Yet that was common in the 1930s and 1940s, when American Jews felt drawn to identifying as "Indians" and "borrowing" their imagined costumes and rituals to create dramatic gatherings (Paris 2008). Rabbis like Mordecai Kaplan denounced those practices, and yet they made a certain cultural sense for their time (Koffman 2018). We live in very different times, and Shabbat has emerged in most Jewish camps as the weekly ritual celebration.

I am not a cultural historian who can explain how those cultural shifts happen over time. Rather, I am an educational ethnographer who has studied contemporary camp life by immersing myself in the details of how Jewish camps today create Shabbat for their campers and staff. I have spent these last years delving into the educational practices of three residential American Jewish camps to explore how they create vital and engaging celebrations of Shabbat. I have discovered that these camps have been working for decades on developing a Shabbat practice that works remarkably well for campers and staff, as Sales and Saxe have noted:

> Everyone—directors, administrators, counselors, campers—tell us that Shabbat at camp is very special. When we were unable to stay for Shabbat, members of the camp community were quick to tell us that we were missing "the best" part of camp. (2004, 87–88)

Yet, to my surprise, there is little previous research on how these camps design and implement Shabbat. That is a great shame, for this is a story that should not remain buried. This is a rare success story that has touched the hearts of generations of campers and staff who have precious memories of Shabbat at camp. These celebrations are a result of careful planning and thoughtful implementation that cross denominational and organizational lines and represent some of the best design work done by camp professionals. It is a story that should be known by camp leaders, parents, and alumni as well as educational leaders and scholars across the community who have much to learn from the ways these camps have created rich opportunities for both Jewish celebration and Jewish learning.

CELEBRATING THE SABBATH

One reason researchers may not have focused on Shabbat at camp is that it is hard to capture. It is difficult to explain both what the Jewish Sabbath entails and how camp leaders have designed Shabbat practices that work well in that context.

It is even difficult to choose the verb that expresses what Jews do on Shabbat. I have chosen "to celebrate," but others might have chosen "to keep," "to observe," or "to mark." Each of these captures an aspect of the Jewish Sabbath. I rely on *The Sabbath* by Abraham Joshua Heschel to guide my choices. Heschel was a leading Jewish thinker, and the publication of this book in 1951 represented a breakthrough in making available to an American audience the many-sided aspects of the Jewish Sabbath. Here are some selections that have guided my writing about Shabbat at camp.

> Three acts of God denoted the seventh day: He rested, He blessed and He hallowed the seventh day (Gen. 2:2–3). To the prohibition on labor is, therefore, added the blessing of delight and the accent of sanctity. (1951, 14)

There are three essential qualities to the Sabbath: resting, taking delight, and making holy. First and foremost, Shabbat entails resting: taking a fundamental break from the world of work. Shabbat asks that you walk away from your busy work life, trust it will not fall apart, and declare that there is more to your life than your work-related accomplishments. Observant Jews follow rabbinic traditions that forbid thirty-nine different types of work on Shabbat, but all who keep the Sabbath seek other foci than work to center this day.

Heschel believes that it will be harder to take that break unless your Sabbath is a delight. Shabbat has to have features that deeply please you: people to be with, meals to enjoy, gatherings to celebrate, time to be with yourself and feel your soul alive with meaning. And that delight cannot be entirely personal. Shabbat is also communal. Shabbat is when we join with others who wish to mark this as a holy day, a time of communal celebration and joy. Shabbat is when Jews greet one another with "Shabbat shalom" (Sabbath peace) and support one another in a mutual quest for establishing a time apart.

Heschel writes that "labor is a craft, but perfect rest is an art" (ibid.). He understood that our society prepares us to be busy craftspeople, but not for the art of finding true rest. The journalist Judith Shulevitz captured this well in her book on the Sabbath.

> When we pine for escape from the rat race; when we check into spas, yoga centers, encounter weekends, spiritual retreats; when we fret about the disappearance of a more old-fashioned time with its former, generally-agreed-upon rhythms of labor and repose; when we deplore the increase in time devoted to consumption . . . whenever we worry about these things, we are remembering the Sabbath, its power to protect us from the clamor of our own desires. (2010, xxix)

Shulevitz is urging her readers to remember the Sabbath for its healing and restorative powers. Heschel asks for even more.

> There is a word that is seldom said, a word for an emotion almost too deep to express: the love of the Sabbath. The word is rarely found in our literature, yet for more than two thousand years the emotion filled our songs and moods. It was as if a whole people were in love with the seventh day. (1951, 15)

Shabbat is more than a day off and weekly celebration. It is a time to feel love: love of the community and its traditions, love of the people with whom you share these intimacies, and love of the life you are blessed to lead. We set this day aside to rest, observe, celebrate, and feel the deepest of our emotions that often elude us. While no single verb can capture all these features that Heschel is describing, I will use "celebrate" to reflect the many-sided nature of doing Shabbat.

To understand the Sabbath is to realize how hard it is to convey this depth of experience to those who have not known it. Heschel brilliantly captures the many sides to Shabbat and helps us realize that there is no comparable occasion in contemporary American culture. Shabbat is not the same as the American weekend, holiday, or day of rest. A child growing up in American society who does not come from a Sabbath-keeping family is not likely to comprehend what Heschel is trying to convey.

Enter the Jewish residential camp. While Jewish camps were *not* created in the early twentieth century to teach about Shabbat, during the 1920s a few gifted Jewish educators decided to create intentional Jewish camps that were designed—among other goals—to give American Jewish children a deeper experience of Shabbat (Krasner 2011). During that first decade, there were only a handful of such camps, but by the 1940s and 1950s that number had significantly increased (J. Sarna 2006).

Today it is probably the case that more non-Orthodox Jewish youth have experienced a full Shabbat celebration at Jewish camps than in any other setting. Camp leaders have developed an expertise in initiating youth into a meaningful Shabbat experience. That expertise does not reside with particular individuals but with the culture of these Jewish camps. Celebrating Shabbat has become so much part of the weekly life of these camps that initiating campers into celebrating Shabbat has become an organic part of the life of Jewish camps.

THE TOOLS FOR CELEBRATING SHABBAT: COMMUNITY, RITUAL, AND MUSIC

American summer camps are designed as a retreat from the furious pace and varied dangers of urban life. Residential camps are safe spaces in rural areas ("manufactured wilderness" is the term that Van Slyck [2006] introduced) for urban and suburban youth to appreciate the beauties of nature and become more skilled in activities that define "the good life" in American society. In the early years, those activities were divided into three main areas: water sports, land sports, and a variety of the arts. Since the 1960s, camp activities have diversified.

Already in the early years of American camping, camp leaders felt the need to devote a day apart for rest and reflection. At Protestant and Catholic camps, Sunday was that day and often featured outdoor religious services as well as the pleasures of sleeping late, visiting with siblings and close friends, and reflecting on the special gifts of camp life. Having a day of rest became part of the culture of American camps (Van Slyck 2006).

The camp leaders who founded the first intentional Jewish camps recognized the substantial cultural difference between what most American Protestants and Catholics mean by a day of rest and what traditional Jews mean by celebrating Shabbat. It took careful design for the early Jewish camp leaders to address that gap. They knew that were Shabbat at camp to feel like a daylong synagogue service, few children would ever return to camp. Yet if Shabbat were only a day of rest and relaxation, where would the Jewish learning agenda be? They worked hard to create a daylong Shabbat experience that simultaneously feels like a time of relaxation and joy while still maximizing the Jewish significance of both celebrating and observing Shabbat (Krasner 2011).

Creating a well-balanced Shabbat requires a fine degree of program design and a highly developed plan for implementation. While it is important to allow campers to sleep late on Shabbat morning and enjoy a relatively unstructured Shabbat afternoon, a traditional Shabbat also involves prayer services that are not easy for children to sit through. How were they going to design those in ways that children and teens would find engaging and joyful? And how would they create *ruach* Shabbat (the spirit of the Sabbath) that would help campers and staff understand that Shabbat time is quite different from weekday time and what one normally does at camp during the week may not be appropriate on Shabbat.

I will explore the details of Shabbat design in later chapters. For now, let me introduce three structural advantages (Sales and Saxe 2004) that residential camps enjoy that make creating Shabbat possible and three tools that emerge from my ethnographic research that camps employ to make celebrating Shabbat engaging and enjoyable.

Control of time and space. Precisely because residential camps are built in isolated settings, they exercise more control over their time and space than urban institutions. No one has to pick up the children at 5 p.m. Thus, camps can decide when to start and end Shabbat and how to build up to that beginning and build down from that conclusion. They can also decide which activities to offer and not offer on Shabbat.

Immersive environment. As immersive environments, residential camps can exert more control over what children are watching and hearing at any given time and can minimize the distractions that compete with attending to Shabbat activities. Because parents and family are not present, familial differences in Jewish observances are less relevant and camps can create a more or less even playing field for what is allowed and not allowed on Shabbat.

Accessible role models. Because Jewish camps often hire counselors and other staff who have a deep familiarity with the culture of these camps, they can train their staff to act as accessible role models for campers for how Shabbat is to be kept and celebrated. Having these young adults in the bunks and at the services on Shabbat helps the campers see what to do and how to enjoy these celebrations.

Building on these structural advantages, these camps have also developed three essential tools to greatly amplify the basic routines of Shabbat celebration.

Community. Camps do all they can to establish a sense of community. The bunk or cabin is the most intimate community in which campers and counselors live together. The division or unit is a community of bunks, and the whole camp is a community of units. Campers spend the most time with their bunks, then with the units, and more occasionally (depending on the nature of the camp) with the whole camp. When the whole camp consistently convenes to begin Shabbat together on Friday evenings, the camp is signaling to all its campers and staff that this is a very special event.

Rituals. Camps ritualize many aspects of shared life, from wake-up to communal dining to bedtime routines. Rituals allow campers to know what to expect and how to behave together at transitional moments of the day. Intentional Jewish camps draw upon a variety of Jewish traditional rituals to complement their daily secular rituals. But on Shabbat the Jewish rituals predominate, structuring the flow of the day. There are the traditional prayer services on Friday evening and Saturday morning, but also invented Shabbat rituals that are specific to camp culture. The camp's ability to create and recreate these rituals keeps the celebration fresh and engaging.

Music. Camp is a place where people regularly sing together. Different camps sing different songs and a camp's songbook is an important part of that camp's culture (J. Cohen 2006). At Jewish camps people sing many different kinds of songs, but on Shabbat Jewish music predominates. There has been a renaissance of Jewish songs, and camps have capitalized on the flow of new music to enliven the rituals and enrich the communal bonds.

There are many other aspects to Shabbat at camp, but the skillful activation of these three tools makes Shabbat most joyous. For many camp alumni, including myself, what stands out as their most powerful Jewish memories are the times when the camp community celebrates traditional Jewish rituals animated by lively group singing and movement.

LEARNING TO CELEBRATE AT CAMP

When children first arrive at summer camp, they are not yet campers. Camps regularly take children who have never before been to camp and, in a matter of a couple of weeks, turn them into campers who know the camp routines and participate in them like old hands. The camps "erase" their memory of ever having been new and unsure, and most children become like eternal campers, born, as it were, into being campers of this camp.

This process works for most, but not all, children. For three summers my daughter Tamara served as a therapist in a Jewish camp and spent a lot of her time working with young campers who were experiencing homesickness. These were the children for whom the camp trick was not working. They could not let go of the emotional grip of their home life and free themselves to learn the routines of camp life. These powerful anxieties stood in the way of new learning, and it was Tamara's job to help ease the grip of those emotions so the children could attend to what camp life might offer and learn how to become campers.

Learning to become a camper is full of challenges. Sometimes those challenges are met with energy and exhilaration and sometimes by severe anxiety. In his memoir of life at a private camp, Michael Eisner (2005) remembers when his learning process was halted by powerful anxieties. He loved canoeing and, to his delight, was selected to be the youngest member of the camp's most rigorous canoe trip. He had learned well the skills of canoeing. Yet, faced with the prospect of this more challenging trip, Michael became "petrified" and "trapped" by these feelings until Brownie, the trip leader, intervened.

> "You know," he began, "I am always nervous before these big trips." I turned and looked at him. "I sometimes think things are more dangerous than they really are, but then I calm myself down and realize I am safe and I'll have a good time." "Yeah," I responded. (2005, 48)

Brownie could read this child's anxieties. By sharing his own anxieties, Brownie opened a door that allowed Michael to get back into action. Soon, "I felt the exhilaration of shooting rapids, creating campsites with no parents or siblings in sight, a nonstop adventure of self-reliance, teamwork, and even leadership" (2005, 49). That is how camp learning happens: with a little help from staff, children get into the flow of camp, recall their skill learning, and are off on new adventures that allow them to exercise "self-reliance, teamwork, and even leadership."

We often associate learning with schools and not with summer camps. But schools and camps have more in common than many of us realize (Zeldin 2006). It is true that schooling is organized around the teaching of specific subjects and camp around what most people identify as fun and games. But that dichotomy is not helpful to understanding what life at these camps is actually like. Camps also have ambitious learning agendas and hire competent educational staff to ensure that campers are learning and practicing skills for activities as diverse as tennis matches, canoe trips, and song session on Shabbat. Campers are not being tested and graded on their learning, but they do display their skills before varied camp audiences and gain the socio-emotional skills needed to live and perform with their fellow campers.

Intentional Jewish camps are also designed to be sites for intense Jewish learning. This is most evident with children who come to camp from areas where they are one of only a few Jews. When those campers arrive, much will be new for them: living with so many Jews, praying on a daily basis, and celebrating the weekly Shabbat rituals. These campers may wonder, "Why does everyone else know so much more about Judaism than I do?" Coming to camp can be overwhelming, and the camp staff may need to help these campers navigate this new environment. As they become comfortable with the routines of camp life, they begin to learn how to practice a Judaism not available in their hometowns.

But even for the majority of campers who come to camp from areas where they know many Jews, the intensity of camp Judaism can feel quite unfamiliar. Every new camper has to learn how to do Jewish in the ways it is done at this camp. That is a primary agenda for these camps: to help their campers—whatever their home backgrounds—get comfortable participating in the Jewish cultural and religious life of camp that affords many opportunities to learn varying facets of Jewish living.

By focusing on Shabbat at camp, I set out to study the opportunities for campers to learn to celebrate Shabbat at camp. Because celebrating Shabbat at camp differs from celebrating Shabbat elsewhere, campers have to learn how to celebrate the camp version of Shabbat. Whether they bring previous experience of celebrating Shabbat or not, they have much to learn about the details of camp observance and celebration. It is my goal to show how the staff works closely with the campers to enable that learning to take place and develop over their years at camp.

CONCEPTUALIZING LEARNING AT CAMP

In exploring how camp staff work with campers to enable that learning, I need to differentiate this study from the work of Sales and Saxe, the one existing comprehensive study of how Jewish camps influence their campers. In their view, the key to understanding the learning process is to view these camps as sites of socialization.

> Socialization is the key mechanism by which groups sustain themselves and bind new members and transmit values and knowledge from one generation to the next. . . . Jewish socialization involves acquiring the knowledge, skills, and attitudes that enable one to be an active member of the Jewish community. . . . If the future of Judaism and Jewish life reside in strong communities, then socialization becomes the core task of the collective. (2004, 5–7)

Sales and Saxe focus on how values and knowledge are transmitted from one generation to the next. At camp that transmission can take place naturally, for camps create a seamless counterworld in which children are "socialized" to the rhythms and values of the place by simply living the camp life, enjoying its intense social life, and identifying with its social messages. Jewish residential camps enjoy a great advantage over other Jewish educational programs because once children become campers, they are living full time in a Jewish environment and can soak up its normative messages.

But, Sales and Saxe warn, camp leadership has to be skillful in how it builds the Jewish elements into the life of the camp so as to set up an effective Jewish socializing environment. First and foremost are the socializing agents: the camp counselors who interact most intensively with the campers. If they have not bought into the Jewish agenda of the camp, they can easily subvert the socializing process. Second are the specialists and educational staff in charge of many of the programmatic elements of camp life. While not as closely linked to the campers as the counselors, they have a secondary influence in that they can either enrich the camp schedule with powerful Jewish content or create programs that have little connection to the Jewish agenda of the camp.

Sales and Saxe view camp as a kind of social psychological experiment in which the conditions have to be carefully set to exert maximal influence. But they know from their observational data that Jewish camps often miss that mark. Here is an example of missing the mark on Shabbat.

> During Friday night services some of the counselors sat in the rows with the campers, while others sat in the back of the chapel and talked throughout the service. The unit heads stood in the back, and the director walked around taking pictures. (Sales and Saxe 2004, 81)

This is a bracing example of missing the basic elements needed to create an effective Jewish atmosphere. Counselors need to realize that on Shabbat they serve as active Jewish role models for campers. Unit heads and camp director also need to be aware that they serve as role models during the Sabbath service, and if they are not visibly engaged with the prayer, they are undermining the sanctity of the moment. Sales and Saxe stress that for Jewish influence to have coherence, it has to be integrated into the daily and weekly life of camp, which requires that staff members be the ones setting the example.

Who can argue with that main point? Shabbat at camp is so different from the way that most campers live their regular lives that if the camp staff is not fully invested, the campers will be lost. They need the staff to establish a clear framework and set of expectations for how the whole camp community will behave on Shabbat. Otherwise, the celebration will lose its coherence and meaning.

Yet, for the purposes of this study, the socialization model is of limited help. Sales and Saxe indicate which elements need to be in place for a camp to have a Jewish influence on campers. Their focus is on transmission, on what camp leaders and staff need to put in place for the campers to absorb the Jewish messaging. But in their work, campers are the passive recipients of the vitality of a staff-led camp. By contrast, my focus is on shared social learning, on how educational staff and campers work together to produce that learning. I accentuate the active role that campers play in this learning process. To conceptualize how that active learning takes place, I will seek other models of learning.

Here is an example of the kind of active learning I set out to explain. At all three camps in this study, the oldest campers have special roles that only they fulfill on Shabbat. One such role is to line up in two rows before certain Shabbat ritual events and with their arms joined in space create "a tent" under which the younger campers pass as they enter. Passing through the tent has become a camp tradition that campers look forward to as part of Shabbat celebration. When younger campers pass through they are actively greeted by the oldest campers and often older and younger will high-five one another. Sales and Saxe might view the older campers as "socializing" the younger ones, but that lens would miss the extent to which this event is cocreated by both sides. Both sides are partners in what learning theorist David Perkins (2009) would call "the whole game" of Shabbat. Both sides are learning to play their active roles in that game. The older campers are learning to greet and create a sense of welcome while the younger ones are learning to be greeted by their older peers.

Perkins (2009) offers these insights. One is that it is helpful to younger participants to see that older participants are playing the same whole game. With chess, for example, it helps young chess players to know that older peers and even adults are still working on their chess game while competing with one another. With Shabbat at camp, from a camper's first Shabbat it is clear that everyone right up to the camp directors is celebrating Shabbat. In contrast to most synagogues, there is no drop-off in celebrating after bar or bat mitzvah. The teens are visibly present on Shabbat greeting the newcomers and demonstrating that celebrating Shabbat is an ongoing endeavor that young people will continue to pursue for all their years in camp.

While everyone at camp continues to celebrate Shabbat, that learning grows more complex as one matures. When chess players move up from one level of competition to the next, they anticipate that their game will have to improve at each successive level. With Shabbat at camp there is no competition, but there are levels of complexity. Newcomers are expected to learn the basic moves, but are not asked to do more. By one's second or third summer, campers are asked to lead parts of the Shabbat service. After they reach bar or bat mitzvah at age thirteen, campers are asked to take on greater service leadership. Finally, in the last year, oldest campers are asked to take on a variety of new roles as leaders of ritual activity. Each time campers move up in this succession, they are asked to learn new roles that require greater ritual skills. Not all campers respond positively to these requests. For those who do, staff at these camps stand ready to work closely with campers so that campers can learn to be more skilled as they move toward fuller participation in celebrating Shabbat.

HOW SHABBAT RITUALS WORK AT CAMP

As these examples illustrate, learning to celebrate Shabbat at camp entails campers' participating in and eventually leading the varied rituals that make up the Shabbat celebration. There is more to Shabbat at camp than ritual celebration, but our focus will be on the communally celebrated Shabbat rituals. First, however, let us clarify what we mean by camp rituals.

For some people, "ritual" carries a negative connotation as a repetitive set of behaviors that people engage in without much thought or feeling. For others, especially those in the observant Jewish community, a ritual is a traditional action that Jews fulfill as part of their religious obligation to observe the Sabbath. But I will use "ritual" in quite a different sense that I have learned from sociologists and anthropologists who study contemporary religious communities in a variety of cultural settings (Ammerman 2014; Luhrmann 2012; Prell 1989).

Many camp people have what I consider to be a static view of ritual. They might say on a Friday evening, "Now it is time to light Shabbat candles." They think of candle lighting as a ritual action that Jews traditionally perform at this given time. They want it done well so campers will remember it fondly. But they are less curious about the performative aspects of the ritual. They do not ask why candle lighting is performed in the particular ways it is at camp—with its communal dynamics and ritual twists. For them, all that is "shtick" and not essential to the ritual itself. But I believe that how the ritual is performed—with all its twists and turns—is what campers and staff learn and subsequently care about.

Camp ritual is rarely a dry affair; it comes with much cultural elaboration—like the hand motions—that matters deeply. In this view, I am deeply influenced by the work of the late anthropologist Barbara Myerhoff, whose study of ritual in Jewish communities (1979, 1992) has informed my analysis. Myerhoff has taught me to attend to ritual as an elastic and expressive medium. Here she is writing about how candle lighting is enacted at the Jewish senior center that she studied in Los Angeles.

> The traditional Sabbath ceremony was rearranged to allow as many people as possible to participate—making speeches, singing songs, reading poems . . . Two or three women were required to light the Sabbath candles—one singing the blessing in Hebrew, one in Yiddish, one putting the match to the wick. (1979, 10)

Never mind that the woman who recites the blessing is traditionally the one who lights the candles. At this center, as in many summer camps, the ritual is both elastic and expressive. It is elastic in providing many more people opportunities to actively participate in the ritual action. It is expressive in that varied participants can express themselves by giving speeches, singing songs, showing off their Hebrew or Yiddish, or simply lighting the wick. The work of the ritual is not to be efficient, but to stretch and shift so that many can get in on the action with their presence and voice. I call these rituals "engaging" and potentially "educational" in that participants may learn to connect the "great tradition" of Shabbat candle lighting with their own personal stories expressed through these cultural elaborations. The more they make the ritual their own, the greater the chance they will find ongoing meaning in performing such rituals.

Shabbat rituals at camp are rarely efficient. They take time and engage many of the participants in roles that allow them to be present and give voice. Campers and staff are encouraged to express themselves by getting involved and bringing to the ritual their youthful energetic selves in ways that would not work in most Jewish contexts outside of camp. Camp Judaism is elastic and expressive in ways that often delight the fancy of the campers and motivate them to want to learn how to participate and even lead the ritual.

But not all rituals at camp work equally well. Myerhoff spells out what it means for a ritual to fail. "A ritual fails when it is seen through, not properly attended, or experienced as arbitrary invention" (1992, 183). Were you to attend a camp where the staff were not much invested in the Shabbat rituals and performed them in a distanced manner, you might not carry away much feeling for Jewish traditions. By contrast, when the Shabbat ritual works well, the people are "drawn beyond words into play, imagination, emotion, and insight and experience a deep sense of *communitas* and fulfillment" (1992, 185).

Myerhoff uses Victor Turner's (1974) term "communitas" to speak of what ritual can accomplish. Communitas is that deep sense of being at one with one's community that is sometimes realized through ritual action. This recalls Judah Cohen's (2008) description of what happened when OSRUI, the Reform Jewish camp, moved Shabbat Shirah—its Friday night song session—from its usual location in a small, cramped hall into its newly built enlarged dining hall. In that cavernous space, the song leaders could not hold the undivided attention of the campers and the event lost the feeling of unity that was essential to its vitality. That posed a crisis and the camp moved quickly to remedy the breach. But the crisis illustrates Myerhoff's point. Rituals are vulnerable to disruption, and it does not take much for that crucial sense of unity to be lost.

I look for that ritual vitality at Shabbat at camp as a sign of engagement. That vitality ebbs and flows. At no camp can one simply assume its presence. Staff work hard to make these ritual events as vital as possible, but there are multiple variables at work that influence how a ritual will work. Ask any song or ritual leader and he or she will tell you about the ups and downs of ritual vitality and how campers can be resistant to being engaged. But for all the ups and downs, these Jewish camps have developed a know-how for making Shabbat celebration come alive with rituals that most often engage their campers' interests and energies and invite their learning through active participation.

SHABBAT CELEBRATION AS OPTIMAL EXPERIENCE

Years before beginning this study I had a conversation with my nephew, Raphael Torn, who had grown up in France but come for summers to be a camper at Eisner Camp. He was describing the power of celebrating Shabbat at camp, and I was moved to record his words in my journal.

> Friday night singing and dancing at camp create a trance-like state that teens have never before experienced and that moves them to tears. It is deliberately created, much-anticipated, and deeply moving. It builds a spiritual ecstasy that Americans otherwise never experience.

These Jewish camps use Shabbat ritual to do more than engage the interest of their campers. They also have developed a set of Friday night rituals that "create a trance-like state" and build "a spiritual ecstasy" that these American campers "otherwise never experience." These ritual moments represent a "peak experience" that is essential to understanding the power of Shabbat at camp.

To give a sense of such moments, let me briefly describe "ReLish" at Camp Yavneh. On Friday evenings, ReLish serves as a transition to Shabbat. ReLish consists of a set of songs that the whole camp sings to the accompaniment of a lively band. Those songs culminate in everyone's having their arms around their neighbors, swaying as a group and singing at full volume. Then everyone breaks from the group embrace to hug one another with the greetings of "Shabbat shalom."

How to understand these ritual moments that characterize Shabbat celebration at Jewish camps? Why have these camps developed these intense rituals, and how do campers learn to participate in them?

The first thing to note is that ReLish draws heavily on the three tools that these camps commonly deploy on Shabbat: community, ritual, and music. ReLish brings the whole camp community together at the very start of the Shabbat to enact this ritual event. The band provides the musical backup to the intense singing and movement. The three tools fit together to create a cultural pattern that is entirely familiar and emotionally arousing for campers and staff.

Second, staff and campers organize themselves into age-specific circles that remain together throughout the ritual. The youngest campers are introduced to the ritual within the safety of their own circle. They may have little idea of what to expect, but they can learn by watching others and being guided into the ritual action with help from staff and fellow campers.

Third, these ritual moments like ReLish exist only at Camp Yavneh. Their purpose is not to be taken home, but to be uniquely and vividly lived at camp. They are particular to camp culture and their intensity distinguishes Shabbat at camp from experiences of Shabbat outside of camp.

Borrowing from the work of psychologist Mihaly Csikszentmihalyi (1990), I will view ritual moments like ReLish as "optimal experiences." Optimal experience happens "when we feel a sense of exhilaration, a deep sense of enjoyment that is long cherished and becomes a landmark in memory." Optimal experiences stand out for the "flow" or "moment-to-moment enjoyment" we derive from having given our all to achieve something that is for us singularly worthwhile (1990, 3–6). By seeing these intense moments as optimal experiences, I can view them as being culturally particular to these Jewish camps, but psychologically akin to the other heightened moments in the lives of American adolescents (Csikszentmihalyi and Larson 1984). They serve a dual purpose of intensifying Shabbat at camp and providing campers with Jewish experiences that are highly focused and intense, and that represent a high point of their Shabbat celebration.

Jewish camps do not merely socialize campers into existing modes of Jewish normative behavior, but they also offer a heightened sense of Jewish celebration. Focusing on these intense Shabbat rituals will lead to exploring the question of why the camp celebration of Shabbat has developed in these directions and what its implications are for educating for Shabbat in other Jewish contexts.

THE THREE CAMPS OF THIS STUDY

In studying Shabbat at camp, I want to give readers an in-depth view of how Shabbat is celebrated and how campers of different ages learn to participate in that celebration. The study could have been an in-depth view of a single Jewish camp, but then the way that particular camp celebrates Shabbat might be seen as the normative way. To avoid suggesting that there is any one best way, I decided that choosing three camps would offer a fair comparative view without losing the in-depth picture that I sought.

By a set of research criteria that I lay out in chapter 3, I chose to study these well-established Jewish residential camps: URJ Eisner Camp in Western Massachusetts, Camp Ramah in Wisconsin, and Camp Yavneh in New Hampshire. Eisner Camp is affiliated with the Reform movement, Ramah with the Conservative movement, and Yavneh is an independent camp with a substantial Orthodox population. I had previously worked professionally with the directors of these camps and had heard from others that each camp offered a robust Shabbat celebration. Those reports would prove true, as readers will see in the forthcoming chapters.

I began this study during the summer of 2015 and kept returning through 2018. Each summer I spent a full Shabbat—Friday afternoon to Saturday night—at the camps and focused on a particular age group of campers and their staff. I began with the youngest campers and had planned to work my way up an age progression until reaching the oldest campers. But it became clear that for the story I was telling, the main action was concentrated at the end points: the newest and oldest campers. That was true at all three camps and needs further explanation.

At all three camps their youngest campers are age eight or nine and their oldest campers are fifteen or sixteen. At each age interval a camper moves up to the next highest division or unit until arriving at the oldest one, which for these camps serves as both a culminating point (last year as camper) and a transitional point (toward many campers eventually becoming camp staff members). During that last summer, the camps offer their oldest campers special opportunities to lead the younger campers, and that is especially evident in celebrating Shabbat.

This age progression creates three primary learning opportunities for campers. During their first summer, campers learn to socially participate in all camp activities, including celebrating Shabbat. New campers look to veteran campers and veteran campers look to oldest campers to figure out how to celebrate Shabbat at camp. They also look to the counselors, who guide their entry into the celebration of Shabbat at camp.

As campers learn to participate in the Shabbat activities, they are given opportunities to move toward more intensive participation. What is interesting is how layered Shabbat participation is at these camps. As campers move from division to division, they are asked to take on more challenging roles in celebrating Shabbat. An obvious example is that after reaching their bar or bat mitzvah at age thirteen, campers are asked to read from the Torah scroll on Shabbat morning, which involves a level of Hebrew mastery that few younger campers possess. A less obvious example are the Shabbat-related rituals to which only older campers may gain access. As campers mature, they are invited to participate in more complex aspects of the Shabbat experience to which they did not previously have access.

During their final summer, a new set of learning opportunities opens up. Oldest campers are asked to take the lead at key moments during Shabbat celebrations. At each camp these opportunities vary in detail, but at all three many of the oldest campers leap at the opportunity to take the lead and model for younger campers how they are celebrating Shabbat. As a participant observer, I was drawn to these moments, paid careful attention to how each camp structured these learning opportunities, and was attuned to how campers explored new ritual roles that were opening to them as oldest campers.

By focusing on these layered learning opportunities, and exploring each layer with the help of learning theorists Rogoff (2003), Perkins (2009), and Csikszentmihalyi (1990), I hope to show that these Jewish camps have found powerful ways to not only engage the interest and energies of their campers but also to expand their horizons by offering increasingly expansive and complex roles in their celebration of Shabbat.

THE THREE RESEARCH QUESTIONS

As I set out to tell the story of how these three Jewish residential camps have created Shabbat celebrations that engage the interest of their campers and promote their Jewish learning, my path was guided by three research questions that illuminate the intellectual journey I have been on for these past years.

What is distinctive about how Shabbat is celebrated at Jewish camps? While a Jewish thinker like Heschel can conceptually describe what constitutes a traditional Jewish Sabbath, North American Jews have created multiple ways of celebrating and observing Shabbat. There are the Shabbat celebrations for the home and the synagogue, for Friday night only and for the full twenty-five hours, and for those that adhere to the strictest and less strict standards in traditional observance. In the 1920s a new variation was created, Shabbat at camp. This new variation has been developing for a full century and has spread from the few initial camps to many different residential camps throughout North America. While this is an in-depth study of only three of those camps, it has given me the opportunity to think about what makes Shabbat at camp distinctive as an initiative designed to engage and educate campers from ages eight to sixteen.

How do the educational staff at these camps create Shabbat celebrations that engage the interests and invite the participation of campers ages eight to sixteen? Creating Shabbat at camp each week is a complex operation involving a variety of educational staff, from the directors to division heads to bunk counselors. Describing how this complex operation is planned, coordinated, and carried out at each of three camps is an ethnographic challenge. Viewing both what each camp distinctively does and what they do in common is important for grasping how these Jewish camps shape Shabbat celebration for its educational purposes and yet offers campers a common Shabbat experience that we call celebrating Shabbat at camp.

What special learning opportunities do these camps provide their campers through their participation in the celebration of Shabbat? These Jewish camps are designed to be sites of intense Jewish learning. On Shabbat, much of that learning happens through camper participation in the ritual celebrations of Shabbat.

That participation is layered as campers move through their years at camp. Describing how each camp offers these learning opportunities and supports their campers to assume expanded roles in the Shabbat celebration is an essential goal of the ethnographic research.

WHAT BROUGHT ME TO THIS CAMP STUDY

My own association with American Jewish camps goes back to my childhood, when for three summers I attended an Orthodox boys camp in New Jersey called Camp Deal. As a teen, I attended Camp Massad Aleph for three summers (1963–65), first as a counselor-in-training and then as a bunk counselor. Those were engaging summers that I have previously written about (Reimer 2007). My most formative experience was as a staff member (1966–1971) at two Ramah camps: Ramah in the Berkshires and Ramah in New England. Those summers—working as a counselor, teacher, and division head of the oldest campers—led me to the Harvard Graduate School of Education to study developmental psychology and then pursue a career as a professor of education with a primary interest in informal Jewish education and camp life. While in graduate school, I spent two summers working with the oldest campers at Camp Cejwin, near Port Jervis in New York.

As a faculty member at Brandeis University, I became the founding director of the Institute for Informal Jewish Education. During those five years (2000–2005), I led professional development institutes for young professionals who saw Jewish camps and youth work as their calling. Their passion for and engagement with Jewish youth deeply influenced my own professional and research interests. From 2006 through 2011 I served as a lead faculty member for the Executive Leadership Institute (ELI) of the Foundation for Jewish Camp (FJC). During those five years, I led seminars for Jewish camp directors on developing their executive leadership skills. During those summers, I visited many varied Jewish nonprofit camps to observe and consult with camp directors. That experience set the stage for this research.

I met two of the study camp directors—Yavneh's Debbie Sussman and Eisner's Louis Bordman—through ELI. They were both members of the first ELI cohort in 2006–07. They were not my advisees and I did not visit their camps at that time. But I kept in touch. Louis and I worked together in 2008 to develop a case study for ELI on the Reform movement's purchase and conversion of Crane Lake Camp. Debbie and I were involved in formulating what later became known as One Happy Camper, a communal program to financially incentivize first-time campers for Jewish residential camps. I consulted with both (and other ELI directors) as I developed my Brandeis course on American Jewish camps.

I met Rabbi David Soloff, the director of Camp Ramah in Wisconsin, in

2001 as part of a research team sent by the Cohen Center to document Jewish education at that camp. I was deeply impressed by the camp and returned in 2008 and 2009 to conduct a study of director vision and camp program (Reimer 2012). Jacob Cytryn—who later succeeded Rabbi Soloff as director—came to Brandeis University in 2007 to pursue his doctoral studies in Jewish education. Jacob was not my doctoral student, but we got to know one another and he asked me to serve on his dissertation committee. It was while he was working on his dissertation research that I began this research.

My involvement over decades with Jewish camps makes me anything but an objective observer of camp life. Nevertheless, I have aimed for what Erik Erikson (1964) has called "disciplined subjectivity." I have worked hard to step back and reflect on my own subjective responses so as to fairly present observations of camp life. I have tried to accurately depict Shabbat at each of these camps and critically analyze their educational goals and implementation. By laying out a comparative portrait of Shabbat, I aim to show how each camp creates a Shabbat that reflects the religious and educational goals central to their mission while also sharing a common design for Shabbat and a devotion to engaging their campers in a robust celebration of Shabbat.

WHAT YOU WILL FIND IN THIS BOOK

I have written this book for two distinct audiences: (1) camp people and alumni who are eager to reflect on their camp experiences and (2) educational leaders and scholars who would like to learn from what camps do well. For both audiences I have a clear message: let's understand how these camps create a powerful model of celebrating Shabbat and what that model can teach us about how children learn to celebrate Shabbat and how we can educate for a vital Shabbat even beyond the context of camp.

This book is divided into three parts: (1) Creating Shabbat at Camp, (2) Celebrating Shabbat at Camp, and (3) Learning from Shabbat at Camp. Part I offers readers in chapter 2 a historical picture of how Shabbat at camp came to be, spread from a few to many more Jewish residential camps, took on the coloration of varied camp settings, and developed into what it is today. Chapter 3 introduces the three camps as distinctive settings for celebrating and learning about Shabbat as well as the rationale for and methodology of the ethnographic study of these camps.

Part II is a report of the ethnographic study of how these three camps celebrate Shabbat. That is presented by the time segments that make up Shabbat at camp. Chapter 4 describes preparing for Shabbat on Friday afternoon. Chapter 5 describes greeting the Shabbat through the Friday evening Shabbat *tefilla* (prayer service) and meal. Chapter 6 captures the intensifying celebration of Shabbat as the camps move from early to late Friday evenings. Chapter 7 describes the Shabbat day from the late rising in the morning to the culminating Havdalah ceremonies of Saturday night. Taken as a whole, part II offers the arc of Shabbat at these camps as campers and staff move from greeting the Sabbath all the way to sending Shabbat off with the Havdalah ceremony.

Part III examines in greater depth two concluding questions: (1) How do these camps engage the interest of their campers and support their learning how to celebrate Shabbat over their years at camps? and (2) What do these cases of Shabbat at camp have to offer other Jewish leaders and educators who are seeking to create robust Shabbat celebrations in their contexts?

Chapter 8 offers a deeper look into how theories of learning can help us better understand how camp staff and campers work together to learn to celebrate a vital Shabbat at camp. Chapter 9 presents a model of three camp practices that may have application to the work of Jewish leaders and educators in other communal contexts.

Abraham Joshua Heschel's book *The Sabbath* gave us a new language by which to explain what is uniquely valuable about celebrating Shabbat. My hope is that this book might give its readers a new language for understanding what is uniquely valuable about Shabbat at camp and an opportunity to reflect on how to bring more of that joy and vitality into the larger American Jewish community and beyond.

Postscript: As this book was going to press, a report by independent investigators was released on sexual misconduct at URJ (Union for Reform Judaism) workplaces. The investigators from Debevoise and Plimpton LLP named two past leaders of URJ camps for multiple reported incidents of sexual misconduct with adult women. While writing this book, I was unaware of these reported incidents. Yet this report should serve as a wake-up call for me and other researchers of summer camps.

Part One

CREATING SHABBAT AT CAMP

LIKE THE QUESTION OF "WHO IS A JEW?" the question of "What makes for a Jewish summer camp?" is not simple to answer. Over the past century there have been different and conflicting answers offered. Does a camp become "Jewish" if a majority of campers are Jewish? Does a camp need to have explicitly Jewish practices to be called "Jewish"? Do the Jewish practices need to be religious or ideological in nature for the camp to called "Jewish"?

Answering these questions requires taking a trip back in time to the early years of the twentieth century, when American Jews first became interested in starting summer camps for their children. That trip will provide an understanding of why those first Jewish camps were established, who they attracted, and what larger educational purposes they served. Jewish residential camps in North America have a rich and varied history that reflects the quite different conceptions that Jews have had of how to structure leisure time for their children so as to prepare them to take their places in the larger society.

This history includes the deliberate initiative undertaken by a small number of camp leaders to create what we call "Shabbat at camp." There was nothing inevitable about Shabbat becoming a regular feature of Jewish residential camps. Many early Jewish camps had minimal celebrations of Shabbat and some had none at all. How Shabbat at camp was created and gradually spread to most Jewish residential camps is central to the history we tell in chapters 2 and 3 that comprise part I of this book.

Today the place of Shabbat at most Jewish residential camps has dramatically changed. During the first two decades of the twenty-first century, the organized North American community came to take a more active role in both supporting Jewish camps and expecting those camps to be actively Jewish. While that support still leaves a wide spectrum of possibilities for how camps can express their Jewishness, most camp leaders are attuned to this communal expectation. One central way that many Jewish camp leaders have chosen to express their camp's Jewishness is through the weekly celebration of Shabbat.

But how does a Jewish summer camp choose to celebrate Shabbat? No camp leaders over the past few decades have had to create de novo Shabbat at camp. They can rely on the rich traditions that have developed at other Jewish camps for how to celebrate Shabbat. Those traditions have been developing since the 1920s and have been passed on from one generation of camp leaders to the next until they have spread to most residential Jewish camps.

2 / DEVELOPING SHABBAT AT JEWISH SUMMER CAMPS, 1920–2000

WHEN JEWISH SUMMER CAMPS FIRST OPENED, around 1900, no one asked the founders, "What makes this a Jewish camp?" They did not have to. In those days of social exclusion, the answer was clear: if a camp had mostly Jewish campers, it was a Jewish summer camp.

It is important to acknowledge how exclusive the early American summer camps were. The first residential summer camps started in New England during the 1880s as a way to bring middle- and upper-class Protestant boys back to the wilderness. White, privileged, Protestant boys were led by young men of the same background who had a vision of a return to nature. Summer camps began when American cities were quickly expanding, absorbing waves of immigrants and building new neighborhoods to accommodate a rising middle class. The founders of the first camps were appealing to a nostalgic sense that something essential was being lost in this transition to city living and that parents could counter this loss by sending their children to this new rustic setting called "summer camp" (Paris 2008; Van Slyck 2006).

These young camp leaders were prescient in vision and limited in social reach. The Protestant camps they started lasted only a few seasons, but what they began soon caught on. By the late 1890s and early 1900s all kinds of people began to value the camp ideal. National organizations started opening camps for a greater variety of campers. When the YMCA and the Boy Scouts opened camps across the Northeast and Midwest, their camps served boys from more diverse backgrounds. After 1910, the Girls Scouts and Camp Fire Girls opened their camps for girls. By these small steps American summer camps expanded to a slightly more diverse, but still socially and racially limited, clientele (Paris 2008).

When around 1900 a few American Jews wanted to send their children to summer camps, it was clear they would have to start their own camps.

Their children were not welcome in most existing camps. The wealthier and more Americanized Jews started private camps where parents paid tuition to private camp owners who recruited from privileged Jewish families like their own. These camps operated a great deal like their Protestant counterparts, yet some private camp directors added a pinch of Jewish flavoring for taste, like a candle lighting, short service, and festive meal on Friday nights (Isaacman 1970; J. Sarna 2006).

By far the larger number of new Jewish camps served a different population: the children of new immigrants. During the 1880s, a huge wave of Jewish immigration started coming from Eastern Europe. This tidal wave was pouring into American cities when the first Jewish summer camps began. Fortunately, there were Jewish philanthropists concerned with the growing number of poor, immigrant Jewish children left behind in the teeming cities. Soon plans emerged to open Jewish Fresh Air camps for these children in communities across the country as a way of protecting them from the illnesses that often spread during the summer months (J. Sarna 2006).

These Jewish charitable camps were quite different from the private Jewish camps. They were run by nonprofit Jewish social welfare organizations that saw camp as way to bring poor kids to the great outdoors, and while there, to teach them to lead a healthier lifestyle. The focus was on food, sun, and water. These camps were created to better young lives and teach Jewish kids to enjoy the activities and habits of life that would help them adapt to the American landscape (Paris 2008). They were organized and financed by Jews, served a Jewish camper base, and sometimes ran a kosher kitchen. Until 1920, one could accurately define a Jewish camp as one owned or sponsored by Jews that served a Jewish population of campers. Nothing more was needed.

The 1920s marked a turning point for American camps in general and Jewish camps in particular. Summer camps entered the American mainstream with a proliferation of many new camps. Jewish camps also began to flourish. As Paris writes in *Children's Nature*, "At the turn of the twentieth century, very few Jewish children attended camps. Within two decades, they were among the industry's most enthusiastic supporters" (2008, 86). Jewish parents could now choose to send their children to a variety of Jewish camps and even some mixed camps like those sponsored by the Boy Scouts. There were Jewish camps that emphasized outdoor activities and socializing with other Jewish children. There were also new camps with more particular purposes, such as sponsoring

Yiddish language and culture or Zionist or Communist ideology. Suddenly the "Jewish" component grew more complex and diverse as Yiddish and Zionist camps offered specific Jewish content. They were claiming that it is not enough to simply serve and Americanize Jewish campers; Jewish camps also need to offer campers a positive model of being Jewish in the evolving American and world context (Joselit 1993; Fox 2019).

Had the directors of these diverse Jewish camps ever gotten together to discuss their similarities and differences, I imagine a fierce debate ensuing. The directors of the charitable camps would have stressed how many Jewish families still lived in poverty and needed these camps as the only chance their children would have to get out of the city and into the outdoors. In their view, their camps were Jewish by virtue of the social services they provided to Jews in need. The directors of the Yiddish camps would have asked, "But why not also use these summer weeks to teach these children to be proud of their native tongue and the rich culture of Yiddish books, theater, and songs?" The Zionists leaders would have objected to the Yiddish and insisted that camps needed to prepare campers for a Jewish future in the Hebrew homeland being built in Palestine. And the Communist leaders would have dismissed all these concerns as mere bourgeois trifle when the urgent agenda was to prepare campers for the coming world revolution. These camps leaders would never have agreed among themselves on what makes for a Jewish camp.

Even more fundamentally, these camp leaders did not agree on the purposes of camping. Were camps primarily to bring youth out of the city to learn new skills and values that were essentially American in nature? Or were camps a vehicle to prepare Jewish children for a particular future envisioned by the founders of those camps? These are very different conceptions of the purpose of camp and lead to creating very different camp experiences.

Noting these fundamental differences, I will focus on the "intentional" Jewish camps, the ones whose leaders were intentional about using the camp experience to transmit a particular cultural or ideological perspective. There is emerging scholarship about the Yiddish camps and how their secular worldviews shaped the camp experiences they provided their youth (Fox 2019; Freidenreich 2010). But to tell the story of how Shabbat at camp arose, spread, and became more normative, I will concentrate on the very few camps that began in the 1920s and became the seedbeds from which Shabbat at camp would grow.

JEWISH EDUCATIONAL CAMPS

Among those discovering the potential of intentional summer camps was a small group of Jewish educators known as "the Benderly boys." They were a tight-knit circle of well-educated men and women who were dedicated to creating a progressive version of Jewish education for the American children of Eastern European immigrants. They were the founders of the Hebrew school movement and firm believers in shaping a next generation of American Jews who would be at home within both the American democratic milieu and their particular Jewish culture.

They were not attracted to either the revival of Yiddish culture or the call to radical politics. Instead, they drew their inspiration from the progressive educational thinkers like John Dewey and cultural Zionist thinkers like Ahad Ha'am and Mordecai Kaplan. They focused their energies primarily on creating new Jewish schools, but during the 1920s some also went into camping. They opened three residential camps: Cejwin (1921), Modin (1922), and Achvah (1927). These were the first Jewish camps to intentionally view camp as "an experience in the art of Jewish living" and the first to create the paradigm for Shabbat at camp (Krasner 2011, 282). Their story is the one I will most closely follow.

Following the lead of Jonathan Krasner (2011), a central figure in this story is Albert Schoolman, who, together with his wife Bertha, founded the first of these camps, Cejwin. Schoolman, a devotee of Rabbi Mordecai Kaplan, was running a large Hebrew school in Manhattan that experimented in 1919 with a two-week summer session at a Catskill farmhouse, where the students took classes in the morning and enjoyed the countryside thereafter. The girls and their parents were so excited by this arrangement that Schoolman could see that this was a scalable experiment: if a few students could gain this much from a short summer experience, why not experiment with more students for more time during the summer? That possibility would call for starting a summer camp—which, by 1920, had become a feasible option. But how could Schoolman raise the money to buy a campsite? Only by convincing the board of directors of his school that a summer site would be the perfect extension of their Hebrew school. So began this new nonprofit venture, a mix of summer school and residential camp, with coed campers attending camp, taking academic classes during the morning and participating in camp activities for the rest of the day.

With many new Jewish camps coming on the scene, could this new mix of school and camp work over time? Schoolman gave it his best shot. It was quite expensive to hire a staff of teachers to teach while also hiring counselors and specialty staff to run the camp activities. Schoolman worked the financial angles to make it feasible. Throughout the 1920s he ambitiously grew the camper base so he could spread the costs over many tuitions. That meant that teachers had to teach campers with very different Jewish backgrounds and come up with new ways to do that teaching. The arts and other experiential modes of learning were adapted to a camp setting and the experiment seemed to be succeeding. However, once the Depression struck in the 1930s and the camper base shrunk, Schoolman could no longer make this work and was forced to let go of his teaching staff. The original model was abandoned and Cejwin emerged as an independent nonprofit Jewish camp with Schoolman as its full-time director (Krasner 2011).

Once he devoted himself to discovering how Jewish camps could educate, Schoolman saw that even without formal classes, Cejwin had developed multiple ways of providing campers with rich experiences in Jewish living. Where else could children live in a bunk with a Hebrew name, enjoy art sessions with serious Jewish artists, attend daily services that were designed to engage them, sing Hebrew songs, and participate in social games focused on the adventures of the *halutzim* (pioneers) in Eretz Yisrael (the Land of Israel)? Schoolman preferred to call Cejwin a "Jewish cultural camp," but he was developing a multisensory approach to Jewish education that we in retrospect recognize as "experiential Jewish education" (Reimer and Bryfman 2008).

Of all Schoolman's contributions, I will single out the creation of Shabbat at camp, a project that he undertook together with his staff and colleagues at the two other Jewish educational camps. Before 1920, with a few exceptions, Jewish camps did not do much with Shabbat. At most private and charitable Jewish camps, celebrating the Jewish Sabbath was not thought of as essential to being a Jewish camp (J. Sarna 2006). Yet, there was probably more ethnic Shabbos celebration at these camps—with festive Friday evening meals, candle lighting, and brief services—than the official record shows. What Schoolman and his peers were introducing was an intentional full-day Shabbat celebration that they hoped would become a defining aspect of intentional Jewish camping (Krasner 2011).

CREATING SHABBAT AT CAMP

For the Benderly group, it was self-evident that Jewish living at camp should include a robust Shabbat experience. They were not Orthodox Jews who would insist upon a fully observant Shabbat, but they were traditional Jews who believed that the Sabbath was a pillar of Jewish communal life. They knew full well that most Jewish immigrants had left behind consistent Sabbath observance when they entered the American workplace (Sarna 2004). But they saw camp as an opportunity for their campers to experience a fuller and more satisfying Shabbat. They dreamed of creating Shabbat as a cohesive day that would still feel like camp. At first no one knew how to design such a Shabbat. There were only a few models to build upon. These leaders exercised their creative resources to gradually design a camp Shabbat that incorporated many of the elements of traditional celebration but in ways that could work for American children in a camp context. As Krasner wrote in *The Benderly Boys and American Jewish Education*, "In a letter to parents written in 1925, Schoolman explained that life at camp was an ideal and romantic adventure into inspiring Jewish feeling, fine Jewish thinking, and beautiful Jewish living" (2011, 284).

Essential to Schoolman's thinking is that camp does not replicate the Judaism that exists at home but creates a more inspiring, thoughtful, and beautiful Judaism. Shabbat was the test case. Schoolman knew that while most of his campers had some Shabbat experience at home, it was often fragmentary, habitual, and non-inspiring. Could he and his colleague create a Shabbat experience that was inspiring, thoughtful, and beautiful, but also worked as a camp day for campers not accustomed to a full-day Sabbath practice?

Jacob Golub, an educator working at Cejwin, articulated two of the essential design elements.

> In an educational institution that which is assumed as unconscious in ordinary life processes must necessarily be made conscious and objective. The camp, therefore, is not merely a Jewish home, but training for a generally finer type of Jewish home that we might look forward to creating. (Ibid.)

First, creating Shabbat had to be a conscious undertaking. Camp could not simply drift into a familiar Shabbat as if everyone were anticipating its arrival and knew how to celebrate its rituals and observe its regulations. Rather, camp had to be structured in ways that created a clear dividing line between

"Shabbat" and "weekday." All elements of camp culture had to be mobilized to make this distinction dramatically clear so campers would realize they were moving from one time zone into another. Second, "Shabbat" had to operate as a special time so campers experienced it as a "finer" space. When Shabbat began, the bunks had to be cleaner, the clothes had to be fresher, the food had to be tastier, the praying had to more dramatic, and the way people related to one another had to be more open. Shabbat had to stand out as unique and elevated to impress the campers with its special nature.

The Shabbat they were creating at camp had to be different than anything the campers had elsewhere experienced. At key moments during Shabbat, camp embraced pageantry for its dramatic effects, with campers playing active roles in that drama. Here is a striking example from Camp Achvah, where Dr. Benderly, the director, led the Friday evening service.

> Benderly introduced the Sabbath by retelling the biblical creation story, with the visual aid of campers dressing up as each day of creation. When the campers began to sing "Lecha Dodi," a hymn from the liturgy, "The Sabbath Queen" herself appeared from the woods. Walking slowly, in time to the singing of the campers, she approached the assembly. Dressed in flowing white robes, her head wreathed in flowers, she was followed by a retinue of the youngest campers dressed as Sabbath angels. (Krasner 2011, 306)

Benderly was quite the dramatist. Where else had anyone enacted greeting the "Sabbath Queen" in this dramatic fashion? In what other educational settings were young children recruited to play her retinue? Who else connected Shabbat's coming so tightly to the first creation story of Genesis? Benderly, in his unique style, captured the dramatic possibilities that camp allowed in initiating youth into poetic aspects of Shabbat celebration. He and Schoolman were setting the precedent that Shabbat at camp was a new creation and needed to be dramatically impressive to engage the children and embed in their memory what Shabbat and Jewish celebration could be like.

Beyond these dramatic moments, Schoolman's most lasting contribution was the Shabbat schedule that he designed for Cejwin that would become a model for future Jewish camps. It became the model because it solved the tough design problem of how to create a special camp day that feels like a traditional Shabbat, allows for Shabbat observance, and yet does not feel overly restrictive for campers of diverse backgrounds. I have laid out this schedule as a series of steps or practices that take staff and campers through the full day of Shabbat at camp (Krasner 2011, 306).

1. Friday afternoon. Regular camp activities end followed by a cleanup period for preparing the bunk and the campers for Shabbat.
2. Friday evening. After cleanup, everyone dresses in white to greet the Shabbat.
3. Friday evening. The camp-wide evening Shabbat service.
4. Friday evening. Following services, everyone enters the dining hall for the festive Shabbat meal.
5. Friday night. After the meal, singing *zemirot* (traditional religious songs) followed by hora dancing.
6. Saturday morning. Late wake-up.
7. Saturday late morning. Traditional prayer service with Torah reading.
8. Shabbat lunch.
9. Saturday afternoon. Relaxed time with visiting siblings and the Shabbat walk.
10. Saturday night. Havdalah service to close Shabbat.

This step-by-step Shabbat schedule is so familiar to Jewish camp people that it seems self-evident and hardly remarkable. But remarkable it was, and not only for its efficient design.

More significantly, this schedule shaped Shabbat at camp to be in many ways quite different from how most Jews had traditionally celebrated the Sabbath. Let me highlight some of these differences.

Cleanup. Placing the weekly cleanup at the break between the regular camp schedule and the beginning of Shabbat accomplishes much at once. It takes a routine activity and gives it special purpose, suggesting that there is an active way that every camper can prepare for Shabbat. It also elongates the preparation for Shabbat, places the whole camp on a single schedule, and culminates in everyone's coming together to begin Shabbat as a single camp.

Dressing in white. Krasner (2011) does not address whether the early camp leaders were explicitly building on earlier Jewish customs in dressing everyone in white for erev Shabbat. But the visual effect of seeing the whole camp dressed as one is striking. At the same time, white dress allows for greater equality, mitigates competing via Shabbat dress-up, and sets off dressing up for Shabbat at camp from other Jewish occasions during the year.

Singing and dancing. Singing zemirot after the Shabbat meal is a traditional ritual that Jews have practiced for centuries. Hasidic males were well known for dancing at their Shabbat gatherings. But what Schoolman and his staff created at camp was new. They skillfully built Zionist elements into traditional Shabbat practices by freely mixing traditional Shabbat songs with newly minted Hebrew songs. They added hora dancing as a way of emphasizing that Shabbat was a time to identify with the Jewish people with one's body as well as one's mind. That this was done in a coed setting was a reminder that they were building what we would call a more egalitarian Jewish community.

Wake-up. The late wake-up and casual Shabbat afternoon schedule were important elements to emphasize that "the most effective way to bring children closer to religion was by first showing them a good time" (Krasner 2011, 305). Schoolman built in other pleasure elements, such as encouraging siblings to visit one another and allowing campers to have free swim on Shabbat. He wanted campers to experience Shabbat as *oneg* or, as we would say, a time of embodied rest and wholeness.

Havdalah. This closing ceremony is traditionally enacted at home and in synagogue by lighting the candle, blessing the wine, smelling the spices, and reciting a short paragraph of separating Shabbat from the rest of the week. It usually lasts about five minutes even with its added songs. But at camp, Havdalah took on a new life and added significance. Cejwin invested heavily in making Havdalah at the end of Shabbat an impressive ritual, using a full range of performative arts to create pageantry that the children would remember as a highlight of Shabbat at camp.

People routinely joke about campers who return from camp and can no longer recite Havdalah without standing around a lake. Cejwin may have been the first site where Havdalah and the lake were joined in children's imagination. Schoolman would likely not have minded the children's objection to saying Havdalah without standing around the lake, for it meant they had internalized this dramatic linkage that camp worked hard to establish. In his view, the goal of Shabbat at camp was to create a model of what Shabbat could be. He had no illusions that the camp experience would by itself change the course of American Jewry. But he did believe that camp, by creating new dramatically impressive Shabbat rituals, could provide powerful, positive Jewish experiences and, in that way, become a model for creative Jewish living (Krasner 2011). Schoolman set a precedent for future camp leaders to continue to build

Shabbat at camp as a memorable experience that may have few parallels in the outside Jewish community but that excited the imagination of both campers and staff members.

HOW SHABBAT TRAVELED TO MASSAD AND YAVNEH

The 1920s were an expansive time for American camps, but the 1930s were a time of constriction. The expensive private camps were hit hard by the Depression (Paris 2008) and so were mid-priced camps like Cejwin and Achvah (Krasner 2011). Given the hard times, one might have wondered during the late 1930s whether this daring experiment was going to last. That is why the opening during the early 1940s of two new intentional Jewish camps—Massad and Yavneh—are of particular interest. They became the sites that adapted and expanded upon the model of Shabbat that began at Cejwin, Modin, and Achvah (J. Sarna 2006).

In 1941, a group of young Jewish leaders came to Albert Schoolman, by then a veteran camp leader, with a crazy idea. They wanted to start an immersive Hebrew-speaking camp. Given all he had been through in keeping Cejwin afloat and with the financial difficulties facing Achvah (which aspired to be a Hebrew-speaking camp), Schoolman was quite discouraging of their dream. Nevertheless, these young leaders managed to raise the money they needed to start an immersive Hebrew day camp, and a year later launched a new residential camp they called Massad—a poetic Hebrew term for a foundation on which to build a shared Jewish future (Benor, Krasner, and Avni 2020).

The key figure was Shlomo Shulsinger. A native of Jerusalem, Shulsinger had come to the United States as a young man and developed a fierce determination to promote modern Hebrew culture among American Jews. He found support from the Histadrut Hanoar Ha'ivri, a Hebrew culture group, and with his peers, Moshe Davis and Sylvia Cutler Ettenberg, approached Schoolman, Kaplan, and others to help fund this new camp. Ettenberg had worked and trained under Schoolman at Cejwin; she too aspired to start a camp that was more intently Hebraic and Zionist than Cejwin. Massad was to have all the features of a Jewish summer camp like Cejwin, but with the added dimension of conducting the life of the camp in Hebrew (ibid.).

As the director, Shulsinger was determined to attract campers who could speak Hebrew. That meant appealing to students who attended Jewish day schools and had the greatest Hebrew fluency. Day school families were primarily Orthodox and expected traditional Shabbat observance at camp. So, from its start, Massad set out to create a more observant Shabbat practice than at Cejwin. Nevertheless, Massad adapted the Shabbat schedule that Schoolman devised, including dressing in white on erev Shabbat and a relaxed Shabbat afternoon with optional swimming available. Shulsinger teamed up with talented artists to use "the performing and fine arts to be a framework for deep emotional experiences" and engage the campers in the great Jewish struggles unfolding during the 1940s (ibid., 66). Their main focus was on a Zionist-inspired national revival through the Hebrew language; that artistic talent also built the Shabbat experience at Massad.

The best available access to what Shabbat was like at Massad comes from the recorded memories of prominent camp alumni who were interviewed years later and asked to recall their camp experiences. We begin with Stanley Sperber, who grew up as a camper and staff member at Massad and went on to live in Israel, where he directed the Jerusalem Chamber Choir and conducted the Haifa Symphony Orchestra. Here is how Sperber remembered Friday evenings at Massad during the early 1960s.

> There was a beautiful outdoor *tekes* [ceremony or ritual] of Kabbalat Shabbat at sunset on Friday. It was a pretty straight Orthodox service and everyone wore white. [Later] the entire *hadar ochel* [dining hall] was filled and we would start singing very quiet, beautiful Shabbat songs. Someone would say Kiddush, the food would come out, and there would be a lot of happy noise . . . I would sing a line and everyone would sing after me. Everyone would sing with a lot of enthusiasm. . . . Even though I was not a music counselor, I would lead the singing on Friday night. We were 400 or 500 people singing traditional Shabbat songs and new melodies for traditional texts. (Sperber 1996, 56)

Sperber's account highlights the intensity of the communal singing. There would be "very quiet, beautiful Shabbat songs" at the outset of the meal. Later, Sperber led a second round with "400 or 500 people singing traditional Shabbat songs." He was leading a mix of songs. There were the traditional zemirot but also "the new melodies for traditional texts," which probably refer to the Israeli songs that he would later record as the director of the Massad Choral Group, which became the Zamir Chorale (Benor, Krasner, and Avni 2020, 68).

At Massad, the music moved easily between traditional Shabbat songs and newer music emerging from Israel.

Robert Hyfler, who became a leading figure in the American Jewish Federation movement, recalled his experience of Havdalah at Massad during the mid- to late 1960s when he was a camper and then a staff member.

> For many years . . . Havdalah was meticulously choreographed. The entire camp assembled in the Machon Szold, the main auditorium. A procession of comely adolescent girls in white robes, holding lit braided Havdalah candles aloft, streamed down the center aisle to the front of the room as the camp sang Tuvia Shlonsky's haunting setting of Shaul Tchernichovsky's poem "I Believe," which begins with "*Sachki sachki al hachalomot.*" Having established an air of wistful solemnity, a member of the senior staff recited the Havdalah prayer. When he concluded, on cue campers and staff rose from their seats and joined in a rousing rendition of Massad's unofficial anthem, *Techezakna*. (Ibid., 75)

Hyfler, in retrospect, characterizes this ceremony as "a bizarre and incongruous yet moving juxtaposition of religion, politics and sexuality" (ibid.). What stands out from our perspective is how reciting the Havdalah prayer is surrounded by this epic choreography, which incorporates disparate elements of camp culture to dramatically highlight the fusing of religious and cultural elements. Massad built on what had already begun at the earlier Jewish camps and brought those trends to a new dramatic height. Shabbat at Massad added two key components that would prove influential in the history of intentional Jewish camps: Shabbat is the time for intense communal Jewish singing and much of that singing should be in Hebrew.

Just two years after the launch of Massad, the Hebrew Teacher's College in Boston opened Camp Yavneh in New Hampshire at the initiative of their president, Louis Hurwich, and his wife, Leah. Years earlier, Leah had worked with Schoolman in starting Cejwin. After marrying Hurwich and moving to Boston, she kept alive the dream of returning to Jewish camping.

While Hurwich took charge of raising the needed funds, Leah served as the camp's first director (Hurwich 1999). Yavneh was a curious mix of Cejwin and Massad. Like Cejwin in its early years, Yavneh required that campers take classes during the mornings before camp activities began. Like Massad,

Yavneh aspired to be a Hebrew-speaking camp. Classes were conducted in Hebrew and all camp activities were to be led in Hebrew. However, without Shulsinger's fierce leadership, Yavneh moved over time toward a compromise position, where "studies were in Hebrew, life in English" (Gamoran 2006, 132).

Louis and Leah Hurwich established a high level of Sabbath observance that attracted a substantial number of Orthodox families. Yet the majority of campers were recruited from the Hebrew schools of the Boston area and were not Orthodox. Yavneh offered a rich panoply of Jewish cultural resources and a lively Shabbat celebration with "extended periods of song and dance" (Hurwich 1999, 240). As a Hebrew-oriented camp, Yavneh attracted staff from Massad, including Stanley Sperber, who brought his gifted musical leadership to Yavneh, strengthening its existing Hebrew singing culture (Benor, Krasner, and Avni 2020).

WHERE SHABBAT DID NOT TAKE HOLD

While focusing on these few intentional Jewish camps where Shabbat celebration thrived, it is important not to lose sight of the many Jewish-sponsored camps where this model of Shabbat at camp did not take hold. What seemed essential to camp leaders like Schoolman, Shulsinger, and Hurwich had little appeal to their peers in most other Jewish camps.

In 1936, the Jewish Welfare Board published a directory of summer camps under the auspices of Jewish communal organizations and listed eighty-eight nonprofit camps in North America (J. Sarna 2006). The awkward phrasing tells a story: what these camps had in common were their Jewish sponsorship and little else. Daniel Isaacman (1970) looked back at this era and counted seven different types of Jewish camps—different by virtue of the organizations sponsoring them and the clientele they served. Writing about the majority of these Jewish camps, Isaacman claims that "a substantial proportion . . . were almost completely devoid of any meaningful Jewish programming" (1970, 133). Although Isaacman probably presented an overly dismissive portrait, it is still important to ask: Why were a majority of Jewish-sponsored camps not invested in promoting an active and meaningful Jewish life?

A first answer lies with what most middle-class Jewish parents wanted for their children in choosing a Jewish camp. Leslie Paris writes of Jewish parents of that era.

> Most important, summer camps allowed American Jews to balance ethnic community and their children's acculturation into American life. . . . Given that many Jewish immigrants had fled anti-Semitism and fears of violence in their home countries, the impetus to assimilate was significant. American Jews tended to be particularly eager to provide their children what appeared to be "American" experiences. (2008, 86)

Jewish camps were attractive to parents precisely because their children would be surrounded by other Jewish children, safe from anti-Semitic encounters, and yet free to pursue activities that seemed most American. Where else could their children be heroes of the baseball league and stars of the stage and dance floor? If those possibilities were safely in place, many parents were less concerned that these Jewish camps provide kosher food or a fuller Shabbat celebration.

A second answer lies with the professionals working for these camps. Camp leadership became more professionalized after 1920 and camps attracted more educators and social workers who brought to their work a greater dedication to the ideals of progressive education. While this was also true of camp leaders like Schoolman and Benderly, in most camps, as Paris explains, this was a move toward greater secularization.

> Progressive camp leaders promised a more secular and scientific "social adjustment." Their brochures and messages to parents were peppered with educational and psychological rhetoric. (Ibid., 238)

Camps aimed to promote greater camper self-direction and social adjustment. While those goals were not logically inconsistent with a focus on Jewish living, often these camp leaders saw them as such. They were second-generation Americans who wanted to free their campers from the old world of parental influence. While Schoolman might have been searching for a more beautiful Jewish expression, the more secular Jewish camp leaders often viewed "old-time religion" as authoritarian and regressive and were not open to celebrating the rituals of Judaism that they saw as having little to contribute to meeting their goals (Isaacman 1970).

At the same time, many camp leaders—Jews and Christians alike—were drawn to an alternative set of spiritual ideals represented by the imagined world of Native American pageantry. The same camp leaders who embraced modernity and its goals sought to create an alternative spiritual world inspired by American Indians. The anti-modern tendencies of the early American camp leaders—their wish to leave behind American city life and pursue a return to nature—blossomed in the 1920s into a full-blown movement to embrace the noble path of the Native Americans and recreate for campers and staff the pageantry and practices of these imagined forbearers. This Indian movement was intense and widespread and, in many Jewish camps, stood as an alternative to Jewish ritual practices (Paris 2008; Koffman 2018).

Some camp leaders took most seriously the Indian movement and its ideals. For these educators, there could be no room for competing Jewish ideals (Roth 2010). But for many other camp leaders, embracing Indian play was less ideological and more a practical Americanized way to engage campers and staff in the life of the camp. "There were dozens of Jewish camps established between 1902 and 1952 with Indian-sounding names. . . . Indian play crossed the secular-religious divide . . . [and] exhibited astounding durability for 30 and 40 years" (Koffman 2018, 15–25). From the 1920s through the 1950s, Jews played Indian at camp as if that were the most natural of activities. Koffman views these practices as providing "a vehicle for Jews to be free . . . not just from Jewish constraints, but from the needs and entrapments of modern life" (ibid., 437). This was camp as a dreamland in which you could be who you wish, free of the constraints of your everyday life. An added allure was that when, at the end of camp, you returned home, you could reenter the very social reality that in your camp play you had been actively escaping (Paris 2008).

At some camps the romance with Indian play lasted for decades and likely fueled resistance to embracing Jewish rituals. However, by the 1950s, many Jewish camps began to shed Indian play as central to their agenda and integrate it with more Jewish content. Sharon Feiman-Nemser, professor of Jewish education at Brandeis University, shared this memory from her years in the 1950s at Camp Maccabee, a private Jewish camp in Wisconsin.

> One night the campers were awakened by a group of male counselors dressed up as Indians (loin cloth clothes over their bathing suits, body and face paint, feathered head bands), carrying torches. The counselors led the campers to a large campfire. I remember the counselors dancing around the fire chanting what seemed at the time to be an Indian war chant. Years later I discovered one Shabbat morning in services that the chant, probably made up by Ben Aronin, the charismatic and creative Jewish program director,

> was actually the opening words of the Shabbat prayer, "Y'kum Purkan." (Feiman-Nemser 2019)

This strange mixing of Indian play with Jewish culture highlights the dream-like quality of Indian play. Campers are woken in the middle of the night to be taken by male counselors dressed up as Indians to a campfire where they witness the dancing and chants. It took Sharon decades to realize that chant was based on an Aramaic prayer and that Ben Aronin was subtly deflating the Indian idyll in favor of a tilt toward Jewish culture. That tilt was not limited to Camp Maccabee. By the 1960s, more Jewish camps began to actively embrace their Jewish identities.

> As the Indian play became less relevant . . . a camp dining hall became a *hader ochel* rather than a "longhouse," Hebrew liturgy or Labor Zionist songs replaced indigenous incantations, and campers imagined themselves into the bodies and minds of partisans or *halutzim* rather than Sioux or Apache. (Koffman 2018, 417)

By the mid-1960s, American Jewry was largely ready to tilt in another direction. Surely the Six-Day War in 1967 helped fuel that shift. Many Jewish camps were getting ready to enact a more inclusive Jewish drama. That path had been prepared for them by the rise of a new phenomenon in Jewish camp life: the denominational camps.

THE RISE OF RAMAH

Cejwin was a large single camp with separate boys and girls sides. Massad began as a single camp and within a few years established a Massad Aleph and Bet, two Hebrew immersion camps in the same region under a single management (Benor, Krasner, and Avni 2020). Ramah was different. Ramah began as a single camp in Wisconsin and, within a few years, there were Ramah camps from New England to California. All (but California) were affiliated with the Jewish Theological Seminary, the hub of the Conservative religious movement. With Ramah begins the rise of denominational Jewish camps: networks of camps affiliated with a single religious movement and united in a clear and unambiguous Jewish mission and spirit. This development would prove a turning point in the rise and spread of Shabbat at camp.

The Ramah story begins at Massad. Two of Shulsinger's close collaborators—Moshe Davis and Sylvia Ettenberg—were working at the Jewish Theological Seminary (JTS) and ready for a new camp venture. They wished to create new Jewish camps whose daily life would be guided by the principles of their Conservative movement, with a focus on serious religious practice, textual study, and progressive educational programs (Ackerman 1999; Schwartz 1987). They loved the Hebrew and cultural life of Massad and wanted to keep that alive at Ramah (which is Hebrew for "heights," as in the heights of aspiration). But they found that Hebrew alone was not a sufficient basis for all they hoped Ramah would accomplish.

They saw their opening when in 1947 a group of Chicago-based Conservative leaders purchased a campsite in Wisconsin's Northwoods. That purchase began a complex negotiation between that local Jewish community and the leaders of JTS over who would own and guide this new camp. Davis and Ettenberg were effective in convincing JTS chancellor Finkelstein to move ahead with the unorthodox arrangement. Their argument was that Ramah camps could become the Little Leagues for developing the future leadership of the Conservative movement. They could see that campers would become staff and the staff could be guided to think of their work at camp as a preparation for future Jewish leadership (Brown 1999).

JTS appointed a Jewish educator to direct the camp and Davis and Ettenberg flew in to help. Together they muddled through. By 1948 there was a second Ramah camp in Maine. By 1961 there were six Ramah residential camps across North America. That growth was due in part to the many clergy and lay leaders in the Conservative movement who were prepared to invest in Ramah and recruit campers for these new camps (Brown 1999). With the spread of Ramah came a leap in the number of campers and staff celebrating Shabbat at camp.

During the 1950s and 1960s, Ramah's leadership was ambitiously reimagining what Jewish camps could accomplish. That reimagining began in 1951 with the appointment of Louis Newman as director of the Wisconsin camp.

> Though Newman had never before run a camp, he had some highly developed theories of education to guide his new undertaking. His ideas were highly influenced by those of John Dewey, and the Progressive approach to education permeated many elements of his thinking . . . [He] was the first to attempt a synthesis of Progressive and Ramah ideology. (Schwartz 1987, 33)

Newman picked up the Progressive threads that Benderly and Schoolman had introduced and updated them for the 1950s. He found camps like Massad too authoritarian, regimented, and competitive and wanted Ramah to be more democratic, cooperative, and child-oriented. He threw out bugle blowing, social dances, and color war. He introduced camper choice for many daily activities and taught counselors to think of themselves as educators-in-the bunk. Newman gathered about him a group of JTS rabbinical students who embraced his approach and would emerge as the leaders of the Ramah movement over the next two decades. The most dynamic of these was Seymour Fox, who became the dean of these camps from the late 1950s through the late 1960s. The story of how the Ramah movement developed has been told elsewhere (Brown 1999; Fox 2000). I wish to highlight one key aspect of Fox's leadership and then focus on how Shabbat developed at the Ramah camps.

In a retrospective account told many years later, Fox describes the vision of Jewish camp that the Ramah leaders were developing in those years.

> We wanted to create an educational setting where young people would be able to discover their Judaism and learn how to live it in their daily lives. We hoped this would nurture Jews who were both deeply committed to their tradition and actively involved in American society. . . . We wanted to create a real and total society that would respond to the whole person, twenty-four hours a day, even though for no more than eight weeks at a time . . . We wanted to pay equal attention to emotional and spiritual issues and to the articulation and living out of Jewish values. (2000, 15–16)

It is impossible to miss the ambition of this vision. Even though Ramah was sponsored by the Conservative movement and supervised by the JTS faculty (on which Fox served), the educational goals are broadly aspirational. Ramah is not primarily about promoting denominational affiliation or simply supplementing what children learn in their homes and synagogues. Rather, it primarily aims to create "a real and total society" that "would respond to the whole person" and allow young people "to discover their Judaism and learn how to live it in their daily lives." Yes, these camps depended on its movement for recruitment and financial support; nevertheless, Fox was boldly stating that "they sought to accomplish what the family and the community were no longer willing or able to do" (ibid.). In short, this was to create a living Judaism that felt real and compelling to its young staff and campers.

Fox would have made my task easier had he also spelled out Ramah's vision for Shabbat at camp, but he only briefly mentions that "we enabled campers and staff alike to experience as close to a total Shabbat as possible within the public areas of camp life" (ibid., 41). From its start, Ramah incorporated a full day of Shabbat celebration and observance (by the standards set by the JTS faculty). But to what extent did these camps develop a distinctive Ramah Shabbat?

Because there is no verifiable historical record, I turn to the memories of Ramah alumni to gain a sense of how Shabbat at Ramah was experienced over time. These are the recorded memories of alumni who were invited to reflect on their years at Ramah (Cohen and Kress 2010). A few directly recall their Shabbat experiences at a variety of Ramah camps. I present these memories and two accompanying photographs to give a preliminary sense of how Shabbat developed over time at these Ramah camps.

Let's begin with Rabbi Shelly Switkin, who remembers the first summer at Ramah Wisconsin in 1947. Switkin came to camp as a ten-year old boy from Chicago. At camp his bunk counselor was a JTS rabbinical student and he was "asked to memorize the Camp Massad Hebrew dictionary" (Switkin 2010, 391). Here is how Switkin remembers Shabbat at camp.

> Shabbat eve was special with all of us wearing white. *Tefillot* at the lake were inspirational; the folk dancing after dinner was a time for everyone to participate. Shabbat day was a continuation of Friday night, with services, study, and informal recreation. Havdalah was a moving closing ceremony to the twenty-five-hour period that served as a high point of the week. (Ibid., 392)

Most striking is how similar this Ramah Shabbat was to Shabbat at Cejwin and Massad. Everyone is in white; they pray outdoors; Israeli folk dancing (and presumably Hebrew singing) follow dinner. If there is a distinctive feature, it is the brief mention of study on Shabbat day. Switkin's reference to the Massad dictionary clues us to the ways that the Massad culture had a large influence on early Ramah practice (Schwartz 1987).

A black-and-white photograph from 1950 at Ramah Wisconsin (Cohen and Kress 2010, 166b) reinforces this sense that Shabbat in the early Ramah years looked much like what we saw at Massad. It is a picture of the camp assembled, everyone dressed in white, seated at an outdoor service on the lawn near the lake. The picture was likely taken on Friday eve immediately before Shabbat began. An adolescent male stands with his back to the camera, facing the camp, and seems to be leading the service. The assembled camp is seated on rows of benches and divided into males on one side and females on the other. The girls are wearing white dresses or skirts and blouses. The boys are wearing white pants, shirts, and *kippot* (skullcaps). Those sitting in the first row are holding books that look like prayer books. Ramah is mostly adapting the Shabbat practices it inherited from earlier camps.

Rabbi Ronald Levine recalls the first Shabbat celebrated at the first full summer of Ramah in California in 1956.

> One hundred and fifty of us, probably dressed in white, sat nervously on the benches in Kikkar Tziyyon, as that area of camp had been named, waiting for Kabbalat Shabbat to begin. The candles were lit. As we held orange-colored Shiloh siddurim in our hands, the service began. At some point during the service, a regal man strode to the small wooden lectern. He was Simon Greenberg, then the vice chancellor of JTS. Pointing to the Ojai Valley to his left, he intoned, "This is the first time these hills and valleys have ever heard the sound of Jewish prayer." (Levine 2010, 365)

The Shabbat service sounds much like what Switkin described. Like at Massad, the prayer site is named for a famous location in Israel. The *siddurim* (prayer books) in use are Shiloh—a traditional, all-Hebrew prayer text. Standing out in memory is what Simon Greenberg said, a comment that fits well with Prell's (2006) claim that Ramah was situating itself as a pioneering force bringing Judaism to the far corners of North America.

At roughly that same time, a twelve-year-old from Milwaukee arrived at Ramah Wisconsin. His name was Elliot Dorff and he would become a rabbi, philosopher, and force in the Conservative movement. But Dorff remembers being wholly unprepared for what he would experience at camp. He had come to Ramah expecting "to drop out of Jewish religious life after my bar mitzvah" because he experienced his religious school as "meaningless and boring." But camp changed that.

> Even at age twelve, I was impressed by the fact that Judaism was truly a way of life for the people at camp. It was not restricted to prayer and study . . . Judaism affected every aspect of life at camp, from discussions with friends to evening activities to the sports field. I loved the singing and dancing, the Hebrew I was learning, the beauty of the traditional Sabbath observances.

> It was all so natural and unselfconscious. For the first time Judaism was a source of joy and guidance and not simply a burden I carried as a member of a minority in a Christian culture. (Dorff 2010, 335)

These memories evoke a common theme among Ramah alumni of that generation. They attended synagogue religious schools that often alienated them from Judaism. They thought of Judaism as only "prayer and study," which never engaged their imagination. Then they came to Ramah, where they encountered a Judaism that "affected every aspect of life" and served as "a source of joy and guidance." Judaism at camp was experienced as a whole package of which Shabbat was one important aspect. Dorff does not offer memories of singular spiritual moments on Shabbat; what he found beautiful were "the traditional Shabbat observances." No mention of soaring music or drama, not even of Havdalah by the lake.

Ramah borrowed culturally from Massad, but was doing different educational work. Their primary mission was to rescue bright, motivated youth like Dorff from the tedium of their local schools. That rescue came from a different educational approach.

> The intellectual stimulation grew by leaps and bounds as I became older. Indeed, the most exciting and mind-stretching conversations I had took place at camp . . . We were encouraged to ask questions that we had never dared to discuss and the leaders themselves raised issues none of us had ever thought of. (Dorff 2010, 336)

Many of those "mind-stretching conversations" took place on Shabbat. Ramah was turning Shabbat into a time of serious reflection as well as religious celebration. The leaders privileged intellectual challenge in ways that grabbed the attention of bright campers like Arthur Green, who would become a leading scholar of Hasidism and Jewish mysticism.

> The level of learning and intellectual conversations taking place at camp was utterly beyond anything I had experienced in my rather mediocre high school. It became clear to me that exploring Judaism was the most intellectually stimulating thing I could do. (Green 2020, 297)

The same summer as Dorff arrived at camp so did a rabbinical student named Neil Gillman. Like Dorff, Gillman would become a rabbi, philosopher, and force in the Conservative movement. Gillman learned an important lesson in his first week as a counselor.

> My bunk played basketball against a neighboring bunk. Using my color war experience (from other camps), I urged my campers to be more physical and use their elbows under the basket. David Mogilner took me aside and murmured, "That's not how we play basketball at Ramah." (Gillman 2010, 347)

Gillman was learning what had become the Ramah ethos: we do not play sports to win, but to give every camper a chance to shine. Gillman concludes that at Ramah, "there was a Jewish way of playing basketball, of eating and of speaking to your campers" (ibid.). While at Massad "the Jewish way" was embodied in speaking Hebrew, at Ramah what counted more was how you treated your bunkmates. Ramah was developing "Judaism as a code of private and public behavior of extraordinary ethical sensitivity" (Ackerman 1999, 15).

I doubt whether the leaders imagined that this Ramah way of playing sports would also come to define how Shabbat was observed at camp. But that is what Rabbi Matthew Futterman remembers about his first Shabbat in 1966 at Ramah in the Berkshires.

> I had my first inkling that Ramah was different and special during my first Shabbat baseball game at Ramah. When we arrived at the field, we were informed by our counselors that we would not be keeping score. Being eleven years old, that did not make sense to me. But sports on Shabbat was not about competition—it was about playing ball just for the fun of playing ball. That lesson was driven home later that day at the weekly Shabbat staff game. The counselors, who also did not keep score, made sure that every male staff member who wanted to play was given a chance no matter how skilled or unskilled at baseball. Until that day, baseball had always been about athletic prowess. That was the day that I learned that doing the right thing was more important than doing things right. (Futterman 2010, 339)

Futterman captures something distinctively Ramah—the Shabbat baseball game—a regular Shabbat event that I also remember. I came that year from Massad to be a counselor at Ramah. At Massad, we did not have organized sporting events on Shabbat and I was surprised at Ramah to be invited to play in the staff game. As Futterman recalls, its distinctive feature was its inclusive nature and lack of scoring. This game grew from the soil of Ramah culture.

The campers and counselors wanted to play ball on Shabbat afternoons and were looking for a way to do so. Someone probably came up with the idea that if they played the game in "the Jewish way," it could fit the spirit of Shabbat at Ramah. These games may never have been officially sanctioned, but they caught on and persisted for years. These Shabbat games would not likely have been played at either Cejwin or Massad.

Shabbat at camp is often described in terms of its religious rituals or intellectual conversations, but there is more to Shabbat than that. There are also the hours of free time on long summer afternoons. The creation of this game came to fill that free time in a way that distinctively reflected the Ramah culture of the 1960s. By creating and enacting these games, the staff and campers adapted Ramah culture for their purposes. The eleven-year-old Matt Futterman took note of this surprising practice and remembered it as "my first inkling that Ramah was different." Shabbat at Ramah became distinctive both by design from above and by creative fashioning from below.

DEVELOPING SHABBAT AT RAMAH

The formative years of the Ramah movement came to a close in the late 1960s, when Seymour Fox left for Hebrew University in Jerusalem and the movement was hit with a series of financial setbacks. Neither the 1970s nor the 1980s were growth decades and a general sense of retrenchment set in (Brown 1999). Yet the movement bounced back in the 1990s (Dorph 1999) and more recently has hit its stride in opening new camps and programs in both North America and Israel (Cohen and Kress 2010). As the Ramah movement has regained its vitality, important changes have been introduced to how Shabbat is celebrated at camp. The whole Ramah movement shares a single *halakhic* (religious legal) framework for observing Shabbat, but each camp has developed its own traditions for celebrating Shabbat. The camp that has recorded those changes is Ramah Wisconsin. We will use that record to describe how Shabbat celebration has developed there in more recent decades.

Rabbi David Soloff, who served for many years as the director of Ramah Wisconsin, did not believe in highlighting Shabbat as a unique aspect of the Jewish camp experience. Rather, he invested in strengthening other aspects of the camp's cultural program that impacted the Shabbat experience. A clear example is with arts at camp. By the late 1980s, Rabbi Soloff believed that

Ramah's art programs needed more investment. He brought the well-known Jewish artist David Moss to camp to be the artist-in-residence. Moss brought the arts more centrally into the cultural life of camp and introduced new artists to work with campers and staff on public art projects (Moss 1999; Soloff 1999).

A second innovation was introduced by Eli Garfinkel, a rabbinical student, who noticed that although Ramah required that teen campers hear a full Torah reading each Shabbat morning, most campers were not attentive. Wondering how to change that, Eli realized that camp handed out a traditional printed Torah text that was impenetrable for teens. Why not create an accessible guide to the Torah reading to capture campers' interest? With Rabbi Soloff's backing, Garfinkel developed a first version that underwent rewrites until camp published *Mikraot Ramah*, a camp commentary that employs humor, illustrations, and a variety of Torah commentaries to address a teen audience (Garfinkel 1999).

The third and most consequential change was introduced in 2000 when two young Torah scholars, Josh Cahan and Aryeh Bernstein, were invited to initiate a Bet Midrash program at camp. In conception, this development had little to do with Shabbat. Rather, it made available to older campers a more text-intensive, interactive, and intellectually challenging weekday Torah study option. This began as an optional alternative for older campers and attracted more and more campers for the decade that it lasted.

Along with this study option, Cahan and Bernstein initiated a Thursday night singing and study program, called *mishmar*. At mishmar

> the singing is intense, the *divrei Torah* [Torah commentaries] are simple and provocative, the atmosphere is one of deep connectedness to God and to each other. Mishmar offers an experience that many participants did not know they were seeking but has become the highlight of their week. It has fostered the kind of powerful spiritual awakening that we have long sought. (Cahan 2010, 231)

The key here is linking intense singing with a "powerful spiritual awakening." Cahan and Bernstein were among a small number of Ramah alumni who had gone after college to study at Orthodox yeshivot in Israel. There they encountered models of Torah study and spiritual engagement that they found deeply inspiring. They sought to bring that back to camp and found in Rabbi Soloff a willing backer. Mishmar began primarily with staff. At first, only a handful of campers joined, but soon many more were attracted. Most campers were unfamiliar with this style of intensive singing, but the spirituality of the experience attracted them (Bernstein 2020).

The more intensive singing led as well to the transformation of *seudah shlishit*, the third meal served late in the day on Shabbat afternoons. This had been a quiet meal. Around 2001 a small group of staff decided to remain in the dining hall after the campers left to sing the slow, spiritually rich Hebrew songs that concludes the third meal. That staff group slowly expanded. Eventually, older campers heard the singing and asked to join. By late in that decade there were almost two hundred participants singing together (Cahan 2010). By participating in either mishmar or seudah shlishit, older campers were experiencing a deeper intensity of spiritual singing. Shabbat had taken on a level of spiritual intensity that was new to Ramah.

These many changes are reflected in a striking color photograph of a 2007 Shabbat evening service at Ramah Wisconsin (Cohen and Kress 2010). Remarkably, this service takes place on the same spot that had been photographed in 1950. But much else has changed. Gone is the uniform dressing in white and in its place everyone is dressed in his or her version of Shabbat dress-up. Gone is the sitting in rows and separate sections for males and females. Now the benches are arranged in a semicircle and seating is mixed by gender and age. Gone is the male camper standing up front leading the service. Now there is a teenage girl leading the service from the middle of that semicircle. Gone are the standard Shiloh siddurim and in their place are the pamphlets the camp designed for this erev Shabbat service. There is also colorful public art spread throughout the prayer space where none was visible in 1950.

What do these changes signify? Over time, the way this Ramah camp celebrates Shabbat has undergone notable cultural shifts. Let's begin with the egalitarian practice that slowly spread through these camps after 1980 and changed the role that girls and women play in leading services. Camp Judaism had been dominated by men from the 1920s through the 1970s. It took years for Ramah and other Jewish camps to fully embrace gender equality. Nevertheless, by the early twenty-first century that equality was in place at Ramah and many other intentional Jewish camps (Prell 2007). That a teenage girl camper is leading the all-camp Shabbat service is now an accepted norm that no one at this camp any longer questions.

Equally noticeable is the move away from the standardized dress and arrangements so evident in the early years. In this 2007 photograph some people are seated, others are standing; some hold prayer books, others do not; some face the center and others look elsewhere. Prayer has become less regimented and more open to variation. As we will later see, the singing has grown more intense, there is now dancing mid-service, and most campers and staff will end the service by hugging their neighbors with wishes of "Shabbat shalom." For all the evident continuity between 1950 and 2007, Ramah has moved into the new century by embracing cultural changes that make for a more participatory and spirited Shabbat service.

THE RISE OF REFORM JEWISH CAMPS

The rise of the Conservative movement's Ramah camps was certain to catch the attention of the Reform Jewish community that faced similar calls to enter Jewish camping. For both of these Jewish denominations, the 1950s was a time of enormous expansion into the emerging suburban communities where Jews were moving in large numbers. Some of the same families who were joining suburban congregations were also open to sending their children to a regional Jewish camp affiliated with their chosen religious movement (Prell 2011).

There are notable similarities and differences in how these two denominations entered camping. One similarity is that the first concrete move to start a Reform Jewish camp came from Chicago, where in 1951 a group of lay and professional leaders identified a site to purchase in Wisconsin. But the details were different. The local Reform leaders did not turn to their rabbinic seminary for help, but to the UAHC, the umbrella organization of Reform congregations. Nor at first did they open a summer camp for children, but an "institute" to house two-week encampments for teens and young adults. Third, the leaders were not much influenced by the models of camps like Massad and Cejwin. They had not attended those camps and the Reform movement at that time was less engaged by Israel, Zionism, and Hebrew culture. They were more engaged by a quest to develop an American, English-based Jewish spirituality (J. Sarna 2006).

While Ramah benefited from the precedents established by earlier camps like Cejwin and Massad, the founders of the Union Institute in 1952 had to develop their own understanding of what they were building. It made sense to start with two-week institutes, for that is what the rabbinic leadership knew how to run. But as they moved to develop a full summer camp, they had to ask: What will a Reform Jewish camp for children look like? No one quite knew. Yet the call for new Reform Jewish camps quickly spread. By 1958 there were five UAHC camps. All over the country clergy and lay leaders developed these new camps in conjunction with the movement and saw a tremendous potential to offer their youth this powerful source of Jewish pride and learning as Reform Jews (Lorge and Zola 2006a).

Celebrating Shabbat was a key element of these camps. In their volume on the rise of Reform Jewish camps, Lorge and Zola (2006b) provide black-and-white photos of celebrating Shabbat in the early years of the Union Institute. In the first from 1960, campers and staff are lighting Sabbath candles (2006b, 117). Two teenage girls, dressed in white tops, are reaching up to light the candles in front of the ark in the camp's outdoor chapel. Flanking them on each side is a line of teen boys and girls watching their lighting. A second photo from the early 1960s (ibid., 118) is of a larger gathering of campers and staff arrayed in a semicircle in front of the "Big House" welcoming the Sabbath. A mix-aged group of campers, dressed up, are holding hands and facing forward toward the camera. A third photo from the mid-1960s (ibid., 123) is an indoor shot of camp director Irv Kaplan leading a Shabbat song session on a Friday night. Kaplan is standing while the teen campers are seated around him. All are dressed for Shabbat. Kaplan is clapping his hands, as are all the campers. The feel is warmer and more dynamic with campers smiling widely as they clap and sing.

Judah Cohen provides the background to these photos and a more in-depth portrait of how celebrating Shabbat developed at the Union Institute circa 1960.

> Friday evening would begin as the freshly showered and dressed campers would gather to greet the Sabbath, singing songs specifically for Friday night. A choir of campers joined the song leader in leading the music of the Kabbalat Shabbat service, which ended with the blessings over the wine and bread to indicate the start of the Friday evening meal. After dinner, there would be a much longer and more enthusiastic song session, occasionally including songs led by and identified with specific members of the staff. Israeli dancing would follow . . . A snack, more song leading, and bedtime concluded the evening. (Cohen 2006, 187)

The order of the celebration follows practices at the earlier camps. What is different is the central role played by the song leader, who leads both the Kabbalat Shabbat service and the song session that follows dinner. Cohen (2006) explains the emergence of this key figure.

The rabbinic founders of the Union Institute faced two key problems in trying to develop a Shabbat celebration that would work for their camp. The first was that their youth had grown up in Classic Reform congregations where the music was formal and sung by the cantor and choir. That synagogue-based music was not going to work well at camp. Second, their youth knew very little Hebrew and had little familiarity with Hebrew songs. Yet, most of the other intentional Jewish camps relied on folk-like Hebrew songs as the basis of their communal singing repertoire. The founders knew that successful ritual relied on accessible music and vibrant communal singing. Their camp would have to develop that vibrant communal singing to ignite their Shabbat celebration.

They found an initial spark plug in William Sharlin. A classically trained cantor, Sharlin was willing to do what few other cantors would: pick up a cheap guitar, bring it to camp, and lead teens in folk singing. There is a picture (ibid., 120) of Sharlin leading singing in 1953. He is working a room of youth playing his guitar and singing as they sit on benches, arm in arm, singing along. They are singing "silly" songs like "Blue-Tail Fly" along with simple Hebrew songs like "Bim Bam/Shabbat Shalom" and brotherhood songs like "We're in the Same Boat, Brother" (ibid., 182). The response was electrifying. As one future song leader recalled, "People used to say, 'The music is the highlight of camp. Wait until you sing with Bill Sharlin' . . . Sharlin wanted us to sing well, to have a good time, to be a vehicle for Jewish expression" (ibid., 183).

Sharlin introduced the guitar, the mix of songs, and the energy of the song leader. As a cantor and song leader, Sharlin began the tradition of the song leader leading both song sessions and services, building a connection between singing in the dining hall and the chapel. That was perhaps the biggest break from common Reform practice. Services at camp became a place for everyone to sing along rather than listening to the cantor and choir sing (ibid.). Communal singing led by a song leader emerged as a signature camp practice. Campers and staff sang every day, and on Shabbat they enjoyed the most intense song session of the week. Through the 1950s, the mix of songs that Sharlin introduced held, with new songs being introduced each summer.

With the 1960s came three major changes in song leading. First was the arrival in 1961 of Shmulik "Sam" Alpert, the first Israeli song leader. Alpert transformed the mix by adding far more Hebrew songs from the contemporary

Israeli songbook. Second, Irv Kaplan, who was appointed director in 1963, saw a need for multiple song leaders at camp and empowered bunk counselors with the right musical skills to be the song leader for their unit at camp. Third, with the wider rise of American folk music, more staff and campers brought guitars to camp and soon song leaders were offering *chugim* (electives) in folk singing. Camp was now alive with the sound of folk music.

Irv Kaplan was a key figure in developing the Jewish culture of this Reform camp. In his six years as director he introduced many innovations. He expanded the programs for campers, created the camp's first counselor-in-training program, built new buildings, and initiated an immersive Hebrew language program for teens (Lorge and Zola 2006a). He also invigorated the Shabbat celebration on Friday evenings. At the erev Shabbat song session, he would take over.

> Toward the end of the evening, the campers would call individual counselors up to lead songs identified specifically with them . . . Finally, after repeated rhythmic shouts of "We want Irv," the camp director would finish up with a rousing and nearly bombastic version of "*Chiri-Bim*." Working without a guitar, he would jump on tables and run in and out of doors to create "not song as much as energy" and "a passion of celebrating Judaism." Of all the musical experiences at camp, Friday night thus became the event seen as the most "spiritual" and exciting of the camp experience. (Cohen 2006, 192)

The move from Sharlin to Kaplan is fascinating. As charismatic as he was, Sharlin was focused on the music and singing. He was not there to arouse passion or place himself at the center of the action. Kaplan was not so much a song leader as a passion builder. He broke the restraints that Sharlin had established and got up on the tables to arouse passion for celebrating Shabbat. The campers loved his energy and found his style exciting and spiritually engaging. Kaplan set in motion a tension that will accompany us throughout this study of Shabbat at camp. The break from restraint jolts campers and staff out of their routine and arouses them to the passion that makes Shabbat at camp truly memorable. Yet passion and charisma wear down over time. Camps need a flexible structure that engages campers without overwhelming them. Irv Kaplan—much like Seymour Fox at Ramah—was a man for his times. These charismatic male leaders were crucial for making denominational Jewish camps a significant force in American Judaism. But their intensity could not be sustained over time (Reimer 2010).

DEVELOPING SHABBAT AT URJ CAMPS

Irv Kaplan announced in 1968 that he would be leaving camp to make aliyah to Israel. In 1970 a young new director, Jerry Kaye, was appointed to run this camp that would become known as OSRUI (Olin-Sang-Ruby Union Institute). Kaye became the longest-serving camp director in the history of Reform Jewish camping (which in 2003 changed its name and became known as the URJ camps). Kaye made a significant contribution to celebrating Shabbat at camp when in 1972 he invited a young songwriter, Debbie Friedman, to be a song leader at camp.

Friedman was a twenty-one-year-old songwriter who had been composing original folk melodies to Jewish prayers as part of a group of young song leaders in the Reform movement. Before coming to camp, she had "embarked upon a complete setting for the Friday evening service . . . titled 'Sing Unto God'" (Cohen 2006, 197). At camp her goal was to prepare the teen campers to perform this service.

> Friedman led most of the service, remaining front and center throughout the ritual; nearly every prayer had a new musical setting, shattering the traditional model of services at camp; and at least two of Friedman's pieces followed a radical new format, combining English and Hebrew within the same composition. It was an exciting and revolutionary introduction that would change the face of camp worship for years to come. (Ibid., 198–99)

Never before had a song leader done anything like what Friedman did. From Bill Sharlin on, the music that campers sang had been imported from sources outside of camp. (That was usually true as well at Cejwin, Massad, and Ramah.) Here was a twenty-one-year-old local song leader with the courage and drive to compose original music for a full service performed at camp. With the subsequent release of her album *Sing Unto God*, that music quickly spread to the other Reform camps and beyond. Debbie became a model for other young song leaders to compose their own melodies for traditional prayers and songs. She inspired younger song leaders, like Jeff Klepper and Rob Weinberg, to bring their own "sense of meaning to a particular text" (ibid.). Soon their songs were being sung at camp alongside those composed by Friedman and other musicians.

Why did this matter so deeply to Reform Jewish camps? Debbie Friedman and those who followed were homegrown composers. Their songs were the fruit of this culture.

> First, they indicated the song leader's emergence within the Reform movement as a person who not only transmitted musical culture, but also created it. Second, they suggested that the musical values fostered at OSRUI had to some extent solidified into a unique, recognizable, and idiomatic style. Most importantly . . . this style was maturing into an important indicator of identity within the Reform Jewish youth culture—the voice of an empowered and idealistic young population. (Cohen 2006)

Debbie Friedman and her peers were taking Reform Jewish youth into new musical and spiritual territory. Friedman's songs grew more personal and soon her followers were singing about the role of women in Judaism, the quest for bodily and spiritual health, and the need for healing (Lipstadt 2014). The leaders of Reform camps—Jerry Kaye and others—grasped the significance of this breakthrough and created the conditions for Jewish song leading to flourish by training successive generations of song leaders.

What does one need to learn to become a song leader? It begins with the compendium of the most popular Jewish songs sung at camp. That repertoire is what the apprentice song leaders practice through group sessions. The songs fall into two general categories: music for religious rituals and for song sessions. The former consists of settings for liturgical texts while the latter is more varied. The teens learn to play both types. They are not learning to become performers but to lead their peers in singing. They are taught to become aware of their audience, draw them in, and teach their peers to sing with feeling and comprehension.

How did this song leading tradition help shape Shabbat celebration at camp? Cohen (2008) returned to OSRUI to study Shabbat Shirah, the Friday evening all-camp song session. This song session extends back to the early days of the camp. There were years when it took place in the dining hall and Irv Kaplan led everyone in a frenzied session. That frenzied style continued through the

1970s. By the 1980s concerns grew that "the dancing sometimes went beyond the spirt of the event" and Shabbat Shirah was redesigned. The session was moved out of the dining hall into a nearby hall where campers sat in a dimly lit space. Only Hebrew songs in the Shabbat spirit were led by the song leaders. Even within this tight space, "campers came to see the event as an almost magical time" (ibid., 328).

There is far more to celebrating Shabbat at Reform Jewish camps than Shabbat song sessions. Yet Cohen correctly observes that the URJ camps have invested most heavily in their song leading capacities. This is a very different investment than has been made at Ramah and, as a result, Shabbat celebration looks and sounds quite different in these settings. The song leader at Reform camps is the primary mediator between the campers who have little Hebrew knowledge and the Hebrew-rich traditions that camp culture draws upon. This musical repertoire moves fluidly back and forth between Hebrew and English and allows English speakers to infuse their songs with Hebrew terms drawn directly from traditional sources. Doing so in song allows this back and forth to be embedded in their musical memories and become a portable camp tradition that Reform youth can draw upon whenever they gather together for celebration.

THE 2000S: THE RISE OF THE FIELD OF JEWISH CAMPS

For all their differences, the denominational camps during the second half of the twentieth century became the main shapers of Shabbat at camp. They, along with Zionist camps, kept investing in how Shabbat would be observed and celebrated at Jewish summer camps. At the same time, Shabbat at camp also spread to many other Jewish residential camps. Why that spread happened is the final question for this chapter.

Had social scientists surveyed Jewish camps around 1990—a task that no one actually undertook—they would have found a puzzling picture. On the one hand, there was a lot of continuity. Many of the camps that began as charitable camps were now functioning as communal camps and serving mostly Jewish children in need of financial aid. The Zionist camps were still around, though small and divided by movement. Private Jewish camps had grown after World War II and were still serving the more affluent Jewish families. The denominational camps had expanded and spread to new locations, with the Reform camps growing more steadily (Sales and Saxe 2004). On the other hand, there was no actual *field* of Jewish camping: no organization that oversaw the growth of camps, no unifying themes that cut across the camps, no shared research about camp life, and very little professional development. The individual camps or clusters of camps had each maintained themselves—and in some cases, grown—but the *field* had never developed.

That was the puzzle that struck a pair of young philanthropists—Rob and Elisa Spungen Bildner—when in the late 1990s they were deciding to create a foundation to support "Jewish continuity." They saw their philanthropic peers investing in diverse areas of Jewish education, but Jewish camps seemed invisible to that philanthropic community. To fill that gap, the Bildners in 1998 began a public foundation called the Foundation for Jewish Camping (FJC). Its mission was to enhance nonprofit Jewish camps in North America. They sought to convince the larger philanthropic community that Jewish camps were providing Jewish youth with powerful Jewish experiences and needed their support to grow, improve, and reach more Jewish youth (Reimer 2011).

Another Jewish foundation, AVI CHAI, was open to exploring an investment in Jewish camps. First, however, they needed basic information. How many Jewish camps were there? How many Jewish campers did they serve? How "Jewish" were these diverse camps? How open were they to Jewish enrichment? AVI CHAI turned to the Cohen Center at Brandeis University in 2000 to conduct a survey of Jewish residential camps in the United States. This was the first comprehensive survey of Jewish residential camps in many years and the first social scientific survey of how "Jewish" those camps were.

Sales and Saxe (2004) reported interesting findings. First, in terms of numbers, they found there were 191 residential American Jewish camps (not including ultra-Orthodox ones). Of these, 100 were nonprofit and 91 were for-profit camps. Jewish camps were still heavily concentrated in the Northeast, with a second concentration in the Midwest and sprinklings in the South and West. These camps served 83,000 Jewish children and employed 18,000 Jewish adults. Two-fifths of the campers attended private camps while three-fifths attended nonprofit camps. (These numbers have been updated by the FJC. By 2018, there were 81,146 campers attending 166 nonprofit residential Jewish camps throughout North America [FJC Overnight Camp Census 2018]. We do not know the comparable numbers for the private camps.)

We had seen that during the 1930s and 1940s most communal and private

Jewish camps had little investment in Jewish practices. That had changed by 2000. The most visible change came in relation to Shabbat at camp. This study found:

1. All the private Orthodox and nonprofit denominational camps reported (as expected) celebrating Shabbat on Friday nights (defined as lighting Shabbat candles, serving a special meal, and conducting a religious service) and on Saturday (defined as conducting a morning service and concluding with Havdalah).
2. Almost all the communal camps reported that same level of Shabbat celebration.
3. The private non-Orthodox camps reported much lower levels of Shabbat celebration. Yet, 65 percent reported that they lit Shabbat candles and 49 percent that they served a special meal on Friday evenings (Sales and Saxe 2004, 38).

These numbers reflect what camp officials reported to the Cohen Center. While there is no way of knowing exactly what those reports mean in terms of actual practices, one thing is clear: by 2000 most of these camps were celebrating Shabbat in their own way as part of how they defined themselves as Jewish camps. For the communal camps, that represented a dramatic shift from where they had once stood. While the shift was most pronounced in celebrating Shabbat, it extended as well to other Jewish markers, such as serving kosher food, flying the Israeli flag, and using Hebrew names for places at camp (Sales and Saxe 2004, 40).

Future historians will hopefully chart more fully how nonprofit Jewish camps came to adopt more Jewish practices during the last decades of the twentieth century. Yet I can point to three clear contributors. First, the historic mission of providing "fresh air" to poor Jewish immigrant children had mostly run its course by the 1960s. Jewish camps that had been founded to serve the children of immigrants needed to find a new mission. After the Six-Day War in 1967, they became increasingly attracted to providing Jewish culture as a point of pride for the campers and staff (Woocher 1986). Shabbat became a time to highlight those cultural features.

Second, whereas early in the twentieth century, Jewish children were excluded from attending many American camps, that exclusion had largely ended by the 1960s. Jews were increasingly welcomed in the growing market of summer programs for youth. That meant that Jewish camps had to provide parents with a positive rationale for choosing one of these camps.

As more parents became concerned that their children were not getting all they could from the synagogue schools in which the children were enrolled, they looked to Jewish camps to provide enriching, immersive Jewish experiences like Shabbat at camp. Camp leaders sensed that need and responded with enriched Jewish programming (Reisman 1990; Rothenberg 2016).

Third, by the late 1990s, committed American Jews—much like their Christian and Muslim neighbors—were open to "a new spirituality of seeking" and "returning to ritual observance by making it a locus of personal meaning" (Cohen and Eisen 2000, 8). While few American Jews outside the Orthodox community were regularly observing Shabbat, they were seeking new ways to experience the joys of Jewish celebration. Synagogues were changing their Shabbat services to meet this new spiritual openness (Wertheimer 2018) and camp leaders likely also felt a push to enliven Shabbat celebrations and intensify the singing and movement within their services.

FJC became a partner in helping Jewish camps strengthen their Jewish offerings. They invested heavily in professional development for camp staff; convened the leaders of the field to a Leadership Assembly; and helped camps gather and share data on their campers, staff, and parents. Their consistent message was that by coming together as a field, Jewish camps could not only help one another but also present themselves to the larger North American community as an essential player in providing thousands of Jewish youth with joyous Jewish experiences. As part of that mission, celebrating a lively Shabbat became a way to showcase the camp's commitment to that Jewish vitality.

CONCLUSION

Jewish residential camps in North America have come a long way since their founding in the early twentieth century. What began as a way to get Jewish youth out of teeming urban life during hot summer months became a context for the transmission of American Jewish life. Wishing to provide their youth with more intensive Jewish experiences, these camps have seized on Shabbat as a most accessible way to celebrate being Jewish together. That choice would have deeply surprised and even disturbed many earlier Jewish camp leaders. But as ideologies like Yiddishism and Communism have fallen away and practices like Indian play have lost their appeal, the celebration of Shabbat has emerged as the Jewish symbolic practice that allows campers and staff a weekly opportunity to express their Jewishness and explore the spiritual possibilities that a day of rest offers in an age of hyperactivity.

3 / SHABBAT AT THREE JEWISH CAMPS

SHABBAT AT CAMP has a long evolving history that forms the backdrop to how Jewish camps today celebrate the Sabbath. To tell that contemporary story, I have chosen to focus not on a single camp, but to offer a portrait of Shabbat at three different Jewish residential camps: URJ Eisner Camp, Camp Ramah of Wisconsin, and Camp Yavneh. I want readers to get a vivid sense of what these camps share in common and how each puts its own stamp on Shabbat celebration. Campers, staff, and alumni treasure the particularities of the Shabbat celebrated at their camp, but often lack a comparative sense of how what they experience overlaps with and differs from what their peers at other Jewish camps experience. That is what a comparative lens can provide.

One might ask: Aren't all these Jewish camps essentially aiming for the same goal of showing campers and staff that celebrating Shabbat can be meaningful and enjoyable?

The answer is clearly yes; at the same time, camps—like families—enact a particular version of Judaism and highlight that version through how they celebrate Shabbat. Our goal is to show both the shared goal and the particular ways that each camp arrives at that shared goal.

Before introducing these three camps, I will explain how I chose them and the research methodology for studying their celebration of Shabbat.

CHOOSING THREE CAMPS TO STUDY

When starting this research, I was looking to study American Jewish nonprofit residential camps where campers and staff participate in robust but varied communal celebrations of Shabbat. To chooses the three sites, I developed three criteria. First was religious variation. I wondered how different religious stances would play out in celebrating Shabbat at camp. Second was stable sponsorship and leadership so that the Shabbat practices I would be observing would have been developing over a long time period. Third was cooperative leadership.

From my earlier study of Jewish camps (Reimer 2012), I had learned how important it is for the camp director to be a partner in the research, sharing an interest in the topic and opening the doors of the camp. Without that cooperation, it is very hard to do this kind of ethnographic research.

Looking for religious variation, I could see from the history of Jewish camps that selecting a URJ and a Ramah camp would make a great deal of sense. These were the two large denominational networks of camps that for decades had been celebrating Shabbat in their distinctive ways. For a third site I might have chosen an Orthodox camp, but decided to choose Yavneh for these reasons. Yavneh is one of many independent nondenominational Jewish camps. Yet Yavneh has a substantial Orthodox population and a long history of robust Shabbat celebration. Yavneh combined a nondenominational governance with a strong Orthodox presence. It offered a different religious stance than URJ or Ramah but one they have developed over time without denominational guidelines. That difference seemed important to capture.

To choose among the URJ and Ramah camps, I employed my second and third criteria. I was looking for veteran camps that had stable leadership where I could rely on current leaders to be partners in this research. When the directors of URJ Eisner and Ramah Wisconsin, two veteran camps, agreed to partner in this research, I was pleased to choose their camps as sites for this ethnographic portrait.

These three camps are not representative of the wide range of residential Jewish camps. I am not aiming for a representative picture (if such even exists). I want to capture the richness of these three camps and show how their celebration of Shabbat reflects the Judaism that each camp enacts. I will highlight both what the camps share in common and how they vary in the details of their celebration.

RESEARCH METHODS

This research has been conducted at three American Jewish residential camps where campers would be participating in robust but varied communal Shabbat celebrations. The research was conducted at Eisner and Ramah during the summers of 2015–2018 and at Yavneh from 2016–2018. I observed at Eisner and Ramah for four consecutive summers and at Yavneh for three summers.

The same research methodology was employed at all camps. I contacted the respective camp directors during the spring, explained my research plan, and received their permission to be at camp for a particular Shabbat. I varied the times during the summer that I visited each camp so that I would see Shabbat enacted at different points of the summer season. The visits to Ramah Wisconsin began on Thursday evening and extended to Sunday morning. The visits to Eisner and Yavneh began early Friday afternoon and extended to Sunday morning. Each visit focused on observing a particular division or unit. On Fridays I was introduced to the division or unit head, who introduced me to the counselors. I attached myself to the division and followed it from Friday afternoon through Shabbat (though I did not sleep in the bunk). I observed all the major activities of Shabbat and freely asked questions of the counselors and division head as we moved through.

In 2015 I devoted my visits to Eisner and Ramah to observing their youngest campers and how those campers as a group were introduced to Shabbat celebration at each camp. From 2016 to 2018 at all three camps I focused my attention on the older campers with particular attention to the oldest campers who had special roles in the Shabbat celebration. In 2018, I extended my visit to Eisner by several days so I could observe the longer preparations for Shabbat in both younger and older units and speak with the faculty who were preparing the campers involved.

The decision not to interview individual campers as part of this research is consequential. I am relying on two main sources of data: my participant observations at each camp and my discussions with the staff of each camp. I can carefully compare the way Shabbat is celebrated at these three camps and present the ways the staff understand the rationale for these varying practices. I can report on how campers as a group participate in each aspect of the Shabbat celebration and what I believe they learn from their participation; however, I cannot report on how individual campers make sense of those celebrations. That is a limitation of this research. I will not be drawing any conclusions about the experience of individual campers.

During Shabbat at each camp, when I was not able to take written notes, I took mental notes and recorded those in a recorder on Saturday night and Sunday morning. I transcribed those recorded notes the week after getting home. On the basis of those notes, I interviewed each of the camp directors and other senior staff by phone during the winter months to get greater historical context, hear their views on how Shabbat was celebrated, and understand their rationale for their camp's practices. I checked their historical accounts against the available literature and relied on their views of Shabbat to represent the official policy and educational thinking of the camp leadership. I tried in each camp to understand the Shabbat practices I was observing in the context of an evolving camp culture in which how Shabbat is celebrated changes over time.

In writing about each camp, I call the leaders and senior staff of the camp by the name that they are called at camp. At Ramah Wisconsin, the former director is called "Rabbi Soloff" and I follow that practice. But at both Eisner and Yavneh, the camp directors are called by their first names and I follow that practice.

There is much to tell about any given camp. I will select what is most relevant for understanding how Shabbat is celebrated and introduce each camp by answering these questions.

1. Who are the leaders who have directed this camp over recent decades?
2. What is the Jewish mission that has guided these leaders?
3. Who are the educational staff responsible for implementing Shabbat?
4. Who are the campers who celebrate Shabbat at camp?

URJ EISNER CAMP

When the Reform movement was developing its first camps, it seemed essential to open a camp to serve the greater New York area where so many Jews lived. In 1958 the Camp Institute for Living Judaism purchased a property in Great Barrington at the center of the Berkshires in Western Massachusetts. The Berkshires is a popular destination for New Yorkers and this site was a historic estate. The camp was named the UAHC Joseph Eisner Camp for Living Judaism and opened its doors in 1958 to serve 120 campers (Eisner website).

Rabbi Leonard Zion, the first director, did not have to invent Reform Jewish camping. Eisner was the fifth camp to be affiliated with the UAHC, the umbrella organization that in 2003 would change its name to the Union for Reform Judaism (URJ). Eisner benefited from the pioneering work being done at the Union Institute and its sister camps in California, Indiana, and Pennsylvania. Over time, Eisner developed a strong following in the Reform Jewish community of Long Island. The camp grew, went through a number of directors, and took its place among the growing number of Reform camps.

But Eisner did not gain a reputation for being among the strongest Reform camps, and by the late 1980s the camp was in financial trouble. Movement leaders decided to bring in a new director to turn the camp around. David Friedman came in 1990 with a mandate for change. In his nine years as director, David successfully increased camper enrollment, reorganized and revitalized the Jewish programs, and engaged donors to fund needed new facilities at camp (Grinberg 2020). But David was not successful in turning around camp culture, which had grown wild and unruly. For that task movement leaders turned to Louis Bordman (Bordman 2008).

Louis was an odd choice. He had never attended camp as a child or worked at a camp before Eisner. Louis was a successful synagogue youth educator when in 1995 he was brought in as the associate director with the specific charge to create a more disciplined camp. For three years Louis worked under David's leadership to tighten the discipline and get campers and staff more in line with camp regulations. But when a new directorship opened, Louis left Eisner to become the inaugural director of the newly purchased Reform camp Crane Lake. When a year later David Friedman left Eisner, Louis was asked to return, where he would remain as senior director through 2018. As director, Louis built Eisner into a larger and more developed camp. He expanded the camp's reach to congregations in New England and grew its camper population. To meet that growth, camp hired more staff. Louis undertook a massive development campaign to build new facilities. Eisner became a highly regarded camp with a growing population and a developing physical plant to support its more diversified camp program (Lev 2008).

When Louis describes his early years as director, he focuses on how driven and unyielding he was. He was determined to turn this camp around and believed he needed to be a strict disciplinarian to accomplish that goal. With time he came to realize that this toughness was not enough and his staff were looking to him to be more than their boss. Most had grown up at Eisner and, in his words, "I was almost like a rabbi and they were my constituency." He wished to develop a different relationship with the younger staff and decided to develop the Olim Fellowship, a yearlong program to educate them to the Jewish purposes of camp. This was a bold move, for few camps meet year-round with their junior staff. Louis led the fellowship and developed a more personal relationship with younger staff (Bordman 2008).

In this quest, Louis worked with the Olim Fellows in 2005 and 2006 to craft a mission statement for Eisner. He sought a camp mission that reflected what the Eisner experience meant to these young staff members. When the mission statement was complete, it was widely distributed. Here is that statement as it appears on the camp website.

HINEINI—HERE I AM

. . . I am here to strengthen my own self-esteem and that of everyone in the camp community.

. . . I am here to strengthen my own Jewish identity and spirituality and that of everyone in the camp community.

. . . I am here to strengthen my connection to the Eisner community and the Jewish community and to help everyone around me to do the same.

. . . I am here to do as much as I can, in the time that I have, in the place that I am, and to inspire others to join me in this holy work.

For it is written: "*Lo alecha hamlacha ligmor, v'lo ata ben horin, l'heebatel mimena*."

"You are not required to complete the work, nor are you free to ignore it."
Pirke Avot 2:16

As Wendy Grinberg writes in her dissertation on Jewish education at Eisner, "The mission is more of a pledge, emphasizing the mission of each member of the community than the organization of camp" (2020). The mission places strengthening one's own self-esteem, Jewish identity, and spirituality as core to the Eisner experience. What struck me in observing at Eisner was how often I would see campers and staff wearing Hineini sweatshirts, singing a Hineini camp song, and engaging in group discussions about the values of Hineini. Something in the personal nature of "Here I am" resonates for this camp community (Tecotsky 2017).

Eisner's Jewish Mission

Eisner is deeply embedded in the Reform movement and its Judaism is guided by the tenets and practices of that movement. Yet, Eisner has developed a particular Jewish mission that gives shape and color to the camp's religious practices. To understand how Shabbat is celebrated at Eisner, one needs to see that the Eisner mission has created these special emphases for the camp's Jewish programs:

1. A values orientation
2. Quest for spirituality
3. Increasing camper participation

All Reform camps live their Judaism by sponsoring prayer and song sessions, celebrating Shabbat, using Hebrew names and terms, and teaching campers to live their Jewish values. But not all are as devoted as Eisner is to Jewish teaching and learning. Not all hire staff to supervise the quality of daily *limud* (learning) sessions, invite area clergy and educators to be regular faculty for the camp, and prepare campers to take an active role in leading aspects of the camp-wide Shabbat tefilla (Grinberg 2020).

Jewish learning at Eisner is centered on values. There is little focus on teaching Jewish literacy or history. Campers will not come away from summers at Eisner knowing the books of the Bible, the borders of the Land of Israel, or traditional Jewish commentaries. They will discuss and practice *middot* (Jewish ethical values) and consider their application to life at camp and beyond. On Shabbat they will reflect on camp as a Jewish community and how campers and counselors can live up to the Jewish values that animate this camp community. Shabbat at Eisner is a time for campers to articulate those key values and, in the spirit of Hineini, learn to apply Jewish values to shaping their lives.

Along with a strong values orientation, creating a Jewish spiritual path is another key emphasis. In recent years, Louis made a connection to the Institute for Jewish Spirituality and used their expertise to bring more mindfulness to staff and campers. Eisner is pursuing a path that joins middot to the values of spiritual centeredness and calm. But above all, spirituality at camp is tied to Jewish music. They sing each day from the Reform Jewish repertoire, often moving to the music. Most evenings each unit at camp has its own Ma'ariv (evening) service, led by song leaders. When there is a pause for spiritual reflection, there is communal singing to carry the moment. Learning to sing these songs is the most available path to Jewish spirituality at Eisner.

Eisner invests in its song leaders, who are key figures in fostering camp spirituality. The head song leader supervises the many younger song leaders who are attached to particular units. They operate as a team and make key decisions about the music they will play at the various services. On Shabbat, the services are led by the head song leader and a tefilla coordinator, and the tefilla is carried by the amplified music and voices joined in song. In a camp where Hebrew skills are mixed, the reliance on amplified music, communal singing, and accompanying movement allows campers to join the spiritual action even when their Hebrew literacy is limited.

At the same time, Eisner places an unusual emphasis on camper participation in leading Shabbat services. Campers are asked each summer to contribute in some way to leading the camp-wide Shabbat service. That is a strong ask, especially for younger campers, and requires a lot of staff input to work well. But it is the Eisner way of communicating a key message: everyone can have a Jewish voice and contribute to making tefilla the voice of the whole community.

Staff and Campers at Eisner

During the years of this study while Louis Bordman served as the senior director at Eisner, there was a team of directors who helped run this camp. In 2017, that team included James Gelsey, the director of operations; Laura Gurvis, the associate director; and Liz Hirsch, the assistant director. Rabbi Liz also served as camp rabbi and the tefilla coordinator. Wendy Grinberg served as the director of Jewish education. When Louis retired after the 2018 season, James Gelsey succeeded him as the senior director.

Eisner has seven units (divisions) of campers and each unit is led by a pair of unit heads. These heads are responsible for supervising the cabin counselors, most of whom grew up as Eisner campers and went through the Machon year, training as CITs (counselors-in-training). The unit heads are supervised by the team of directors and members of the camp care team. Eisner also has an extensive array of specialties, including outdoor adventures, athletics, arts, and aquatics. Eisner's Israeli *shlichim* (emissaries) serve as these specialty staff and throughout camp.

Eisner is our largest camp. In 2018, it had 576 campers attending session one and 539 in session two for a total of 850 different campers. Campers range in age from entering second to entering tenth grade. The vast majority of Eisner campers are recruited from Reform temples in New York, Connecticut, and Massachusetts, where they receive their Jewish education. Most are from white, Jewish upper-middle-class families and attend for one session. Session one runs for four weeks and session two for three weeks. The oldest campers almost all attend for the whole summer and many choose to go on NFTY in Israel, the Reform movement's summer experience for those entering eleventh grade. Eisner has worked hard to diversify its Jewish camper population and offers scholarships for families in need. The camp has adopted an "Audacious Hospitality" policy that welcomes "everyone in our community from LGBTQ to children with single, same-sex, or interfaith parents to children of color . . . We are committed to bringing the transformative power of Jewish camp to every child and family who come through our gates" (Eisner website).

CAMP RAMAH IN WISCONSIN

As the first Ramah camp, Ramah Wisconsin's early history has been told before (Schwartz 1987; Brown 1999). Highlights of that history are retold in chapter 2. To understand this camp in its current state, I will pick up that story in 1974, the year that camp director, Rabbi Burt Cohen, was tapped to become the national Ramah director and the camp's board turned to the Jewish Theological Seminary for a replacement. Soon it was announced that Rabbi David Soloff would become the new camp director as of May 1975.

David Soloff grew up attending Ramah in Connecticut and later worked for Ramah in the Berkshires. During college he decided to become a Conservative rabbi, and while he was studying at JTS he was preparing to become a camp director. Ramah Wisconsin was his first opportunity. Moving to Chicago, he realized he knew little about the Midwestern Jewish community and looked to a few influential congregational rabbis to mentor him in how to develop relationships with the Conservative rabbis and congregations whose youth were the potential campers and counselors for Camp Ramah (Soloff 2008).

The 1970s and 1980s were financially difficult decades for Ramah and there were leaders in the movement who were calling for updating the original assumptions of the Ramah movement. Some questioned the primacy of Hebrew as a spoken language at camp. Others thought that sticking with the eight-week summer schedule was a mistake, and that Ramah—like the Reform camps—should shift to two four-week sessions (Brown 1999). Rabbi Soloff opposed those changes.

In his view, this Ramah played a crucial role within the ecology of Midwestern Conservative Judaism. What these campers needed was a long-term immersion experience in a vibrant Jewish life, where they would live in a Jewish community, take daily classes, hear Hebrew spoken, celebrate a full day of Shabbat, and make lifelong camp friends. He did not want to break the summer up into sessions, though he did eventually support a shorter session for younger campers. He was determined to develop a network of lay leaders and supporters who would buy into this traditional Ramah vision and support it financially (Soloff 2008).

Rabbi Soloff was a Ramah traditionalist who would affirm the core purpose and values that Seymour Fox (2000) articulated. At the same time, he believed that camp practices needed to be evaluated and updated each decade. In the 1980s when Ramah was facing headwinds of change from the feminist movement and its nonegalitarian practices in camp prayer were questioned, Rabbi Soloff looked to JTS for halakhic guidance. When halakhic permission was granted, he began to move this camp toward a more egalitarian practice. Soon women and girls were leading tefilla and reading Torah. Some years later, women scholars were serving as scholars-in-residence, bringing to staff and campers a deeper engagement with Jewish thought (Soloff 2020).

Of the many new program initiatives that Rabbi Soloff sponsored, let me cite two most relevant to Shabbat at camp. During the 1990s Dr. Simcha Leibovich came to camp to work on the camp's informal educational programs. After a while, Simcha made the case that most Ramah counselors had no training in educational programming and were running routine, unstimulating sessions for campers. When Simcha proposed developing a *mercaz* (center) at camp dedicated to providing counselors with training and guidance, Rabbi Soloff backed his proposal (Leibovich 2009). That mercaz would develop into the prime location where staff prepare their programming for campers on Shabbat.

Perhaps the boldest proposal for change came from Josh Cahan, a veteran Ramah staff member. As cited in chapter 2, Josh and Aryeh Bernstein proposed to bring the spirit of yeshiva learning to camp in the form of a *beit midrash* (Torah study) for older campers. Even though nothing like this had been tried at Ramah, Rabbi Soloff could see a need for innovative Torah study and backed the plan. What no one anticipated was how this beit midrash would also impact Shabbat at camp. Rabbi Soloff was not seeking to change Shabbat at camp, but the ruach, or spiritedness, that emanated from this style of Torah study spilled over into Shabbat singing. Soon Ramah staff and campers were singing intensely at seudah shlishit, the third meal on Shabbat (Cahan 2010). The beit midrash lasted through 2009.

In his long tenure as camp director, Rabbi Soloff shaped much of the culture of this camp. In planning for change, he would consult with key Conservative rabbis from around the Midwest and work closely with the camp's board to fashion long-term plans for the camp's development. He viewed himself as a facilitator, rather than an originator, of the many changes that took place at Ramah Wisconsin during his tenure (Reimer 2012). One colleague called Rabbi Soloff "a conservative radical," by which she meant that he was slow and deliberate about initiating change, but radical in his determination to see those changes through to the end.

By 2009, Rabbi Soloff had served as camp director for thirty-five years and planned with the camp board for a leadership transition. He accepted their proposal that he become the camp's CEO while they sought a new camp director. They turned to Rabbi Loren Sykes, who had been the inaugural director of Ramah Darom in Georgia. Rabbi Sykes agreed, but was clear that he would stay only a few years. The board felt comfortable with this arrangement because they were planning to hire Jacob Cytryn. Jacob had grown up as a camper and staff member at this camp and made an early decision to prepare to one day become the director. After having set out on this course, Jacob worked his way up the staff structure, learning the ropes of running a camp. When Rabbi Sykes left after three years, Jacob was appointed director in 2012 and his first summer as director was 2013. He was the first director of the camp in many decades to not be an ordained Conservative rabbi.

Everyone at camp calls the new director "Jacob." Like Rabbi Soloff, Jacob is devoted to the founding values of Camp Ramah: Jewish learning through Torah texts, celebrating Shabbat through a halakhic framework, speaking Hebrew, and supporting the staff to become Jewish role models for campers. He is especially devoted to staff development and strengthening the arms of camp, like the mercaz that support staff to provide quality educational programs for their campers. His passion is for camp to be an exciting, challenging place for young Jews to wrestle with their Judaism and imagine leading a life of serious study and action within a Jewish framework (Cytryn 2016).

Ramah Wisconsin's Jewish Mission

Ramah Wisconsin is deeply embedded in the Ramah movement, and its religious practices are shaped by the principles of the Conservative movement. Yet this Ramah has developed its own particular mission within the larger Ramah movement and has emphases that one might not see as much at other Ramah camps. Three of those emphases are:

1. Dedication to its educational mission
2. Close adherence to Conservative halakha
3. Shabbat as a day of learning

Few Jewish camps are as focused on their educational mission as is Ramah Wisconsin. Rabbi Soloff and Jacob are devoted to an ideal of what Ramah education should look like and are dedicated to realizing those ideals. This focus came clear to me the very first day I was in camp in 2015. I was sitting with Jacob over breakfast when a devoted senior staff member came over to discuss with great feeling the shooting in a Black church that had taken place in Charleston, South Carolina. He wanted the camp to highlight the racial hatreds that plague this country. Jacob listened carefully and then asked, "How will that fit in with our mission this summer?" My sense was that Jacob was not saying, "This is not very important." Rather, he was insisting that there is a mission and a plan and camp needs to find a way to include discussing racial inequalities as part of that plan. Mission governs.

Rabbi Soloff knew I was doing comparative camp research and several times asked me about tefilla at URJ camps. He listened to my descriptions, but what bothered him was that the Reform Jewish educators were not distinguishing between *shira* (song) and *tefilla* (prayer). His ideal, he reiterated, was singing that enhanced the campers' appreciation for the nuance of tefilla. He did not want campers to simply sing a prayer or display spiritedness for its own sake. Rather, he hoped they would sing in a way that called their attention to the Hebrew wording of the tefilla. I asked him whether that was a realistic goal for campers, and he answered, "We have to hope so." I understood him to mean that this may be a far reach, but it is what Ramah aims for. That is part of its mission: a deeper understanding of and commitment to the language of the Hebrew prayers.

Celebrating Shabbat is very much part of Ramah Wisconsin's Jewish mission, but only a part. Shabbat is meant to fit into a larger goal of creating religiously committed Jews who will love Shabbat, but will equally pray each day, study Jewish texts, and live a Jewishly informed ethical life. At Ramah Wisconsin, Shabbat does not stand out as boldly as it does at Eisner or Yavneh; by design, Shabbat is meant to reflect rather than overshadow the larger educational mission. Shabbat is designed to be a wonderful experience, but not so special as to suggest that one could live one's Judaism one day a week.

Shabbat at Ramah Wisconsin is lived by the parameters of Conservative halakha. (Halakha is the traditional Jewish legal process that governs many areas of Jewish life.) To illustrate how this halakha works, let's take the example of maintaining an *eruv* (enclosure) that allows for carrying on Shabbat. That eruv is checked each week as it would be at an Orthodox camp. However, I was told that one week someone discovered on Shabbat afternoon that there had been a breach. That could have meant a radical change in what campers were allowed to do that Shabbat, but the camp authorities decided they needed to be flexible and not unduly tax the camp population with restrictions. So there is both strictness and flexibility in halakhic observance.

All Ramah camps sponsor educational activities on Shabbat, but I doubt that any other devotes the same resources that this camp does. Each division at camp develops a Jewish theme for the summer and each Shabbat its staff prepares a series of three informal educational programs to engage campers with that theme. In that way, Shabbat is as much a day of Jewish learning as a day of celebration. This focus on Jewish learning expands campers' opportunity to explore themes in contemporary Judaism that might go unexplored at other Jewish camps. Jacob once joked that this camp is like the University of Chicago among Jewish camps. He was referencing two of the early camp directors (Fox and Cohen) who had done their doctoral work at that university. But he was also acknowledging that even among Ramah camps, this one stands out for its serious educational program. That emphasis leads to a different way of celebrating Shabbat than at our other two camps.

Staff and Campers at Ramah

During the years of this study, Rabbi Soloff served as the CEO of Ramah Wisconsin, Jacob Cytryn as the camp director, and from 2016 Adina Allen served as the assistant camp director. When Rabbi Soloff retired in 2018, Jacob Cytryn succeeded him as the executive director.

Ramah Wisconsin has nine *aidot* (divisions), two of which are for special needs participants. Each aidah has a *rosh aidah* (division head), a veteran staff member who has risen to this supervisory position. The division heads supervise the counselors, most of whom have grown up as campers and gone through counselor training in their first year as junior counselors. Ramah has an extensive specialty staff in areas like sports, waterfront, arts, and outdoor adventure. Ramah also has a staff of teachers who teach daily classes and advisors who work with the staff. The Israeli *shlichim* (emissaries) work throughout camp, with the heaviest concentration in the specialties and teaching.

Ramah Wisconsin recruits its campers primarily from Conservative congregations around the Midwest. The heaviest concentrations come from the Chicago area and the Twin Cities. A bit more than half of the campers also attend Jewish day schools. They come primarily from white, upper-middle-class Jewish families who can afford (with financial help) camp tuition. There were 478 campers in 2018. The campers range in age from entering fourth through entering eleventh grade. The youngest division remains in camp for only twelve days while for the next two summers campers come for a four-week session. Starting with Solelim (entering seventh grade), campers transition to the eight-week program for their last five summers. That remains an unusual setup for Ramah camps, and this camp has worked hard to make the full summer tuition affordable for families. After completing Nivonim, the oldest division, many elect to go on the Ramah Israel seminar before twelfth grade.

"Inclusion" at Ramah Wisconsin refers to integrating special needs campers into the regular camp program. Since 1973, this Ramah has sponsored the Tikvah Program as a division at camp "to provide inclusion opportunities for children with learning, social, and communication difficulties. This includes those with who are higher functioning on the autistic spectrum" (Camp Ramah in Wisconsin 2018). From ages eleven to fifteen, these campers come for four weeks and then transition to eight weeks during their late teen years. For many years Tikvah had a special relationship with Machon (campers entering tenth grade) and the two held many joint programs. More recently, Tikvah campers spend most of the camp day with the division closest to their natural age. Graduates of Tikvah may continue on to Atzmayim, the Tikvah Vocational Program that is designed to strengthen their social and vocational skills. Atzmayim, the ninth division, is open to high school graduates from ages eighteen to twenty-two years.

CAMP YAVNEH

Camp Yavneh, the oldest of the three camps, was founded in 1944 in Southern New Hampshire by the Hebrew Teacher's College of Boston. The camp was the creation of Leah and Louis Hurwich and a throwback to the early years of Camp Cejwin, when Leah had worked alongside Albert Schoolman to begin that camp. Yavneh was envisioned as a "summer study camp"—a mix of a camp and summer school. Campers took Hebrew courses during the mornings while regular camp activities would fill their afternoons and evenings (Hurwich 1999). Yavneh had no denominational ties and served primarily youth from the Greater Boston area.

The camp program resembled Camp Massad, with a strong focus on speaking Hebrew, cultural ties to Israel, and a lively singing culture (Benor, Krasner, and Avni 2020). To find staff who could speak Hebrew, Leah Hurwich made multiple trips to New York to recruit staff from both Yeshiva University and JTS. And while Yavneh would follow Orthodox practices in their religious services and observance of Shabbat, their primary goals were to create a lively Hebrew environment in which "camp life was permeated with song and joy" (Hurwich 1999, 239).

Leah and Louis ran Yavneh only through 1947, when his poor health required a change of leadership. By then Yavneh was well established and was attracting campers from many Hebrew schools in the Boston area. The Hebrew College remained the sponsoring organization and attracted top staff to run the camp. Two of the young men who directed the camp in its early years were Alvin Schiff and Walter Ackerman. Both would go on to distinguished careers in Jewish education and academia. The model of a summer study camp worked well through the 1960s (Ackerman 1999).

Joshua Jacobson, who went on to direct the Zamir Chorale of Boston, described an atmosphere at Yavneh in the early and mid-1960s that he found thrilling. As a teen, he would lose himself in Hebrew music and imagine himself as part of the pioneering culture of Israel. He could sing zemirot on Shabbat, Israeli songs at communal sing-alongs, and Broadway songs as part of the Hebrew musicals they staged each summer (Jacobson 2019).

The original model began to falter by the mid-1970s. The Hebraic culture that once had such allure lost much of its appeal. The rise of the Jewish day schools meant fewer youth attending supplementary education. By the late 1980s it seemed that Yavneh might have to close. Camper enrollment was way down, fewer classes were being offered, and the physical plant was badly depleted. When Shoshana Marcus stepped down as director in 1990, the college was not sure that it could find a new director for this failing camp.

Enter Debbie Sussman. Debbie was a physical therapist who had attended Yavneh as a youth. She met the chair of the Yavneh board at a party and he admitted to her that they were having trouble finding a director. He asked her jokingly, "Might you be interested?" She decided to express an interest. The board chair was thrilled, but not so the president of the college. He could see that Debbie had no credentials to run a camp and was not a fluent Hebrew speaker. But he agreed to give her a try. If her efforts did not work, they would close the camp. With that enthusiastic send-off, Debbie took over as director in 1991 (Sussman 2016; Rubins 2020).

Debbie realized the old model of Yavneh was beyond repair and the camp needed a makeover. Yavneh could offer some classes, but could no longer be a summer study camp. Debbie worked on camper enrollment, staff development, and fundraising to rebuild the physical plant. She deeply valued the Jewish spirit of the camp and worked hard to maintain the base of Orthodox families while also opening Yavneh to more diverse Jewish families. She and her staff built out new specialties to enhance the camper experience and rebuilt the physical plant so that Yavneh would have a new look with up-to-date sports fields and facilities. Over time Debbie rescued Yavneh. She and her senior staff breathed new life into this veteran camp.

As a Jewish camp, Yavneh is distinct and not easy to define. Yavneh has a core Orthodox constituency, but is not an Orthodox camp. It is a Klal Yisrael camp (see below) that is open to all Jewish families while also being sufficiently halakhic to meet the needs of its Orthodox core. For many years, Yavneh has hired a liberal Orthodox rabbi to serve as the *mashgiach ruchani*, or camp spiritual advisor. He has helped Yavneh knowledgeably walk the tightrope of meeting the religious needs of both Orthodox and liberal constituencies while presenting a coherent camp program.

Families who want a Conservative or Reform camp have the option of Ramah in New England or Eisner. Orthodox families could choose Orthodox camps in nearby states. Yavneh has appealed to a special set of Jewish families who want this unique blend. Many of these families also send their children to Jewish day schools. Yavneh has managed to incorporate both a fidelity to Jewish traditionalism and a vivid vitality that draws people in and unites people across diverse religious perspectives.

Over time, Yavneh and Hebrew College have gone their separate ways. Yavneh still has a strong working relationship with the college and its winter office is in their building. But the camp has become an independent nonprofit organization with its own board of directors. Yavneh has developed its own

Israel experience for campers and opened a family camp that meets at the end of each season. After twenty-six years, Debbie decided to retire in 2016. The board appointed Bil Zarch as the next director. Bil has deep roots in Yavneh and served as the director of the high school at Prozdor and as the head of school for two Jewish day schools. Bil returned home to Yavneh with a mandate to strengthen it into a thriving camp.

Yavneh's Jewish Mission

Yavneh began as a camp that offered daily Hebrew classes and created a Hebrew-speaking environment for its campers. When that original mission proved no longer viable, Yavneh retained some of its original features but pivoted to develop a new Jewish mission that could work for the twenty-first century. To understand that new mission it is helpful to grasp these three emphases:

1. Klal Yisrael
2. Ruach Shabbat
3. Orthodox halakhic orientation

"Klal Yisrael" is a traditional Hebrew term that refers to the value of maintaining the unity of the Jewish people. It is commonly used when Jews of different religious movements work together to forge common cause around issues of importance to the larger Jewish community (Conyer 2011, 275). But it is not a term familiar to most American Jews.

When I first asked Debbie about Yavneh's being a Klal Yisrael camp, she said, "Even in the camping world people don't get it" (Sussman 2016). Apparently, that was true as well for many Yavneh parents. In response, Rav Yaakov Komisar, the newly appointed mashgiach ruchani, put out a short document explaining Klal Yisrael. Let me quote from that document.

> Camp Yavneh is a Jewish Klal Yisrael camp that celebrates the diversity of our people by bridging the differences that span the various movements of Judaism . . . The Klal Yisrael community of Camp Yavneh presents an ideal setting for campers and staff to engage across difference through interpersonal connections in order to clarify, strengthen, and evolve our Jewish convictions. (Komisar 2018)

Yavneh is a rare space where Orthodox and liberal Jews learn to live together in a single community. They do so by having multiple options for prayer spaces, but a strong common space for Shabbat celebration. It is a place that honors difference and in which no one is trying to convert others to their persuasion. Yet Yavneh has always recognized that for its Orthodox campers and staff to feel at home, the whole camp has to abide by stricter practices, such as being a *shomer Shabbat* (Sabbath-observant) camp. Yavneh attempts this balancing act to a greater degree than Ramah or Eisner, whose religious policies are guided by a single denominational framework.

Rav Komisar (2018) acknowledges that this arrangement will result in "inevitable values conflicts, which must be handled with care." In my observation, these tensions are visible, but mitigated by Yavneh's emphasis on ruach, or Jewish spiritedness. Yavneh enjoys an abundance of what the beit midrash brought to Ramah Wisconsin: a lively, even fervent communal capacity to sing with intensity. At Yavneh, singing together helps bridge religious differences. An alumna of the camp captured this quality in describing Shabbat singing at Yavneh.

> The entire camp shamelessly singing. Some to God, some for fun, some just because everyone else is, but everyone singing the same words. Nothing else could create such beautiful times. (L. Sarna 2014, 38)

Singing without restraint is the Yavneh way. It matters not whether someone sings to God or for the fun of it. Everyone joins in and gives their all to create ruach Shabbat. Ruach Shabbat is a powerful resource for Yavneh. It unites everyone in a common devotion to a spirited Shabbat celebration. In my view, ruach Shabbat is the glue that holds together these religiously diverse groupings within the Yavneh community.

From its first days, Yavneh has been guided by an Orthodox halakha. Both Yavneh and the Ramah movement share a fidelity to halakha, but there are nuanced differences that could be described as Ramah follows a Conservative halakha while Yavneh follows an Orthodox halakha. That would explain why when Yavneh prays as a whole camp on Shabbat there is always a *mechitza* (partition) dividing the separate seating sections for females and males. But at other times, Yavneh shows a halakhic flexibility that one would not see at most contemporary Orthodox camps. One example of that flexibility is evident on Shabbat afternoon. Like Ramah Wisconsin and most Orthodox camps,

Yavneh maintains an eruv to allow people to carry on Shabbat. But unlike many Orthodox camps, Yavneh follows the Ramah movement's leniency in allowing campers and staff to play on the ball fields and swim in the lake. Thus, on Shabbat afternoons, Yavneh and Ramah Wisconsin look very much alike. So there are ways that Yavneh and Ramah Wisconsin differ in their halakhic observations and ways that they overlap. Both look very different from Eisner, which, following Reform practices, is less particular about what campers and staff may do on Shabbat.

Staff and Campers at Yavneh

When Debbie Sussman ran the camp, she worked for years with a team of senior staff members. At first, Bil Zarch kept that team in place. Gradually, team members left and Bil filled those positions with younger Yavneh staff alumni. One staff leader who remained is Lisa Rubins, who first came to Yavneh as a camper in 1977. Lisa also as an informal historian of the Yavneh experience and has shared much of that history with me.

Yavneh has seven divisions, or *aydot* (spelled differently than at Ramah). Each division has a *rosh*, or head, who is almost always a staff veteran and supervises the counselors, most of whom are former campers who trained as CITs. Yavneh also has a full staff of specialists in the areas of sports, arts, waterfront, and outdoor adventure. The camp has a rabbi who is the mashgiach ruchani, a staff of teachers who teach the Judaica classes, and a group of Israeli staff who work throughout camp.

Yavneh campers range from age eight to sixteen for the regular camp program. Those campers may attend for one three-and-a-half-week session or the whole summer. Yavneh also offers a two-week program for campers entering second to fifth grade. Younger campers tend to elect to attend for one session while older ones tend to stay the whole summer. In 2018, Yavneh had a population of 532 campers, with 343 attending the first session and 354 attending the second.

Yavneh has recruited its campers primarily from the Greater Boston area, but in recent years has spread its recruiting to many different states. The camp draws heavily on Jewish day school students, but actively supports campers who come from different backgrounds. Most campers come from white, upper-middle-class families who can afford (with financial help) the camp tuition. The oldest campers, in Kerem, serve as CITs and spend the whole summer at camp. Many choose to go to Israel on Na'aleh, the Yavneh Israel experience before twelfth grade. Yavneh also has an inclusion program for campers with special needs. In 2018, there were 25 special needs campers at Yavneh (Zarch 2020).

LEARNING TO CELEBRATE SHABBAT

In researching the details of how Shabbat is celebrated at these three camps, I was attentive to opportunities that arose for campers to learn new aspects of celebrating Shabbat. For the youngest campers, those opportunities arose frequently, as they had never before celebrated Shabbat at that camp. For older campers, those opportunities arose when they were asked to participate in some aspect of the Shabbat ritual that was new for them. I set out to investigate how camp staff and older campers provided these learning opportunities and encouraged younger campers to learn to assume new roles in the Shabbat celebration.

By "learning opportunities," I refer to those offered to all campers in a given division or unit. My research focuses on collective opportunities offered and responded to differentially by individual campers. The research focus is not on the differential responses, but on what the camp program offers to campers at different points along their careers. The aim is to provide a portrait in each of these camps of what campers may learn about celebrating Shabbat without attempting to account for what individual campers actually do learn.

All these learning opportunities are embedded in the daylong camp program of Shabbat at camp. A detailed account of how Shabbat at camp unfolds at each of the three Jewish camps is presented in the ethnographic report that makes up part II of this book.

Part Two

CELEBRATING SHABBAT AT CAMP

"CELEBRATING SHABBAT AT CAMP" is an ethnographic report of how the three selected residential Jewish camps celebrate Shabbat. URJ Eisner Camp, Ramah in Wisconsin, and Camp Yavneh provide robust, engaging, and cohesive enactments of Shabbat that differ from one another in terms of Jewish mission, religious observance, and camp traditions. By comparing how these three camps celebrate Shabbat, I show what these different camps share in common and how they use the rituals of Shabbat celebration to communicate their distinctive educational messages and promote camper learning about Shabbat.

Part II divides the Shabbat experience into distinct time segments. Across these camps celebrating Shabbat has a common rhythm. First, the camp ends its regular activities on Friday afternoon and prepares for and transitions to Shabbat. Next, early Friday evening the community gathers as one to greet the Shabbat and eat the erev Shabbat meal. Later on Friday evening, the Shabbat celebration ramps up to a high pitch of engagement and excitement. Then, Shabbat morning represents a slow rise into communal prayer. After Shabbat lunch, the energy level picks up through a relaxing afternoon that includes opportunities for Jewish learning. Finally, on Saturday night, Havdalah lights up a final burst of energy as the camp rallies to conclude Shabbat and start the new week.

Following this rhythm, each chapter in part II describes a particular segment of time as that plays out across the three camps:

Chapter 4. Preparing for Shabbat on Friday afternoon
Chapter 5. Greeting the Shabbat through prayer and meal
Chapter 6. Late evening Shabbat celebration
Chapter 7. Shabbat day from morning through Havdalah

Each chapter opens with a focus on a particular camp and on how that camp undertakes the challenges of that segment of Shabbat. I then compare that camp's approach to what is done at the other two camps. The composite picture offers readers a rich sense of how these various approaches express the distinctive cultures of each camp and the common work they do to make Shabbat vital and engaging for their campers and younger staff.

4 / PREPARING FOR SHABBAT

IN OUR HECTIC WORLD, many Jews who keep Shabbat find themselves rushing on Friday afternoons to get ready. Because Shabbat has a start time, people know by when their preparations must be complete. Still, it often feels like a race to meet that deadline and a relief when you can finally relax into the Shabbat atmosphere.

Camps have the great advantage of long summer days and greater control over time and space. They can do what most American Jews find nearly impossible: gradually prepare for Shabbat's coming. Since the days of Cejwin, camp educators have known that it works best to slowly transition the camp community from the "weekday" to "Shabbat." As a result, these camps structure Fridays so that regular camp activities end sometime in the afternoon and everyone has ample time to get ready for the day of rest. The transition is ideally felt as a letting go of the swifter pace of regular camp life and slowing down for a leisurely Shabbat. This is an artful transition in which every step is carefully choreographed to prepare a range of campers for a mental shift from "weekday" to "Shabbat." For many, this mind-set shift is unfamiliar; they are more accustomed to preparing on Fridays for a secular weekend. So the camp's transition needs to be deliberate and aimed at moving campers and staff toward the special, but unaccustomed, mind-set of Shabbat at camp.

In this chapter, I examine how each of the three camps prepares for and transitions to Shabbat in ways that anticipate the distinctive nature of Shabbat celebration and learning.

PREPARING STEP BY STEP FOR SHABBAT AT RAMAH WISCONSIN

Friday morning at Ramah Wisconsin feels like a regular camp day, with campers busy with their accustomed camp activities. You might not realize that Shabbat is coming unless you were to visit a nondescript room filled with computers that is called the mercaz. There you can find a buzz of activity, with staff working in small groups preparing programs for Shabbat. This rush to prepare characterizes many Jewish camps, but I am told that the mercaz at Ramah Wisconsin is unique. It is an educational resource center with dedicated space and senior staff who work with counselors on developing programs of Jewish substance. Each division appoints a rotating Shabbat committee of counselors charged with developing three programs around a Shabbat theme. The counselors—often accompanied by their division head—work with the mercaz staff, consult a bank of past camp programs, and design new programs that will be age-appropriate, participatory, and reflective of the Shabbat theme. Examples of these programs will be presented in this and coming chapters.

The mercaz operation reflects a changing camp culture. There was a time when counselors were expected to design most division activities by themselves. That has changed in these camps. When I ask why, a mercaz staff member explains that many counselors have no particular skills in program design and tend to plan the same programs they experienced as campers. These standard "fun" programs have their place as evening activities, but not for Shabbat. To prepare educational programs, the counselors need guidance from the mercaz staff (Blitt 2018). The mercaz reflects the investment that Ramah Wisconsin makes in preparing its staff to become "Jewish educators." The process they undergo is as important to the camp as the programs they plan (Cytryn 2020).

While this planning proceeds, the rest of camp is at their morning activities. All this changes at 1:30 p.m., when camp-wide Israeli dancing begins on the *kikar*, the lower lawn that serves as a gathering place for the camp. Standing on an outdoor platform are three women dance counselors. Behind them are the loudspeakers with prerecorded Israeli dance music. These are not the pioneer Israeli songs that I heard at camp in the 1960s and 1970s. Israeli music has diversified and sounds more like hip-hop than hora. But that hardly matters to the scores of campers and staff who line up to dance the steps that the instructors are modeling. The campers and staff seem to know the steps and anticipate the songs coming up. When a favorite song is played, they cheer and dance with added enthusiasm.

Staff and campers arrive gradually from wherever in camp they have been. This is a voluntary activity: whoever wishes may join in the dancing. I am struck by the diversity of people who choose to dance. There are older and

FIGURE 1. Kikar dancing, Friday afternoon, Ramah Wisconsin

younger staff as well as older and younger campers. Bunk counselors dance next to campers, but so do specialists, roshei aidot, and teachers. Some dance the whole time, but many come in and out. Some campers watch from the side and then are drawn in. One group of campers hovers in the background asking for donations to the *tzedekah* (charity) they are sponsoring. The overall feeling is of pleasure and fluidity.

One time Rabbi Soloff stood next to me during the dancing and explained that this was not the traditional Israeli dance time at Ramah. For decades they held Israeli dancing on Friday nights after dinner. Since Ramah does not allow the use of recorded music on Shabbat, they danced to songs that they sang. In the 1990s, he hired a *rosh rikud* (dance director) who dedicated herself to improving the dance culture at camp, and she suggested that they move the camp-wide dance time to Friday afternoon, when they could use recorded music and get everyone excited. Although that rosh rikud has left camp, the change she instituted remains. Lunch has been moved back to 2:15 p.m., and for forty minutes anyone who wishes can freely dance. In a camp where most activity is held by aidah, the camp-wide dance time foreshadows the coming of Shabbat and provides younger campers with a sense of being part of the larger camp. Younger campers can decide whether and when to join the dancing. If they decide to dance, they can be sure that older campers and staff will dance by their side and support their learning the steps.

When the dancing winds down, camp gathers in front of the dining hall for lunch. This is not the usual lunch. Rather, campers and staff enter the dining hall to collect their slices of pizza and cartons of chocolate milk, which they take outside to eat leisurely by bunk. This alternative lunch signals that this is not a usual day but that camp is slowing transitioning to Shabbat.

Lunch is followed by free time or rest hour and then *nikayon* (cleanup). I learned about this cleanup time in 2015 when observing Kochavim, the youngest campers. Their counselors held a nikayon contest to teach the new campers how to do bunk cleanup. The contest had four parts: folding clothes, making beds, cleaning the bathrooms, and sweeping the bunk floor. There were scores assigned to each task and the camper who assembled the highest score won the prize for that bunk. Once cleanup is completed, the campers showered and dressed for Shabbat.

Dressing for Shabbat is a complex undertaking. Long ago this Ramah camp stopped dressing in white for Shabbat. Instead, there is a dress code that focuses on modest dress-up. The typical dress at camp is shorts and T-shirts during the day, jeans and sweatshirts in the evenings and early mornings. That dress is not particularly gendered. But for Shabbat, gender differences definitely emerge. Most girls are wearing dresses or skirts and blouses and the boys wear slacks and shirts with collars. To my eye, the girls are more elaborately dressed than the boys. Because I never observed dressing up, I asked Shira Forester, a division head of twelve-year-olds, to describe the differences between girls and boys dressing up for Shabbat.

> As a rosh aidah in 2019 for entering seventh graders, I learned that the male side of camp sees this time entirely differently. When I would do nikayon checks for my female campers, their cabins were totally spotless and they were eager for my arrival so I could give them permission to begin getting ready for Shabbat. The boys, on the other hand, were often playing Frisbee or other games while their staff pretended to encourage them to clean. I would need to return a few times in order to get their cabin to a somewhat passable level of cleanliness so they could shower and throw on clothing for Shabbat . . . The female campers therefore arrived with fully done makeup

and hair and the male campers arrived with wet hair. I noticed how many male campers arrived in fairly casual clothing . . . I think there is a lot to be said on how Friday night clothing spoke to performance of gender in a way that did not happen at any other time of the week. (Forester 2020)

This gendered discrepancy in dress-up is not unique to Ramah Wisconsin and alerts us to how changing gender norms can clash with camp's rather stereotyped conception of appropriate Shabbat attire. Although this is not my research focus, there are indications that Shabbat dress-up may become increasingly contentious in years ahead.

Once the campers and staff are dressed up and ready to begin, each division gathers at 5:30 p.m. for their formal preparation for Shabbat.

Ramah's Transitional Ritual: Hachana l'Shabbat

When I was a staff member at Ramah camps, campers and staff went straight from dressing up to gathering as a camp for the evening camp-wide prayer. But at each of these camps a new ritual had been inserted as a transition to Shabbat. At Ramah Wisconsin, that is called in Hebrew *hachana l'Shabbat* (preparing for Shabbat) and is held by division. It is meant to be a more intimate occasion for that age cohort before the whole camp gathers together.

Kochavim, the youngest division, held its first hachana l'Shabbat in late June 2015. Thirty-two nine-year-old campers gather with their staff on a beautiful afternoon at the lawn in front of the library. Time is taken for photographs so this precious moment can be captured and shared with parents. Then the aidah gathers and is led by the two counselors who make up the Shabbat committee. They welcome all to their first Shabbat at camp and announce that the theme of this Shabbat is leaving home. The Jewish model for leaving home is the biblical Abraham. They ask campers questions about Abraham, and from the answers they receive, soon establish that Abraham showed great courage in leaving his home to follow God's call to travel to a new land. They draw an analogy to these campers' leaving home to be campers for the first time at this new camp. The counselors then teach the Debbie Friedman song "L'Chi Lach." They explain that the song is modeled on Abraham and Sarah and is about the courage to undertake a journey. Because this is before Shabbat, they play the guitar as they teach the song. The counselors sing the words and the campers haltingly join in.

This is a counselor-led activity that displays the hallmarks of a merkaz-planned educational program. The topic of leaving home to come to camp is encapsulated within a broader Jewish theme of Abraham and Sarah being called to leave their homeland to journey to a new land. The counselors can count on many of these campers having learned this biblical story at school and hence understand on some level the analogy being drawn. Teaching the Debbie Friedman song is a way to engage camper interest and introduce them to the central role that contemporary Jewish music plays in celebrating Shabbat at camp.

Campers then divide into bunk groups to review their first week at camp and talk about what they are looking forward to on Shabbat. The mood is light and humorous. Shabbat, these new campers are told, is going to be fun. They will get to sleep late, have great meals, and enjoy free time tomorrow. Then they go off to eat their Shabbat meal before joining the whole camp for the evening prayer session.

FIGURE 2. Pre-Shabbat cabin circle, Friday afternoon, Ramah Wisconsin

Why have the camps introduced this transitional ritual? I see it as analogous to what happens at many traditional Jewish weddings. Once the guests arrive for the wedding and are standing around schmoozing and eating, they need a ritual transition to prepare them for the wedding ceremony. The transition helps them focus on what is about to transpire and ready themselves for their role in the celebration. At a wedding, this is called the *tish* (the table) and *badeken* (veiling of the bride). The tish and badeken are highly ritualized and work to set up the wedding ceremony, the central ritual event. So too at camp. The transition ritual readies the campers to receive the presence of the Shabbat, which is the central ritual event of the evening.

Returning to Ramah Wisconsin the next summer to focus on the older campers, I climb the *givah* (hill) at 5:30 p.m. on Friday to attend the hachana for the oldest division, Nivonim. First, the aidah recites the *mincha* (afternoon) prayer. Then Aviva, the division head, lists the main dos and don'ts of Shabbat observance, saying there may be some confusion (this being late in the summer), but the rules have not changed. She adds, "On Shabbat, try to act differently, to relax and to love."

As she speaks, a counselor is spreading photographic images around a patio and asks, "Who are these people?" There are a variety of responses until it emerges that these are Israeli leaders. The counselor announces that the theme for Shabbat is Zionism and asks a series of questions: "What is Zionism? Does Zionism have one or many definitions? What are different ways of expressing Zionism?" These questions hang in the air as the campers and counselors spread out to form female and male circles to bless one another with the traditional Shabbat blessing for children. This is a more intimate moment with each person placing his or her hands on the head of the one ahead and reciting the Hebrew blessing in unison. Each person blesses and is blessed. Then, Nivonim heads down the hill as a group to join the rest of camp for the camp-wide Shabbat tefilla.

How do we make sense of this transitional ritual? Its several parts do not hang together well and, in contrast to the youngest campers, there is no singing or joking about how much fun Shabbat will be. How is this ritual preparing these older campers for Shabbat?

Shabbat at Ramah Wisconsin is designed to be a conjunction of three elements: the halakha, the learning agenda, and the group ritual. Both Rabbi Soloff and Jacob have explained several times that the Ramah movement is

FIGURE 3. Blessing the children, Friday afternoon, Ramah Wisconsin

governed by Jewish law as interpreted by the JTS faculty. They hope their older campers will come to appreciate that halakhic element. Historically, the older three aidot at Ramah Wisconsin did not regularly recite the mincha prayer on Friday afternoons. That was added in the early 1980s for halakhic reasons (Soloff 2020). This Ramah also takes seriously the learning agenda that is reflected by the work at the mercaz. An important function of the hachana is to introduce the theme for Shabbat, and this week focuses on Zionism. That theme will be visited three times during Shabbat with varying educational programs. Ramah Wisconsin is unique among our three camps in making this continual type of learning central to their Shabbat agenda.

Finally, there is the act of blessing, the element that most engages these teens. Without a word of direction, they and their counselors form same-gender circles and bless one another. At home this is a traditional blessing that parents may bestow upon their children around the Shabbat table. With no parents around, the staff got creative and reconfigured that traditional ritual to fit the camp context. It is an example of bottom-up change in the culture of the camp (ibid.). For the teens, this moment has a different feel than the rest of the hachana. They are not being directed by their staff but are blessing one another. This intimate moment completes the hachana before they join the larger camp for the camp-wide prayer session.

Mishmar on Thursday Nights at Ramah

This step-by-step Friday afternoon preparation for Shabbat is experienced by all the campers at Ramah Wisconsin and represents the official preparation for Shabbat. In recent years, however, the three oldest teen divisions—Bogrim, Machon, and Nivonim—have added an earlier step on Thursday nights, called mishmar, which adds another dimension to preparing for Shabbat.

Mishmar was introduced to camp in 2001 by the leaders of the beit midrash (see chapter 2), who brought this practice from their yeshiva experiences in Israel. In those sites of intense Jewish study, students hold an extra-late study session on Thursday evenings followed by intense singing that foreshadows the coming Shabbat. Historically, Ramah camps did not have mishmar or start preparing for Shabbat on Thursday nights. At Ramah Wisconsin, some Thursday evenings are dedicated to the Hebrew musicals that each of the older aidot stages for the whole camp (Reimer 2012). In recent years, mishmar has found its place after these plays and become a highlight for the coed campers who choose to be involved.

Mishmar happens in the camp library, a small building off the camp lake. When I arrive in 2017, Jeremy, a senior staff member, is setting up the room. There is a large table in this small room surrounded by rows of benches. There is an inner row around the table and outer rows behind. First, about twenty-five Machon campers arrive. Machon, which is the second oldest aidah, had returned that day from an all-week bus trip around Wisconsin. They fill in the outer benches. At 10 p.m., Jeremy turns off the lights and says, "Let's wait another few minutes." Two minutes later, twenty of the oldest Nivonim campers—who a half hour earlier had finished staging the musical *Chicago*—run in to take their places on the inner benches around the table. Then the singing begins.

Jeremy distributes a song sheet of forty-four traditional Hebrew songs and calls out one of those songs. I watch as the campers get into their singing. Eyes close. Voices start soft and slow. The singing intensifies. Hands bang on the table. Intensity increases: voices rise, the banging gets harder. A second Hebrew song calls for arms around one another. Every camper assumes that position. Eyes close. Voices rise. Only Jeremy bangs on the table as the singing intensifies and concludes. For the third song, everyone around the table bangs as hard as they can. Jeremy then introduces a counselor to give a short *dvar Torah* (Torah teaching). After the dvar, Jeremy calls out three more songs. The last has a chorus and multiple verses. Different campers lead the verses. For the chorus everyone sings and the banging is even more intense. At the end, Jeremy wishes them "Shabbat shalom" and at 10:35 p.m. the campers move out.

After they leave, I ask Jeremy why mishmar has become this intense moment of traditional singing. He tells me that moment used to be at seudah shlishit (the third meal) on late Shabbat afternoon. But that has faded and mishmar has taken its place. He is not sure why. His body language communicates, "This is camp. Take it as it comes." But I want to know more. First, I was moved by the intensity of the singing. These oldest campers had come from performing *Chicago* and voluntarily ran over to sing at mishmar. What does this kind of singing mean to them? How does mishmar help prepare them for Shabbat at camp?

I asked a variety of camp staff and learned the following. The camper investment in mishmar has been voluntary and cyclical. Mishmar was widely attended after it was first introduced, but then interest fell off as the older campers were more attracted to singing at seudah shlishit on late Shabbat afternoons (see chapter 2). When interest in seudah shlishit began to wane, some counselors revived mishmar singing for the oldest aidah, Nivonim. This newly revived event drew interest as well from some campers in the next oldest divisions, Machon and Bogrim. Then mishmar took off—so much so that one week in 2016 when there was an electrical storm that cut the camp's electricity, the older campers insisted there still had to be mishmar. They held mishmar on the porch because it was too dark in the building. On another occasion, a Bogrim group was scheduled to be on a canoe trip on Thursday night and some insisted the counselors bring the musical sheets so they could sing these songs at the appointed hour. Mishmar was introduced and revived by staff members, but it has been kept alive by camper energy and persistence—though not all campers choose to attend.

When I asked staff members what motivates this intensity, they believe that these campers like the lateness of the hour and the ice cream treat at its conclusion. These staff are cluing me that these teens can be motivated by varied reinforcements. I take their point. Yet what interests me is that mishmar is an example of what I have seen at all three camps: older campers have become highly invested in certain ritualized moments of Jewish celebration. They attend them with alacrity and have learned to sing and move with full hearts. Mishmar is one of several examples of how a certain kind of intense communal singing has taken on new spiritual significance at these camps. That is a point to pursue in this study.

I return in 2018 to witness mishmar again. It takes place at the same time, in the same room, and with Jeremy still leading. But three things have changed. This time Bogrim campers (age fourteen) also attend. The dvar Torah is given by a Nivonim camper and not a staff member, and the singing concludes with the ice cream treat I had heard about. But the pacing and intensity of singing are as before. Then I notice a pattern in the seating. The inner ring of seats around the big table is reserved for Nivonim. The Machon campers sit in seats once removed from the table, and the youngest Bogrim campers sit in the back. Each year the younger aidot move up a notch and get closer to the table. When they become Nivonim, the oldest campers take this prized position at the center of the ritual action. One counselor told me that when he was in Nivonim his group was late one week in coming. The counselor in charge let the Machon campers sit in their places. His peers were so upset that they refused to enter. Some even broke down in tears. When they did return the next week, they rejoined the action but never forgave that counselor for breaching the sacred order.

At each camp there is a sacred order. No one calls it that, but certain honorific roles are reserved for the oldest campers alone. Only Nivonim campers can sit around the table and bang at mishmar. If you are a Machon or Bogrim camper, you have to wait your turn and then guard the honor. It is hard to describe the emotional significance of these matters at camp. That sacred order reflects how seriously older campers take these camp rituals and how wholeheartedly they learn to fulfill their expected roles.

Mishmar anticipates Shabbat at Ramah with its focus on this intense Hebrew spiritual singing. There are plentiful occasions during the week for campers to sing. But they do not generally sing with this kind of intensity. By participating in this intense singing on Thursday nights, the campers are learning to be ready for what Shabbat at Ramah now offers.

PREPARING FOR SHABBAT AT EISNER

Rabbi Liz Hirsch occupied a unique role at URJ Eisner Camp. Having grown up as a camper, staff member, and song leader, Liz attended rabbinical school, was ordained as a Reform rabbi, and returned to camp as an assistant director and camp rabbi. In that role she had overall responsibility for planning and coordinating Shabbat services. Liz was my guide for how Eisner prepares for Shabbat. I learned that at Eisner there is no one moment—like the mishmar at Ramah—when preparing for Shabbat begins. Rather, there are multiple moments that involve different campers and staff members at different points during the week (Hirsch 2018). For the camp at large, the first full indication that Shabbat is coming arrives at the end of lunch on Friday. Until that point, Friday has seemed like a normal camp day, but soon that will change.

At 4 p.m. all regular camp activities cease. Campers and staff return to their cabins to clean the space, shower, and dress for Shabbat. Then at 5:15 all gather for the transitional ritual that they call Kabbalat Shabbat.

In July 2015 I accompanied a boy's bunk from K'tanim, the youngest unit at Eisner, as they leave their cabin on a beautiful Friday afternoon to attend Kabbalat Shabbat. The eight-year-olds are freshly showered and wearing shorts and a white shirt. This is their first Shabbat at camp. One boy asks his counselor why they are wearing white. The counselor answers, "Because it is Shabbat." A second counselor chimes in, "Shabbat is like a bride and we are going to a wedding." They meet up with the girl bunks and the girls are wearing varieties of white: white summer dresses, skirts, or shorts with white blouses. Here too girls are more elaborately dressed.

The campers and counselors arrive at a grassy hill for Kabbalat Shabbat. All the bunks coalesce, forming a unit circle. Around them on the hill are other circles representing each of the other units at camp. Campers can see that they are part of their unit, and their unit is part of the whole camp, and the whole camp has gathered to greet the Sabbath. They will do so by singing selected songs (from the Reform repertory), which they have previously heard at song sessions. Standing within each circle is the song leader assigned to that unit. At Eisner all the song leaders work together as a team under the leadership of the head song leader. They each play different roles at camp, but one important role is to teach the songs selected by the team to their unit.

FIGURE 4. Kabbalat Shabbat circles, Friday afternoon, Eisner Camp

The K'tanim song leader, playing the guitar, opens with the simple and familiar standard "Shabbat Shalom, hey." Most of the campers join in. Then they sing "Over the Mountain," which has hand motions that the campers all know. Everyone is singing. The third song, "Shiru Shir Chadash," is less well known and has more Hebrew. Here it is mostly the counselors singing. The final song, "Lecha Dodi," is sung with vigorous hand clapping. The counselors sing and clap and the campers clap along.

Note the progression of songs. The song leader leads from simpler to more complex songs, from more English-based to more Hebrew-based songs. By the fourth song, few of the youngest campers are singing, but they are engaged through the hand clapping. At Eisner there is a consistent message to campers that there are many entries into Shabbat celebration. If you do not yet know the words, learn to clap along.

This fifteen-minute transitional ritual is the Eisner parallel to Ramah's hachana l'Shabbat. This ritual makes aspects of Shabbat visible to these new campers so they learn what to anticipate. The song leaders with their guitar-based Jewish folk songs embody the camp's "Reform Jewish song book" (Cohen 2006) and invite campers to participate in Shabbat by singing and clapping along. When this ritual ends everyone heads down to the hadar ochel (dining hall), where the whole camp will be seated to begin the festive erev Shabbat meal.

The Longer Shabbat Preparation at Eisner

Each week at Eisner two units begin their preparation for Shabbat as early as Tuesday evening. These rotating units are preparing to learn their special roles in leading Shabbat services. A younger unit learns to lead the erev Shabbat service while an older one the Shabbat morning service.

Preparing these campers entails a large-scale operation involving senior staff, faculty, and counselors. This operation has been in place for years, but Rabbi Liz recently redesigned it for greater efficiency. There used to be a lot of last-minute staff work to get this operation going, but during the winter of 2018 Liz developed themes for each Shabbat at camp for each unit that will lead a part of the service. Each theme is rooted in an aspect of the Torah portion for that week but is also related to what that unit is learning with the faculty during the week. In this way, faculty—who at Eisner are visiting clergy and educators from area synagogues—can step in when they arrive at camp for their week and know how to prepare the campers for Shabbat (Hirsch 2018).

Campers also now know in advance when their unit will be leading Shabbat services. Coming from different backgrounds and having varying strengths, campers are asked to select one of four ways of participating in Shabbat services: through the spoken word, a song, a dance, or an artistic project. When camper choices are known, the staff divides the unit into four groups. Each group works with a specialist or faculty member to learn their part in leading the service.

Each of the first three groups performs their roles on the *bimah* (leader's stand) during the Shabbat service while the campers' artwork is displayed nearby.

To make sense of this preparation, one has to understand how differently Eisner views camper participation at Shabbat services. While all three camps give campers leadership roles at tefilla, each does so in a different way. At Ramah, older campers are preparing on Fridays to individually lead parts of their Hebrew-based tefilla. They may be a prayer leader or a Torah reader or even, on special occasions, give a dvar Torah. But only at Eisner do whole units of campers learn to lead the service through performing a dance piece, singing a composed song, and offering their thoughts on a weekly Torah theme. They do so in the spirit of the creative services that have characterized tefilla at Reform camps for decades (Splansky 2006).

I was planning in 2018 to observe how Rabbi Liz puts this operation into action when it was announced that she would be leaving camp to assume a Reform pulpit in the area. In her place, Wendy Grinberg, the educational director at camp, took over that operation. In August, I observed how Wendy, members of the Eisner faculty, and other specialists prepare the campers in Chalutzim (age eleven) and Tzofim (age fourteen) for their Shabbat leadership roles. Preparation happens in three sessions: the first is briefly learning about the *parsha* (Torah portion) with the faculty. The second is devoted to learning the part each group will play and the third to rehearsing that part. Once rehearsed, the group of campers will be ready to ascend the stage during the camp-wide Shabbat service and perform their part.

On Tuesday in 2018 each unit learns from the faculty about that week's Torah portion. The faculty are not actually teaching the content of this portion from Deuteronomy, but are following the theme that Liz selected—*emet* (truth) and *chesed* (kindness)—and deriving those Jewish value concepts from chosen verses in the parsha. As Wendy has written elsewhere, the focus of Jewish learning at Eisner is almost always on ethical values derived from Torah (Grinberg 2020).

By Wednesday morning Chalutzim has been divided into the four groups and each group is working with faculty and camp specialists. A cantor is teaching those who will sing a song she composed, a dance specialist is preparing a dance to an Israeli song that she choreographed, and, in another location, art specialists are guiding those fashioning visual representations of the weekly theme. I am observing the faculty working with the campers who are now writing their thoughts on emet and chesed. Some campers are addressing the theme in relation to life at camp and some are relating the theme to the evening prayers. They work in small groups and primarily consult with one another and occasionally with the faculty. They are expected to write a short paragraph. When they finish, the faculty collects their pieces, which the staff will type and slightly edit for clarity. Wendy tells me it is important for the campers to speak in their own voices.

On Friday morning these same groups of Chalutzim campers meet in the camp social hall. Wendy is working with the campers who will be reading their pieces. She explains that they will be rehearsing to be heard and inspire the audience. "You are leaders of a service. It is not a show. You're inspiring others to pray." They go up to the mike to rehearse their pieces. The feedback is mostly directed at being clearly heard. The content of their pieces focuses mainly on how to speak truthfully but with kindness. Their examples are derived from life at camp.

When Chalutzim finishes, in comes the older group of Tzofim. They follow a similar routine of rehearsal. The Tzofim theme is taking responsibility, which they address with more depth than their younger peers. The unit is then introduced to Naomi Less, a visiting songwriter and performing artist. Naomi teaches these campers a musical version of *Etz Hayim Hi* that she has composed. Tzofim are the first to learn her version so they can help Naomi introduce it to the whole camp at Shabbat morning services.

This Eisner preparation for Shabbat is so different from Ramah that it is easy to overlook the similarities. First, both camps invest significant staff time and talent in preparing for Shabbat.

Second, both use themes as a way of educating campers on topics of Jewish content. Third, both have senior staff overseeing the operation and ensuring a level of quality. Rabbi Liz stressed what I heard from the mercaz staff at Ramah. If the preparation were left to regular camp staff, they would do this on the run squeezed between many other camp obligations. The results would be rushed and choppy, and it would be far less likely that the campers involved would learn much from this experience (Hirsch 2018).

For all the similarities, it is the differences that stand out. To begin, Ramah and Eisner have varied conceptions of what Shabbat tefilla should be. A Ramah service is always in Hebrew, and while it is common to add prayers in English, the basic tefilla is in Hebrew. Even the songs they sing at Ramah are in Hebrew. That means that those who lead services or song sessions have to be fairly fluent in Hebrew usage. This limits who can lead, but that is the Ramah ideal (Benor, Krasner, and Avni 2020).

Matters are very different at Eisner. Over the decades, much Hebrew has been added to the Reform liturgy, but the service is a flowing mix of Hebrew and English. The cultural assumption at Ramah is everyone should know enough Hebrew to pray and sing in Hebrew. The cultural assumption at Eisner is that everyone should know enough Hebrew to participate, but there are many avenues of participation that do not require Hebraic fluency. Eisner clearly promotes Hebrew usage, but not at the cost of excluding those who have not yet gained that fluency.

Beyond language, a Ramah service has a "required choreography" (Gillman 1989). That refers to when one sits and stands, bows and stands straight, but it extends as well to the order of the prayers. At a Ramah Shabbat service there is an obligation to recite the prayers in a required order and no one may interrupt this order with other cultural performances. That does not mean no one gets up to speak, dance, or sing, but it does mean that the cultural performances that Eisner campers prepare would have no place at a Ramah tefilla. At the Eisner Shabbat services, interspersed between the siddur-based prayers are dance and song performances as well as campers sharing their prepared thoughts on the theme of that Shabbat.

At Eisner what matters most is not the Hebrew you know or the Judaic knowledge you can draw upon, but a willingness to get up in front of camp and express yourself in a medium of your choice. That can be speaking your English words, singing the song, dancing the Israeli dance, or displaying the artwork you created. All have an honored place within the Shabbat service at Eisner. With the exception in 2018 of K'tanim, the youngest unit, every camper at Eisner has one opportunity per summer session to participate in these ways in leading a camp-wide service. Not all Reform Jewish camps follow this practice. Eisner stands out in its own movement for its commitment to educating through this participation in the Shabbat services (Grinberg 2020).

PREPARING FOR SHABBAT AT YAVNEH

Of our three camps, Yavneh has the shortest preparation for Shabbat. Given Yavneh's more observant Jewish population, it makes sense that transitioning to Shabbat would take less time. Yet in that shorter time, Yavneh follows the same sequence of steps as do Ramah and Eisner.

At 4:45 p.m. on Friday afternoons, the regular camp activities end. Immediately after, the kitchen staff brings out freshly baked pizzas. You can stand in the front of the dining hall and watch as campers and staff stream in to feast on hot pizza. That is the most definite signal that Shabbat is soon approaching and that dinner will be served later than usual.

There are earlier signals. The dining hall is already set up for the more elaborate Shabbat dinner. There are staff members and older campers preparing to lead prayers and read Torah. Invited guests have been arriving to give Shabbat talks. The *kolbo* (canteen) opens at 2:30 for campers to get treats for Shabbat. The small signs accumulate until serving the pizza is the clarion call no one can miss. Everyone returns to the bunks to clean up, shower, and dress for Shabbat.

Shabbat officially begins at 6 p.m. Yavneh is our only camp to have flagpoles and a *mifkad* (lineup) ceremony. Campers' dress-up at Yavneh looks much like Ramah Wisconsin, with the female campers dressed up more elaborately than their male counterparts. At the flagpole, the Israeli and American flags are lowered, tzedekah is collected, and "Hatikva" is sung. This is a quick ceremony and then the whole camp heads over to the adjacent *beit am* (social hall) for the transitional ritual of ReLish.

ReLish—standing for *Ruach Lifnei Shabbat* (spirit before Shabbat)—was created about a decade before this study began as a way "to grab attention" and "engage kids in singing before Shabbat" (Rubins 2018). Senior staff felt something was lacking in moving directly from the mifkad to tefilla and turned to their musical staff to create a transition ritual. ReLish always follows the mifkad and involves the whole camp in the social hall.

As you enter, a four-piece band is set up on the side. At a given moment the band begins to play a set of four Jewish songs, three in Hebrew, one in English. The words are projected on the wall. Campers and staff stand in circles by aydah (division) with arms around one another. As the songs progress, the singing grows steadier. Then comes the last song, "Minyan Man," a ballad performed by Shlock Rock about a Jew who arrives in Mobile, Alabama, to become the tenth man for making a *minyan* (quorum) for Shabbat prayer. Now everyone is singing and swaying. As they reach the final chorus, campers and staff explode with sound. The moment the singing ends everyone starts hugging one another and wishing "Shabbat shalom" (Sabbath peace). Then all head to the whole-camp Kabbalat Shabbat service, with some stopping along the way to light Shabbat candles before the tefilla.

ReLish works by placing at the center the spirited communal singing that characterizes Shabbat at Yavneh. Everyone is invited to participate in the singing and then the hugging. As at Eisner, the ritual is set up so that campers are grouped by division, with all the divisions visibly present. Individual campers hold one another tightly while joyfully shouting out the words of "Minyan Man." They are then released from that grip to hug one another and make their way across the large room and hug others from across the camp. Yavneh is a smaller camp than Eisner. ReLish is structured so that the whole camp feels like an intimate community in which all warmly greet one another on their way to welcoming the Shabbat.

At Eisner, the song leaders with their guitars accompany the campers

FIGURE 5. Boys' circle, Friday afternoon, Camp Yavneh

FIGURE 6. ReLish, Friday afternoon, Camp Yavneh

through Shabbat; at Yavneh, following a stricter level of observance, the band leaders (and everyone else) put away their instruments until after Shabbat. That difference is subtly hinted at in the ballad "Minyan Man." The speaker in that song—following Orthodox practice—becomes the tenth man who can complete the quorum for a traditional minyan. Yavneh is the only one of our camps that follows (though not exclusively) Orthodox practices. Campers need to be mindful that Shabbat at Yavneh entails both joyous celebration and stricter observance.

Yet Yavneh thinks of itself as a Klal Yisrael camp that welcomes diverse Jewish families (see chapter 3). When I ask Lisa Rubins, the veteran camp leader, about this discrepancy, she tells me that when ReLish was being put together and the musical staff proposed "Minyan Man" as the concluding song, others on the staff team were reluctant. Here is an English ballad told in a male Orthodox voice. Some questioned whether this was the right song for Yavneh. But they decided to try it, and in Lisa's words, "It took off." The older campers loved it and "took it to another level" (Rubins 2018). That is a wonderful reminder that at these camps staff may experiment with new ritual forms, but the ritual only takes hold and becomes a camp tradition when the older campers and younger staff grow excited and make the ritual their own. Now no one at Yavneh could imagine another way to transition to Shabbat other than through ReLish and "Minyan Man."

THE IMPORTANCE OF PREPARING FOR AND TRANSITIONING TO SHABBAT

When travelers embark on a trip for a few days, they know to prepare: plan an itinerary, buy tickets, secure lodging, pack clothes, and notify family and friends of their plans. Travelers do this so routinely that they may not even think of it as preparation. Even less do they think of the transition rituals: the goodbyes, the trip to the airport, lining up for security, and finding the gate. Travelers do not simply get on a plane to fly. There is a clear set of steps they take to transition from home to travel. Only when these steps are disrupted do they become aware of how much they emotionally rely on a smooth transition.

Moving from weekday to Shabbat at camp is another kind of trip: a communal, spiritual journey. It too requires both preparing and transitioning, which are distinct from one another. Preparing is what one does to get ready and transitioning is how one moves from one mind-set to another. Camps have standardized the steps for preparing the whole camp: end regular activities; offer a special meal or snack; and get everyone back to the bunks to clean up, shower, and dress up before assembling at a set time. These are universally practiced each week in ways that clearly communicate: Shabbat is coming, get ready.

As for the deeper preparations, they vary by camp. Ramah Wisconsin has the mercaz, which supports teams of counselors to prepare the themes and experiential educational programs for each aidah. Eisner has the two units preparing with faculty for their special roles in helping to lead the Shabbat services. Yavneh has older campers and staff preparing to lead various parts of the Shabbat service. Shabbat is a complex operation, and in each camp some people are preparing in advance to make sure there is a high quality to the central events of the Shabbat celebration.

Transitioning is a shorter process than preparing, but of equal importance. These camps have learned from experience that it is disorienting for campers to move too quickly into the Shabbat evening prayer. It would be like wedding guests going straight from the parking lot into the wedding ceremony. That is too sudden a transition and would not prepare the guests for the seriousness of the wedding ceremony. So too at camps, where the campers need to properly transition from one state of mind to the next.

But how do campers learn to properly enter the Shabbat? Eisner and Yavneh have come up with similar responses and created transitional rituals that are quite similar. Both rituals highlight the role of instrumental music and communal singing, take campers through a few select and familiar songs, and structure the event so each camper is nested within his or her division (unit) within the larger camp body. Both rituals communicate that at this camp singing and moving together will be a primary mode for the Shabbat celebration. That is what newcomers need to learn to be part of their unit and their camp.

Ramah Wisconsin has taken a different path and prepares their campers for a different state of mind. First, they structure the ritual transition as an aidah event and thereby highlight the centrality of the division as one's community for celebration. Then they highlight the Shabbat theme over the musical experience. While Ramah as a camp sings throughout Shabbat, the camp leadership invests first in Shabbat as a Jewish learning opportunity. The leadership gives up a little on the ruach (spiritedness) of Shabbat to highlight the importance of conceptual learning on Shabbat. They are trying to create a mind-set that balances the cognitive learning and emotional singing dimensions of Shabbat.

I never heard staff explicitly say to campers, "This is what we value most about the Shabbat experience." That is not how these camps operate. Rather, the camp staff help create these rituals of transition that communicate these messages. Because the messages are embedded in the symbolic language of the ritual, when the rituals do their work well, the campers learn how to enter Shabbat prepared for what will come next.

5 / GREETING THE SHABBAT

THERE IS SOMETHING MIRACULOUS about that moment each week when the whole camp gathers to greet the Shabbat. How did everyone get here on time? How did camp people manage to put aside other agendas to celebrate together? How beautiful it is to pray and sing together as a whole camp greeting the Sabbath Queen and welcoming her arrival at camp.

> At 6:15 every Friday . . . a miracle happens. Everyone in camp is at the same place at the same time. No one is carrying a cell phone or car keys. We are all dressed in our finest summer threads; and with the well-known approving smile of our director, the community opens their siddurim and begins to chant. (S. Cohen 2010, 333)

Our goal in this chapter is to more clearly understand how our three camps design and implement the weekly welcoming of Shabbat into the life of the camp. When thinking about this moment, it is helpful to consider the analogue to a traditional Jewish wedding. After the transition rituals, all the wedding guests gather together to witness the wedding ceremony to affirm the couple's transition from single to married adults. Then they proceed to a *seudah*, or special meal, that celebrates the couple's being joined together. So too at camp the whole community gathers to greet and welcome the Shabbat as a bride who is joining with her partner, the house of Israel, as embodied by the camp community. By gathering together in the spirit of Shabbat, the camp community feels for that moment like an *edah kedosha*, or holy gathering. After the prayer service the community usually celebrates the Shabbat's arrival with a special meal in the *hadar ochel* (dining hall).

That is what Jewish camps hope will happen each week. Our focus is what actually does happen on Friday evenings at our three camps. This is a critical moment in celebrating Shabbat. The camp leaders have invested much thought and preparation in structuring this all-camp tefilla to convey to staff and campers their conceptions of what Shabbat should be. They each adapt

FIGURE 7. Outdoor Friday evening tefilla, Eisner Camp

FIGURE 8. Setup of benches for Friday evening tefilla, Ramah Wisconsin

the liturgy that is familiar from their denominational context and modify it to communicate to staff and campers the values and practices that animate the Jewish life of their camp. This is not done through discursive messages, but through the ways that they design the erev Shabbat experience.

To illustrate this point, let us take the most evident modification of Shabbat service that these Jewish camps have made: holding prayers outdoors. From early years, American camps have brought campers into the great outdoors to experience the spirituality of natural settings (Van Slyck 2006). Jewish camps follow suit, especially on Friday evening. Weather permitting, camps provide campers and staff with the moving experience of welcoming the Shabbat while watching as the surrounding natural world moves toward evening. While services at a synagogue are almost always held indoors, camps intuitively understand they can add to the beauty of this experience by holding the session outdoors.

To accomplish that move, camps have to designate an outdoor space for this service. It will not work to move from space to space each week. Many Jewish camps have put careful thought into the design of that space. Of our three camps, Eisner has the largest and best equipped space that they call their *beit tefilla* (house of prayer). Yavneh has a smaller designated space that they call Gilboa. Ramah Wisconsin has a temporary space near the lake that they put together and take down each week. On Friday afternoon, campers and counselors from the oldest unit bring out the benches and place them in a special design that transforms this spot into a "holy space." These different spatial arrangements reflect how the camp leadership thinks about Shabbat, the communal tefilla experience, and the camp values that they wish to communicate.

At Eisner, what catches the eye in their beit tefilla is the magnificently sculpted metal Tree of Life that stands in the middle and holds the ark for the Torah scrolls. The movable bimah is located about ten feet before that sculptured tree. Those who will lead the service stand there and, with their instruments and voices, set the pace and tone for the service. At Yavneh the space is a smaller amphitheater designed for tefilla. What catches the eye is how this space divides between the male and female sections. The *mechitza* (partition) that separates the sections is made up of short trees that could easily be taken as a decorative feature. So there is a mechitza, but it looks nothing like the standard mechitza. This spatial arrangement perfectly reflects Yavneh's culture: there is a separation so Orthodox Jews can pray here, but the mechitza gives little offense to liberal Jews who want the whole camp praying together as a single community.

When I asked Rabbi Soloff why Ramah Wisconsin had not built a separate prayer space for the whole camp, he said that building a centralized space to be used only for Kabbalat Shabbat would give this prayer service more weight than it already has. While Shabbat is central to the camp experience, its celebration cannot stand alone, but needs to be integrated into a wider conception of Judaism at camp (Soloff 2016).

Each camp has constructed a spatial configuration that reflects their leadership's conception of how Shabbat should be celebrated. What is true of spatial configuration is also the case with who leads the service, how music and communal singing are deployed, and what is expected of the staff and campers who participate in the tefilla. This is one ritual event where the leadership has invested heavily in conveying their messages about what Shabbat at this camp should mean.

Yet no camp ritual is simply what the leaders hope it will be. There are many factors that influence how the event will play out. Weather is a first factor, because it often rains during the summer. There are the staff whose many roles are critical to success of this ritual. There are the campers whose minds and hearts are to varying degrees engaged by the ritual. While it is true that tefilla is a high point of all-camp Shabbat celebration, the details of how it is implemented matter greatly to understanding Shabbat at camp. What follows are my observations and analysis of the Friday evening tefilla at all three camps during the summer of 2017. The goal is to understand both how these camps design their distinctive prayer ceremonies and how those rituals actually play out when everyone is brought together to greet the Shabbat.

SHABBAT EVENING DINNER AND TEFILLA AT EISNER

The Friday afternoon I arrive at Eisner in July 2017 is cloudy and cool. As late as 4:30 p.m. Louis Bordman is unsure whether the evening tefilla can be held outdoors or will have to move indoors. At 5:15 the whole camp gathers outdoors on the grassy hill for the transitional ritual of Kabbalat Shabbat. Many are wearing jackets or sweatshirts over their white tops. Kabbalat Shabbat is sung as usual and then everyone heads down to the hadar ochel for the Shabbat dinner.

Eisner is a large camp and their dining hall has been enlarged that year. Walking into the massive space can be disorienting, especially on Friday evening. For while seating is usually assigned by cabin, on erev Shabbat seating is open and many seek new places to sit. Campers are encouraged to sit with their siblings and buddies from other parts of camp. I sit with staff I know and close to the youngest campers, who remain seated together. The tables are covered with white tablecloths and each of us has a little plastic cup for the grape juice.

Standing in front on a raised platform are Louis and select members of the faculty. They begin by leading everyone in singing "Shalom Aleichem" to a familiar tune. A female faculty member lights the Shabbat candles and everyone chants the blessing with her. For the blessing of children everyone at the tables holds hands and recites the blessing in Hebrew and English. Everyone raises cups of grape juice as the faculty recite the Kiddush. A faculty member holds up a giant challah and staff raise the small loaves at the tables. Everyone recites the Hamotzi and then pieces of challah are passed around for everyone to enjoy. Then the meal of chicken soup, chicken cutlets, and vegetables is served; vegetarian portions are available for those who wish.

For a camp that proudly announces its support for nontraditional families, Eisner projects a "traditional" family image with a woman lighting Shabbat candles. At all these camps there is a nostalgic pull toward an unspoken "traditionalism" that pervades the Shabbat dinner ritual. Yet eating dinner before the communal prayer is a break with camp tradition. Louis made the decision to reverse the order before this study began. He had previously found that many campers were hungry and fidgety at services and he believed they could get more out of the tefilla if they have eaten first (Bordman 2018). Ramah Wisconsin allows its two youngest divisions to eat before the tefilla and Yavneh serves hot pizza late in the afternoon to offset hunger. But the Eisner decision changes the usual order and creates a different dynamic.

Shabbat dinner at Eisner concludes with the singing of grace. Near my table I watch with fascination as an older camper leads the younger girls in an elaborate set of hand motions to accompany the singing of the Birkat Hamazon. James Gelsey announces after Birkat that the camp-wide service will be held indoors in the nearby *beit am* (social hall). He directs some of the counselors to leave first so they can help campers find their seats. Two song leaders play Shabbat songs as the counselors leave. James then calls each unit in turn to go to the tefilla. The exit is quick and efficient. James later tells me they made the indoor call for fear that it might start raining during the service. It is a hard call when it is not actually raining; most things at camp—and especially services—happen best outdoors. DJ, the head song leader, tells me that he always prefers the outdoors because indoors the chatter reverberates in a way it does not outdoors.

The social hall is very large and its primary function is to house the camp's theater productions. It has a full stage and well-developed sound system that are employed when services move indoors. When entering you receive a four-page mini-siddur with the prayers printed. You find your seat and wait while everyone else is seated. Up front on the stage the two song leaders—DJ and a male counselor—are playing their guitars. The chatter is audible.

Erev Shabbat tefilla at Eisner is quite different from the more Hebrew-based tefilla at Ramah and Yavneh. The guitar-playing song leaders standing on the stage—with their sound amplified throughout the hall—are the first sign of difference. But even more significant is the structure of the service. While Ramah and Yavneh follow a traditional Hebrew liturgy (Gillman 1989), Eisner opens that liturgy to include other cultural elements. That allows for a degree of camper involvement in leading a service that has no parallel at the other camps.

Rabbi Liz Hirsch, serving as the camp rabbi, carefully planned this tefilla with Daniel Fortine (universally known as DJ) and worked with Wendy Grinberg, the director of education, to prepare the campers for their roles in leading the service. This Shabbat the unit of Ofarim (entering seventh grade) will help lead the service. They have prepared all week and now are seated up front waiting their turns to go up on the stage to lead.

Louis greets the guests—especially the visiting board members—and the tefilla commences. Rabbi Liz explains that the *parsha* (portion) this week is *Pinchas* and the theme that the campers will explore is gender equality. The campers go up in small groups and read clearly what they have written. Their turns are interspersed between the prayers that are led by DJ. Participants can follow in the mini-siddur, printed in Hebrew with transliterated English. But, I notice, few campers have even opened their siddur.

The song leaders begin with "Lecha Dodi," but few campers are singing. They move on to Borkhu and follow with "Roll into Dark" by Noam Katz, a former

FIGURE 9. Shabbat dance group, Friday evening tefilla, Eisner Camp

head song leader. Many more campers and staff know this song and respond with hand motions and singing. This song builds on the first paragraph of the Ma'ariv service. Many also join in for the Sh'ma and V'ahvata. That is followed by the Ofarim dance group dancing to a prerecorded Hebrew song. Soon after, a camper group comes up to sing at DJ's direction. Then comes a lively tune to V'Shamru and the place responds: staff stand and sway and campers join in as well. The Amidah is quietly chanted and followed by a pause for reflection. Louis gives a short Torah talk. Then concluding prayers—Aleinu and the Mourner's Kaddish—with everyone standing, bowing, and responding.

DJ and Rabbi Liz explain that they plan the music to build on what is familiar to campers, but also introduce less familiar music. They close the service with two well-known, rousing songs to prepare the campers for the song session that will follow (Fortine 2017; Hirsch 2017). This week the Ofarim group ends by singing "What Makes You Glow" by Jacob Spike Kraus (another former head song leader) and gets the strongest response of the evening. That is followed by an old favorite, a lively Debbie Friedman song. The service ends on that high note. Campers are then invited to line up outside for their weekly treat, Shabbat brownies.

FIGURE 10. Shabbat song, Friday evening tefilla, Eisner Camp

Making Sense of the Eisner Tefilla

If we view celebrating Shabbat as a series of steps, campers at Eisner go from singing on the hill to a family-style meal to gathering (indoors or out) as a unified camp body. This tefilla presents the camp as a whole for all to see. I was made aware of this from speaking to a young camper. After my first observations in 2015, I sought out Rabbi Todd Markley, rabbi at Temple Beth Shalom in Needham, Massachusetts, to make sense of the Eisner experience. My good fortune was that Rabbi Todd's eight-year-old daughter Mia was also present. Mia had been a camper in K'tanim and, with her father's permission, I asked Mia a few questions. Here is what she said about Shabbat services at camp: "I just love to look around at all the people doing all different things: talking, praying, and just sitting there" (M. Markley 2015).

"Looking around at all the people" is part of what this ritual accomplishes. The visual aspect of everyone in white is important to Mia. Rabbi Todd added, "For most of our kids, the key is to be surrounded by an entire camp together." He reminded me that even for children like Mia who at home attend Shabbat services, "the experience is sporadic and isolated." Only at camp do they have the experience of "Shabbat is what everyone is doing" and that makes Shabbat at camp "a Jewish battery charger" (T. Markley 2015).

I had missed how powerful the simple gathering each week must be for campers. Seated in the social hall, campers are surrounded by a sea of peers and staff wearing white, who have come together to pray. Where else but in summer camp do they see this? Where else are they part of an ongoing, surrounding community of peers who celebrate Shabbat? Louis said at one of these services, "This is Shabbat, Shabbat is holy, and that is why we wear white." The wearing white conveys something special to a camper like Mia.

Beyond the optics, Eisner staff invest heavily in the unique structure of their tefilla. I am told by senior staff informants that this is how Eisner tefilla has been structured for as long as they can remember (Grinberg 2020). I can see that the songs and prayers are thoughtfully selected, the music is artfully arranged, and a unit of campers is carefully prepared to contribute their input. But why put the service together this way?

Donald Splansky (2006) helps us understand that Eisner is building on a long tradition of "creative services" that goes back to the early days of Reform camps. A creative service "will have readings interspersed between the prayers" that "are expressions on a theme" and serve to "create a mood of seriousness about that theme" (ibid., 164). The readings are not themselves prayers, but their purpose is to build a connection between the formal prayers and the concerns expressed by the campers. In earlier years the creative services had been more episodic: "a camper or staff member" would be moved to offer "an

FIGURE 11. Outdoor Friday evening tefilla, Camp Yavneh

innovative prayer" that "addressed an issue at camp or in the world at large" (ibid., 160). Their inclusion was meant to show the many ways that Judaism speaks to the everyday concerns and aspirations of campers and staff.

Eisner has taken that older tradition and transformed it. These readings, songs, and dance performances are not episodic, but planned and expected. Louis clarified in an interview what Eisner is aiming to achieve. While synagogue services highlight the rabbi's understanding of Judaism's relevance, camp turns that around and asks the clergy on faculty to help the campers express *their* view of what Judaism means for them. Camp positions these campers to experience a personal connection to the weekly parsha and learn that they have the words or actions to express what that connection means to them (Bordman 2018). Eisner has taken an older tradition of creative services and distributed the "creativity" so that even younger campers can have their say and hopefully feel Jewishly connected. As such, Shabbat tefilla plays an important educational role of empowering campers to present their personal statements to the assembled community.

During the service I was sitting near Rabbi Matt Cutler, a congregational rabbi and longtime Eisner faculty member, who commented on how hard it is to build a prayer service around these camper statements. These campers "have no sense of ritual" and are "writing short essays" that do not really fit the service. Rabbi Matt put his finger on a central tension of the Eisner structure. Eisner is melding together two strands of Reform camp traditions—the creative service and the folk music liturgy—and interlacing them into a single Shabbat service. The diverse elements of this service do not organically fit together, and that lack of fit places a heavy attentional burden on the assembled campers.

How do the campers handle that burden? Eight-year-old Mia was accurate in noting that there are three things that campers do during the service: they talk to their neighbors, sit there quietly, and sometimes join in the singing and praying. From my observations, most campers—but not all—are drawn into the tefilla at two key points: when there is an engaging song and for central prayers like the Sh'ma, Amidah, and Kaddish (prayer for the dead). Otherwise, they retreat into their habitual talking or reverie. What is most likely to draw them out is familiar music that engages them.

Counselors also play an important role. They sit among the campers, especially in the younger units, and model what more active participation looks like. But there are a few key staff that play a crucial role. They are what I call the ruach rousers. When there is a lively tune, they are the first to rise, sway, and move to the music. They actively model and draw campers into the ritual action. They signal to others to stop talking, come back from their reverie, and attend to the ritual action. They are a key to making the service feel more engaging. They wait for the songs that move them, quickly rise from their seats, and get the ritual action rolling. That happened three times during this tefilla: for "Roll into Dark," "V'Shamru," and "What Makes You Glow." These are familiar, up-tempo pieces that allow the Eisner tefilla to reach high points of engagement. When the music lifts these staff up, their ruach ignites the crowd. Talking abates, reverie is interrupted, and the community is roused to actively participate. At those points tefilla is most alive at Eisner, and *aliveness* is what these services aim to accomplish.

But at Eisner the tefilla has an added function: to bridge between the calmer Shabbat meal and the more stirring song session. DJ explained that the song leaders intentionally end the tefilla on this high note to prepare the campers for the coming song session. Song session on erev Shabbat has a very special place in the history of Reform Jewish camps (see chapter 2). If music and song are the integrating forces that hold the tefilla together, they take the main stage in song session and provide campers and staff with their most intense Shabbat celebration.

SHABBAT EVENING TEFILLA AT RAMAH WISCONSIN

The late July Friday afternoon that I am at Ramah Wisconsin is sunny and mild. At 6:15 p.m. I follow the Nivonim campers down the hill from their transitional ritual. They are marching to the lower kikar, where two hours earlier they had set up the benches for the camp tefilla. Now the Nivonim campers take their place off to one side, line up in parallel rows, and create a tent for others to pass through. As the younger campers pass through, Nivonim campers sing a soft Hebrew song, smiling and handing out the Ramah siddur booklet for erev Shabbat. This is their special role at erev Shabbat tefilla, which they see as modeling for the younger campers.

The benches are set up in a semicircle with campers and staff facing into a central space from which the *shleichei tzibbur* (service leaders) will lead the service. This is the only weekly tefilla where the whole camp prays together. Seating is "family style" and participants are encouraged to sit with family

FIGURE 12. Nivonim siddurim, Friday evening tefilla, Ramah Wisconsin

FIGURE 13. Friday evening tefilla, Ramah Wisconsin

members or friends from other parts of camp. In a camp that is heavily division centered, family-style seating adds a special treat for campers.

Before the tefilla formally begins, Josh Warshawsky steps to the center with his guitar. Josh is the primary song leader at Ramah. He pursued the same musical training as the URJ songs leaders as well as rabbinic ordination in the Conservative movement. Josh is a pioneer in building a Ramah version of song leading and composing. Today he leads a group of Bogrim campers in a song that he composed. This is his way of introducing new music to camp (Warshawsky 2018).

At Ramah the older divisions take turns leading the tefilla. This week is the turn of Tikvah, the special needs aidah. Of our three camps, Ramah has the most ambitious inclusion program for special need campers (Blas 2010). Tikvah has been a special aidah within camp for many years. Tikvah members in years past would co-lead the tefilla with Machon campers, but now Tikvah staff prepares selected campers for these leading roles: chanting a chapter from the Song of Songs, lighting the candles, and leading Kabbalat Shabbat and then Ma'ariv. All tefilla leading is in Hebrew, and since the 1980s, boys and girls have equal access to leading (Soloff 2016).

This evening a girl camper chants a chapter of the Song of Songs, a group of girls lights the candles, and boy campers lead both Kabbalat Shabbat and Ma'ariv. Over my four years I have seen gender variation in all these roles. From his much longer perspective, Rabbi Soloff is amazed at how Tikvah participants have taken on more varied and active leadership roles at camp. He counts that as one of the camp's proudest achievements (Soloff 2018).

Seated outdoors I can watch the sun sparkle on the surface of the lake. But being outside without amplification makes it harder to hear the leaders leading. Two division heads stand on either side of the camper leader, yet the three voices are still hard to hear. The difficulty is amplified by the many campers who are chatting away. The counselors mostly carry the singing. They sing along with the leaders and model what active participation looks like. But most campers come in and out of the tefilla. They join in for the most engaging singing and familiar prayers, like the Borkhu, Sh'ma, and Amidah. Otherwise, they are either deep in conversation or drift away in silence.

The tefilla itself follows the traditional Hebrew liturgy for Kabbalat Shabbat and Ma'ariv. There is ample communal singing modeled on the style of the Jerusalem-based Shira Hadasha congregation. There is dancing for Psalm 96, the second paragraph of Kabbalat Shabbat. Male and female staff and campers rise to dance in a mixed line around the sides as many others sing the lively tune. After Kabbalat Shabbat, Jacob addresses the camp in Hebrew and welcomes the guests who have come. There are a generous number of guests from the Midwestern congregations that support Ramah. At the end of Ma'ariv, Adina Allen, the assistant director, also speaking in Hebrew, thanks all who participated in the service and makes a few announcements. When the service ends, the Shabbat shalom hugs begin. I can feel joy rising in this interlude between prayer and the Shabbat meal. The Machon campers are breaking down the benches and returning them to the social hall. Younger campers are running around and letting off steam. Most everyone else is mulling around and chatting before heading into the hall for Shabbat dinner.

Making Sense of the Ramah Wisconsin Tefilla

Ramah Wisconsin uses the whole-camp format sparingly for special events that the camp leadership wishes to highlight. Besides erev Shabbat, the whole camp assembles for the Zimriyah (music festival), Yom Sport (a day of sporting events), the Thursday evenings when the older campers stage their musicals, and the eve of the Tisha B'Av fast. Having studied the Ramah musicals, I learned that the whole camp attends these productions to show their appreciation for the work that went into them and the pride that the aidah feels for making it happen. After the play, the whole camp rises for a rousing singing of "Himnom Ramah" (the camp anthem) in an unabashed display of camp pride. Staging the play before the whole camp represents what I call an optimal experience for the Ramah campers involved (Reimer 2012).

Assembling the whole camp each week for the erev Shabbat tefilla clearly signals the centrality of Shabbat to the Ramah experience. Yet, it could not be more different than the Thursday evening musical productions. Jacob put this clearly to me: "It is an honor to lead Kabbalat Shabbat, but not a big deal" (Cytryn 2017). Unlike the leads in the musical who are celebrated by the camp for their performance, the campers who lead this service are acknowledged, but not celebrated. They are not budding song leaders, but *communal leaders* leading a prayer service.

This point was brought home to me when I met a colleague from Israel who had been at Ramah for the Shabbat of staff week before the campers arrived. He told me with excitement that Josh Warshawsky had led the tefilla for the staff and what an exceptional experience it had been. Josh had set a standard for beautiful leading. But when I asked Josh whether Ramah should be aiming for that high standard in tefilla leading, he said no. Ramah should aim for educating many campers to lead the tefilla. Then he honestly acknowledged that doing so means the musical quality will suffer (Warshawsky 2017).

The contrast with Eisner is telling. DJ, the head song leader, is a trained musician and a cantorial soloist during the year. While he is certainly not performing as a cantor at the Eisner tefilla, he is working with Rabbi Liz to arrange the most musically satisfying service that could work in a camp setting. But that is exactly what this Ramah is *not* doing. They are not trying to create the most musically satisfying tefilla. Rather, their explicit educational goal is to show that the older campers can adequately lead the service. In the view of Jacob and Rabbi Soloff, tefilla is not a performance like the musicals on Thursday nights. Tefilla is communal prayer where the camp joins together to greet the Shabbat. While the aesthetic quality matters, it is not the dominant concern (Soloff 2016).

All this reflects Ramah Wisconsin's educational goals. Of course, the leaders want Shabbat at camp to be special and beautiful for the campers, staff, and guests. But they do not want Shabbat at Ramah to feel so different that it feels unique. Quite the opposite. Their goal is to teach campers that they can develop the skills that would enable them in other Jewish contexts to participate in and lead a traditional tefilla both during the week and on Shabbat.

In this regard, the exclusive use of Hebrew is striking. Not only is the prayer in Hebrew, but Jacob and Adina also address the camp in Hebrew. When I asked Jacob why he greets the guests in Hebrew when he knows many do not understand, he told me that Hebrew is the official language of the camp and all public addresses need to be in Hebrew. His hope is that as campers get older and hear more spoken Hebrew, they will come to understand more of what is said (Cytryn 2016). Hebrew is another of the Jewish norms that Ramah is trying to cultivate in their campers. I know from my travels to other Ramah camps that they are not as insistent on Hebrew usage as Ramah Wisconsin is. Jacob is a true believer in the traditional Ramah values, which include hearing and understanding Hebrew (Benor, Krasner, and Avni 2020). He knows that speaking Hebrew comes at a cost. Not only many guests but also many campers do not understand what he is saying. But he is willing to pay that cost to maintain that value.

How does all this engage the campers? How do they respond to the particulars of this tefilla? Having observed erev Shabbat prayers several times, I see little difference between the campers at Ramah and Eisner. Yes, the Ramah campers have greater facility with the Hebrew, but most never open the camp siddur. They willingly come to Shabbat tefilla and seem happy to be there. They eagerly seek out friends and family members from different parts of camp. They drift in and out of engaging with the service. Many chat with neighbors for a good deal of the time. When the service ends, they come alive with an energy that shows that Shabbat is a happy time for them.

How to reconcile this Ramah's lofty educational goals with the camper response? Jacob offered a clue when he said, "I do not think of Shabbat as a centerpiece of camp, but marketing does" (Cytryn 2017). Jacob knows that Shabbat is a special time when guests come to camp and enjoy being there. It is what the alumni remember most fondly. Many campers look forward to having this special time to be with friends and family. For these key stakeholders, Shabbat at camp is a wonderful time of rest and togetherness. Shabbat in that sense markets the camp experience. Yet Jacob believes that this version of Shabbat cannot be "a centerpiece of camp." He believes that the "ideal Ramah alumni are people who get joy from serious engagement" (ibid.). They enjoy speaking Hebrew, keeping traditional Shabbat practices, and engaging in Jewish intellectual pursuits. What makes this Ramah distinctive, from Jacob's perspective, are the educational goals that distinguish it from Eisner, Yavneh, and most other Jewish camps.

The Friday evening prayer at Ramah Wisconsin is shaped by these distinctive values. The tefilla follows a traditional liturgy, is led by prepared campers, and is all in Hebrew. Yet the modal camper response is not that different from Eisner. What most campers seem to love about the service is its being the weekly moment when the whole camp comes together to joyfully celebrate Shabbat in their beloved community.

SHABBAT EVENING TEFILLA AT YAVNEH

The Friday I arrive at Camp Yavneh in early August of 2017 is cloudy and overcast. As the camp prepares for the coming Shabbat the first drops of rain begin to fall. By 6 p.m. it is coming down steadily and there will be no flagpole today. A few minutes later I watch as the campers—now dressed in rain gear—head to the social hall for the transitional ritual of ReLish.

It is sad to forego an outdoor service in the Gilboa amphitheater, but the Ben Zvi theater building awaits them. Ben Zvi is set up differently than at Eisner or Ramah. When Yavneh prays as a whole camp, they follow Orthodox practice and use a mechitza that divides males from females. While the mechitza in Gilboa is barely noticeable, in Ben Zvi it is a more conventional divide. The females find seats on one side and the males on the other. It is a tight squeeze to fit the whole camp within this space.

This is Bil Zarch's first summer as director and his role is to open the service with reading the letter from Na'aleh, the Yavneh trip to Israel. The participants are the young alumni who were last summer's oldest campers. Their letter tells of their journeys during the last week in Israel and their anticipation of being back in camp for the last Shabbat. Bil is reading in English. While the tefilla at Yavneh is all in Hebrew, the other spoken parts of the service are in English.

A female staff member comes up to light the candles and recite the blessing. She is followed by an a cappella group that sings a short piece in Hebrew. Then Kabbalat Shabbat begins. Talya—who is the co-division head of Kerem, the oldest campers—rises and stands alongside the mechitza on the women's side. A few years earlier Yavneh introduced a new practice of Kabbalat Shabbat being led by a woman. They were following the halakhic guidance of Rabbi Dov Lerea, their *mashgiach ruchani* (spiritual advisor) at the time. Ever since, women staff—and sometimes Kerem campers—have led this tefilla (Rubins 2018).

Talya has the voice and skill to lead well. She is leading in the Shira Hadasha style. Liturgically, this is the same Kabbalat Shabbat as at Ramah Wisconsin, but with a difference. Standing at the side is a group of staff members who are singing antiphonally with her lead. They are moving their bodies and gesticulating with their hands as they sing and encourage camper participation. The result is an active camper response with many singing along in Hebrew. Twice during the tefilla people rise for dancing. Male staff on one side and female on the other form same-gender circles and many campers join in. There is an aliveness to this Kabbalat Shabbat.

After Kabbalat Shabbat someone is usually invited to share a story. This week a visiting rabbi comes up to tell a story about Jews trusting Jews. Ma'ariv is led by a male staff member. Camp moves quickly through this tefilla with much less singing. To conclude the service Yavneh in recent years decided to move the singing of "Shalom Aleichem" and reciting of Kiddush to the tefilla space, where the leaders can be heard more clearly than in the hadar ochel (Rubins 2018). The camp sings "Shalom Aleichem" together, and a girl from Kerem comes forward to recite Kiddush. Then everyone heads directly for Shabbat dinner.

Making Sense of the Yavneh Tefilla

Camp Yavneh walks a fine line between being a Klal Yisrael camp open to all Jewish families and serving a modern Orthodox clientele whose halakhic standards are carefully maintained. Making sense of this erev Shabbat tefilla requires attending to how that fine line plays out at Yavneh as compared to what happens at Ramah Wisconsin.

Both Yavneh and Ramah have been coeducational camps from their inception and encouraged full female participation in most areas of camp. Yet these camps have differed on the place of women in tefilla. Yavneh has historically followed modern Orthodox practice in tefilla. That meant using a mechitza to divide the tefilla space into male and female spaces and having only males leading the tefilla. Ramah, following the practice of the Conservative movement, has never had a mechitza and has evolved on the question of female leadership of tefilla.

While Yavneh is independent of any denominational affiliation, it has had modern Orthodox rabbis serve as their halakhic guide. For many years all prayer services were governed by Orthodox practices. In more recent years, Yavneh has distinguished between all-camp and other services, where older campers are offered a choice of options, egalitarian or mechitza. But when the whole camp prays together, they follow modern Orthodox practice. When a few years ago some modern Orthodox rabbis ruled that women could lead certain tefillot, Yavneh decided a woman could lead Kabbalat Shabbat. In 2016, their Orthodox advisor also allowed women to recite Kiddush for the camp and Yavneh gave that honor to their oldest girl campers.

Two recent trends are noteworthy at Yavneh. First, Orthodox staff and campers have become more open to egalitarian values and welcomed women to lead where their halakha permits. Second, while everyone comes together for this tefilla, there are tensions around these decisions. I happened upon a group of young staff who were loudly arguing this point. One counselor asked why if the majority of camp is not Orthodox does the camp impose these rules on them. The other, voicing an Orthodox perspective, responded that some people have no idea how liberal this camp's Orthodoxy is and how many compromises he personally has to make to be at this camp. I had the sense this was an ongoing tension that bursts into the open from time to time.

From my comparative perspective, another difference becomes evident during the Kabbalat Shabbat dancing. At Ramah Wisconsin the dancing is mixed gender. Whoever wishes to dance gets up and joins the line of dancers. This includes male and female staff and campers. But at Yavneh they dance in two different spaces: males dance in their way and females in their way. The intimacy of same-sex dancing is quite different from the mixed-gender dancing at Ramah.

That Yavneh dances twice during the tefilla points to a larger difference with Ramah Wisconsin. While both camps employ the same traditional liturgy, the Yavneh tefilla is strikingly more spirited. Yavneh generally positions talented staff members to lead Shabbat tefilla. When someone like Talya leads, she brings a skill that few campers have yet developed. But perhaps even more significant are the staff members who step up as ruach rousers. They lend their voices and bodies to the tefilla and rouse the campers to fuller participation. They draw campers into singing and dancing. Their actions create a spiritedness that is not as much in evidence at the Ramah tefilla that I witnessed.

I have witnessed other Shabbat services at Yavneh where the staff are quieter and the campers recede into the same distanced responses that one can see at Ramah or Eisner. The staff play a critical role in creating the ruach of tefilla. Yet the ruach at the erev Shabbat tefilla is a warm-up for the more intense display of Yavneh ruach that will come after the Shabbat meal.

WHAT THE EREV SHABBAT TEFILLA COMMUNICATES

When Jewish camps market camp Judaism to prospective parents, they love to show images of the whole camp gathered outdoors on a beautiful Friday evening with everyone dressed up and smiling in anticipation of the coming of Shabbat. When I remember back to my days as a camper and staff member on erev Shabbat, it is always in my memory sunny and beautiful. Neither marketing images nor nostalgic memories provide us with an accurate guide for understanding Friday evenings at these camps. For that we need the observed details of celebration across the camps.

All three—and most other—Jewish camps intuitively understand the need to bring the whole camp together for the Friday evening tefilla. There is a majesty to wholeness and a sanctity to the whole at rest. This is the moment that creates the aura of camp as an everlasting Jewish community that has always celebrated Shabbat in these ways. For young people living in ever-changing social conditions, tefilla on erev Shabbat can feel like a Jewish version of Turner's communitas. Yet, how do the camps use this precious moment to communicate about celebrating Shabbat? At these camps, tefilla is carefully designed to convey particular images of what celebrating Shabbat entails and what roles campers and staff can play in that ritual celebration.

At Eisner, Shabbat tefilla primarily consists of a particular type of communal singing that asks campers to join with words and movement. That tefilla could not happen without the leadership of the song leaders, and yet, the song leaders are doing all they can to encourage campers to join in the singing. Additionally, the staff spread throughout the prayer space are both modeling that participation and at times rousing others to join them in a more spirited singing and moving to the music. Everything about this service invites campers to join in and participate in whatever ways feel most comfortable. Not all campers respond enthusiastically, but Eisner makes clear many forms of participation are welcome.

Eisner also identifies what leading a service entails. It means coming up before the camp and "creatively" connecting with the themes that are expressive of the Jewish values of this camp. When it is your unit's turn, campers are asked to help lead parts of the service by speaking, dancing, singing, or making art to the Jewish theme of the week. While Hebrew is encouraged, the creative contribution is through the spoken English word or the modalities of song, dance, and art. Through these modalities, Eisner campers learn to help lead the service in ways that are distinct from their peers at Ramah and Yavneh.

Shabbat tefilla at Ramah Wisconsin is all in Hebrew and follows a traditional liturgy. Campers at Ramah learn that to participate in the camp tefilla they need to develop the Hebrew facility that will allow them to recite and sing the words of the tefilla. They also learn the shape of the traditional liturgy so they can participate knowingly. Finally, once campers have reached their bar or bat mitzvah, they are requested to help lead the camp tefilla. If campers are willing, the staff will help prepare them to lead one aspect of the tefilla. To lead at Ramah entails standing before the camp and leading that part of the Hebrew-based Shabbat tefilla.

At Yavneh, the Shabbat tefilla asks of campers much of the same as at Ramah plus two other distinctive features. Because a majority of Yavneh campers do not come from Orthodox homes, many are asked to learn how to participate in a modern Orthodox mechitza service. They are also asked to step up to the ruach that animates this service. Yavneh's ruach-rich tefilla provides opportunities for campers to get involved in the singing and dancing in ways that may feel quite different from what they know in home contexts.

Few campers come to camp knowing how to participate in a camp Shabbat tefilla. Many have some experience with communal tefilla at their local synagogues and schools. But these camps design their Shabbat tefilla to be distinctive, with novel features that all new campers will need to learn. The erev Shabbat tefilla is designed to make clear what that learning entails. Most campers who I have observed have become familiar with the moves of the tefilla and know how to participate in the major parts of the service.

At the same time, campers at all three camps have learned that there are acceptable degrees of tefilla participation. Some campers are enthused and want to participate as actively as possible. Others seem indifferent and wish to do the minimal; most are somewhere in between and respond differently to various parts of the tefilla. When they are drawn in, they engage actively. When they are not drawn in, they sit back quietly or talk to their neighbors. These varied camper responses reflect a gap between what the camps ideally project and what the campers are ready to accept. That gap sets up a challenge for each camp: how to engage the campers who can be drawn in to participate more actively in the tefilla.

Engagement of campers is primarily the work of the staff and can be divided into two parts. The first is how the senior staff design the tefilla and the second is how the junior staff interact with the campers during the tefilla. At camp there are a few basic rules of thumb that the designers of tefilla know. Campers grow increasingly restless and distracted as the tefilla goes on for longer. Keep the service short. Vary the pacing and the music. End on a high note. The designers are always struggling between the wish (or halakhic requirement) to add more to the service and the sure knowledge that length kills camper attention and participation. Every Shabbat tefilla lives in the tension between these two poles.

It is the younger staff who play the active role in engagement. At all three camps many counselors are active role models for tefilla participation. They sit among their campers, keep their siddurim open, sing along, and get up to dance and move when appropriate. They communicate with their campers, trying to keep them engaged even when it is clear that camper attention is waning. Each tefilla is an uneasy balance between the staff who are doing their best to keep the service alive and the campers who are growing increasingly restless when not actively engaged. That is where ruach rousers come in. These staff volunteer to inject spirit into the tefilla. They stand, move, and sing loudly. They actively draw campers into the liveliest parts of the tefilla. They have a special skill that is very helpful for camper engagement in Shabbat tefilla.

Why are there more ruach rousers at Eisner and Yavneh than at Ramah Wisconsin? For all their denominational differences, Yavneh and Eisner live by their ruach (spiritedness) in a way that Ramah does not. Ruach at Eisner is tied in with the Reform tradition of song leading. Yavneh does not have the tradition of song leading and yet it has created its own special spiritedness, which then becomes an ideal of Shabbat celebration for its campers. By contrast, at Ramah the ideal is a lively but measured level of participation in tefilla.

In summary, gathering the whole camp on erev Shabbat to greet the Sabbath queen is a unique moment of great significance. Campers look around and see they are surrounded by a camp full of dressed-up peers ready to celebrate Shabbat together. But that moment of wonder is followed by a seventy-minute tefilla where questions of engaging camper attention naturally emerge. The junior staff are charged with the tasks of engagement and many do their best through role modeling and ruach rousing. Yet, in truth, every Shabbat tefilla is a delicate balance between the staff's efforts and the campers' limited capacity to engage with prayer. For that reason, erev Shabbat celebration never ends with tefilla but is always followed by later Shabbat activities that more fully engage camper energies.

6 / INTENSIFYING SHABBAT JOY

THERE IS A RHYTHM to celebrating Shabbat at camp. It begins with preparing for Shabbat, the whole camp's greeting Shabbat, and the relative calm of eating Shabbat dinner. But after dinner (or the brownie break at Eisner), the pace of celebrating intensifies. Like at a traditional Jewish wedding, when it comes time to sing and dance, one can expect exploding youthful energy as an expression of communal joy. Camps design Shabbat rituals to channel that energy and give it shape and meaning. These rituals deserve our careful attention because they are the medium through which older campers and young staff members express their love of Shabbat at camp.

How did these camp rituals arise? Their story goes back to the earliest intentional Jewish camps. When the leaders of those camps were creating Shabbat at camp, they designed Friday nights to culminate with active after-dinner activities that would be in the spirit of Shabbat. As strong Zionists, they wished to infuse Shabbat celebrations with the spirit of Eretz Yisrael. So they created active song and dance programs that imported songs and dances from the Yishuv (pre-state Israel) to accomplish the double goal of celebrating Shabbat and involving campers in Hebrew song and Israeli dance (Krasner 2011). Generally, they sang in the dining hall and danced outdoors. That pattern of post-dinner celebration remained normative for many camps over many years. It is what I remember from my years on the staff at Massad and Ramah and probably what I expected to see at these three camps.

It therefore came as a great surprise to discover how dramatically the after-dinner Shabbat activities have changed. At Eisner and Yavneh there are now Shabbat celebrations much wilder than what would have been possible in my day. At Ramah there is some of the wild, but also a seriousness to the formal activities that was also unfamiliar to me. That surprise led to these questions: (1) How have these camp rituals changed over time? (2) What do these changes tell us about how celebrating Shabbat at camp has changed?

There was yet another change that captured my attention: the role of the oldest campers at each camp. At Ramah I had been a counselor, teacher, and rosh aidah of the oldest campers. Yet I cannot remember those campers playing special roles on Shabbat that differentiated them from the younger campers. But at all three camps the oldest campers are now singled out for leadership roles on erev Shabbat. That change is an important clue for understanding how learning to participate in and lead Shabbat rituals has changed over time.

Shabbat at camp is always a shifting balance between what the staff envision and the campers want. The senior staff have a vision of what Shabbat should be, but campers and younger staff are the ones enacting the celebration. Their energy and investment are crucial for making Shabbat the joyous occasion that everyone is hoping for. This shifting balance is particularly evident on late erev Shabbat at camp. For while the Friday evening tefilla and dinner are closer in style and form to what one observes in other Jewish communities, once arriving at post-dinner celebration, camps feel freer to innovate and come closest to what makes Shabbat atcamp uniquely powerful for campers and staff. Let's pay close attention to these Shabbat rituals at each of our three camps to understand their power for the older campers and the staff.

LATE EREV SHABBAT AT EISNER

The oldest unit of campers at Eisner is called Olim—those who go up. These 113 campers are entering tenth grade, and almost all spend the whole summer at camp. They are given special housing, assigned the most experienced counselors, and play leadership roles on Shabbat at the song and dance sessions. They are asked to step up and provide younger campers with a model of what Shabbat celebration can be. And step up they do, as reflected in these notes from July 2017.

Like the rest of camp, Olim comes to Kabbalat Shabbat dressed in white shirts or blouses and remains in these finer clothes through dinner and tefilla. Immediately after, when the younger campers are getting their brownies, the Olim campers and staff go up to the gym and quickly change into gym clothes. They hold a pep rally there and then line up in front of the adjacent social hall. With their arms extended, they form a tower over all those coming for song session. Campers and staff are high-fived as they pass through.

Olim campers are the last to enter the social hall. The other campers and staff have already distributed themselves around and leave space for Olim at

FIGURE 14. Song Session, Friday evening, Eisner Camp

the center of the hall. The song leaders (DJ and his number two as well as a percussionist) are set up on their platform. Olim place themselves as a group standing squarely in front of that platform. The song leaders have planned the music for this session and prepared the words of the songs to be projected on the wall. The songs come from the same Reform Jewish repertoire that has been featured all evening. As soon as Olim is comfortably in place, the music begins.

By any measure, the sound is highly amplified and loud. The Olim campers throw themselves into the music. They are tightly bunched together into a formation they call "the mosh pit." They jump up and down to the music, thrust their hands into the air, and sing along with intensity. They move as a unit, bumping into one another as they jump up and down. They exude great energy, song after song. In contrast to the earlier tefilla where their participation was mixed, here they are devoted to song session, thrusting their bodies and souls into the music. This is a picture of teen rapture, a group giving itself up to sound and movement.

Then, at some preassigned moment, the Olim campers fan out throughout the hall looking to dance with their buddies. Each Olim camper is assigned a ten-year-old camper as his/her buddy and they spend time together during the week. In the midst of song session, they break away to seek out their buddies to dance together. Then they come back together for the last songs of the session. They know that song session is scheduled to run for only thirty-five minutes. Still, they ask for more songs, but DJ declares the session over. They cannot resist, for they need to change again before dance session. This time the boys put on long skirts while the girls put on colorful boxer shorts. In these costumes they rush down the hill to the dance session and occupy the central space during Israeli dancing. This is all done with total dedication.

Dance session is held outdoors and led by an Israeli dance instructor standing on another platform. Next to her stand a few campers who demonstrate the steps. Prerecorded dance music plays throughout the session. All the participating campers and staff are standing in lines waiting to do the line dancing. The costumed Olim campers stand in the front row before all the other campers. Dance session runs much like song session. There are a preset number of dances and everyone seems to know the order. They also seem to know the dance steps, which they perform with vigor and high energy. Everyone in Olim dances every dance. The younger units are called out, and after each dance, another unit is sent back to their cabins. By the end it is just Olim and staff dancing. Olim holds the floor to the end.

In what sense have the Olim campers served as leaders during song and dance sessions? Surely not in any usual sense, for in actuality the music and dance staff lead these sessions. I would describe the Olim campers as standing at the center, throwing themselves into the song and dance, and modeling total camper devotion. In their eyes, and apparently those of the younger campers, that is an important role to play. They model Shabbat joy. This is not an idealized spiritual joy that adults might seek on a spiritual retreat. Rather, it is a loud, crude joy that teens may feel when, clad in gym clothes, they jump up and down until sweat pours from their bodies. It is the joy of being part of your group shouting Jewish songs whose words most barely understand. It is the fun of dancing to steps of Israeli dances while cross-dressing. It is zany, outrageous, and can happen only at camp—which is exactly why this ritual joy matters so deeply to these teens and why they throw themselves into these sessions with such abandon.

On Embodying the Joy of Shabbat at Eisner

Abi Oshins is the unit head of Olim in 2017. A veteran Eisner staff member, Abi has been working with this group of teens for the past few years. She is proud of them and of her staff, whom she calls "the best of the best." She describes how her campers are "learning to become Olim" and "to deepen their Judaism" through their study of *middot* (Jewish ethical values) and raising serious questions about Judaism in conversation with their counselors. This group has a history of cliques; this summer, however, campers are "looking beyond their cliques," wishing to get to know more of their peers and "leave their legacy" on the camp (Oshins 2017).

Abi wants me to hear directly from the campers and organizes on Shabbat morning a group of twelve campers to answer my questions. While this is only a small group, they leave me with these distinct impressions. First, what most stands out for them about Shabbat are the song and dance sessions on Friday evening. That is where they can be camp leaders, where the younger campers can look up to them, and where they can leave their legacy. Second, they take seriously the buddy system. They remember how much it meant to them when they were younger campers and now want to help their buddies with things like finding new social relationships. It is a new experience for them to be doing for others and not just for themselves.

After the group conversation, Abi stresses how intensely these kids feel "the obligation to enjoy Shabbat" and "to embody that joy" for all the other campers (ibid.). I get a clear sense of Abi's investment in this being the case, and that recalls what I had seen the night before. When Olim campers are changing into their gym clothes, the staff also change their clothes. Then campers and staff gather for a pep rally in a packed room at the back of the gym. The staff lead with chants to psych everyone up for what is to come. My sense is of staff helping Olim transform themselves from their camper status into role models for the younger campers. For when the campers leave the gym and line up in front of the social hall, they seem fully invested in welcoming the others and high-fiving their younger peers.

Eisner's Song Session

Song session began in the earliest days at Union Institute, the first Reform Jewish camp. The practice of holding a late Friday evening song session became normative at URJ camps, with each camp having its own nuanced way of enacting the ritual. No senior staff I spoke with at Eisner could remember a time when erev Shabbat did not include a song session run by song leaders. But they also recounted how the Eisner song session has evolved over the past two decades.

Until 2005, song session took place in the dining hall. In those days, the camp would first pray together, then eat Shabbat dinner in the hadar ochel, and then push back the tables after dinner to hold song session in the vacated space. The Olim campers played a leadership role, but not what we saw in 2017. What changed this arrangement was building the *beit am* (social hall) and the availability of an alternative, larger space outside the dining hall. Here is how Louis describes what happened when he made the decision early that summer to move the song session to the social hall.

> There was an Olim uprising. They complained, "How can you do this during our Olim summer?" I sat with 120 kids and 18 angry counselors. We had a conversation. I asked, "What is the tradition? That we sing in the dining hall with chicken bones, forks, and knives?" They threw different things at me and I kept insisting that the real tradition is that we have song session on Friday night . . . I gave each a T-shirt that said "Singing in the Beit" and they came out that first Friday night. Olim led the camp into it. That worked. Everyone was happy. (Bordman 2018)

There are a few things to note in Louis's telling. First, it was not only the Olim campers but also the staff who were up in arms about this change of location. That is often the case at these camps, for the staff are in most cases former campers, and it is their tradition as well that he is messing with. Second, from Louis's perspective, the fact that participants during song session were still holding on to "chicken bones, forks, and knives" was a negative, but from the participants' perspective those were as much part of the ritual as any other detail. Third, while it might sound as if Louis was buying them off with T-shirts and a new role as greeters, that role has become very important for both Olim and the younger campers.

DJ describes how song session has evolved since 2005.

> In the early years in the beit am, Olim were not so dominant. There is a photo [that hangs in the entrance to the social hall] that shows that the song

> leaders were on wooden blocks and Olim were seated before them. Then they introduced the higher platform in 2014 and Olim began to stand in the front. (Fortine 2017)

DJ is relating this history to explain how Olim became so dominant in song session. From his perspective that dominance is a problem. He carefully prepares the songs for song session, but "they throw me off." In fact, at the song session that Shabbat, DJ had planned to end with a softer song, but felt he had to change his plan and end with a louder one so that Olim could conclude the session with their full energy on display. There is a big difference between a song session where the campers are seated and moving in place and one where the teens and their staff are in mosh pit formation, jumping up and down as they shout out the words. DJ recalled that in earlier years when the song leaders were positioned on lower wooden blocks, the Olim campers rose from their seated positions and began rushing the blocks and beating upon them. That was a sign of the changing times in terms of how teens respond to their music. So Eisner introduced the higher platform, which is safer for the song leaders. But that platform invited the mosh pit, which the teens soon formed and which has become the tradition for song session.

This evolution of song session shows how this ritual is affected both by decisions made by camp leadership (the move from the dining hall to the beit am) and by changing patterns in how teens respond to their music. From a management perspective, it makes great sense to move song session out of the dining hall, which is cramped and in need of cleanup. But a move like that is deeply disruptive to the oldest campers and their staff and needs to be carefully negotiated. In that negotiation, Louis empowered Olim to become leaders of song session. That move over time would have an unanticipated consequence, for the teens also felt empowered to change where they locate themselves in the social hall. They pressed for the mosh pit formation in which they dominate the session with their wild throwing of their whole selves into the singing and movement.

It is hard to convey the shock of my first encounter with this wild song session. Before beginning this study, I had carefully studied Judah Cohen's (2006) account of the history of song session and also knew that at a local Reform temple a young rabbi had introduced a rock-band service once a month for young adults. So I was not expecting to see a folk song session like in the days of Debbie Friedman. Still, I was woefully unprepared for how song session had evolved at Eisner. That summer of 2015 I was observing the youngest unit, K'tanim, during their first Shabbat at camp. After brownies, we went up to the beit am, where the Olim campers were lined up outside to greet us. The little ones seemed genuinely pleased to be high-fived by the big kids. Then we went inside. The Olim campers took up their position near the platform while the K'tanim were mostly on the side of the room watching. When the loud music began, I kept my eyes on the little ones and saw two reactions. Some continued to watch the older campers from afar, seemingly amazed by what they saw, but not drawing near. Others sat down at the edges of the social hall and joined other young children in playing games. The latter seemed to be shutting out the loud music and movement by focusing on board or card games. As I stood there, I felt assaulted by the loud music and teen exuberance. Here is a passage from my notes:

> The dancing was ecstatic. The moves were straight out of a contemporary dance floor. The teens and staff danced with abandon. It was very loud and intense. No one was out of control, but the intensity was very unusual and (for me) frightening.

I met a rabbi there whom I knew from home and asked him what was going on. He responded with a story about a prominent Reform rabbi we both knew. That rabbi had been a song leader at Eisner when he was young [during the 1980s] and had not been back in years. He recently returned and was completely taken aback by song session. "What is this?" he asked. Then he heard one of his teens say that this is what made him love Shabbat at camp, and he felt, "This is what it takes now." When I later asked Louis about song session, he replied, "I do not love our wild song session; however, they do. You have to meet the kids where they are" (Bordman 2018).

If this is where the kids are, I had a lot of catching up to do. I did not even know what the term "mosh pit" meant. I later found this dictionary definition helpful: "An area in front of a stage in which audience members mosh—knock against others intentionally while dancing" (*American Heritage Dictionary* 2001). I was relieved to realize that the campers knock against each other rather gently, but they had imported from their outside musical lives the moves that they find most expressive of their youthful enthusiasm. In their world when you move with music, you have to be up on your feet, bunched together, jumping up and down, knocking one another, and thrusting your arms in the air as you sing/shout the words of the songs.

This style of song session has created a problem for some campers. In Louis's words, "Eighty percent of the kids are into it and 20 percent are not" (Bordman 2018). I had first noted that in 2015 and then again in 2016, when my notes read: "Sitting alongside one side of the gym were groups of younger campers—mostly boys—quietly playing cards. They seem to ignore song session and use the time for their playing." Louis was not pleased that these campers were opting out of song session. "When I first came," he related, "everyone had to go to song session. Some kids cannot handle it . . . [Song session] is not to be a rock concert, but something more sensitive" (Bordman 2016).

By 2017 Eisner had created a second option. They now offered "wild" and "mild" song sessions that ran concurrently. Campers were expected to choose one. When I went to see the mild session in 2018 I found a single song leader with a guitar leading gentle folk singing in Hebrew and English for about two dozen campers and their staff. To my surprise, more of the younger campers were now participating in the wild song session and no campers were off to the side playing games. When given a choice, more campers opted for the wild song session.

There is a striking contrast in leadership's attitude toward tefilla and song session. Louis, Rabbi Liz, and DJ relate to tefilla as a camp-wide service that needs to reflect the camp's values and ways of praying. But with song session, their attitude shifts to "you have to meet the kids where they are." DJ may have planned to end with one song, but he accedes to the wishes of Olim. Visiting rabbis may find song session disturbing, but if their teens love it, they say to themselves, "This is what it takes now." The leadership acknowledges that at song session, Olim dominates. Shabbat at camp works best when those crucial players can safely go wild for Shabbat. Then the older campers can feel "this is *mine* and I love it." Camp-wide tefilla will never be that for the older campers. It takes a wilder, louder, and more expressive mode of celebration for them to feel that ownership. And without that ownership—that feeling that this is *my* camp and here I can really celebrate *my* Judaism—the camp loses their engagement and wish to model that joy for the younger campers. No wonder Olim dominates at song session. Camp leaders know that joy is essential to Shabbat and begins with the oldest campers.

Communal joy is the most salient ingredient for making erev Shabbat at

Eisner work. At a time when so much of shared life is mediated through a screen, many young people come to camp seeking a more immediate togetherness, body to body, which generates that feeling of joy.

This is a generation of campers that seems more comfortable celebrating with both body and heart. At Eisner, that moment comes at song session as they jump up and down, bumping against one another while shouting the words of the Jewish songs. As bizarre as this might seem, campers and staff alike interpret that shared joy as loving Shabbat at camp. For many, this is a culminating moment of Shabbat celebration.

The Skirts and Shorts: An Evolving Eisner Tradition

Dress-up matters greatly to Shabbat at camp. When noticing that Olim campers wear three different outfits during erev Shabbat—white tops, gym clothes, and long skirts or colorful boxer shorts—I wondered: What could this change in outfit tell us about Shabbat at Eisner?

First, it tells us that Olim is unique. They alone go through these outfit changes. Second, it tells us that song session will be wild and sweaty and hence the gym clothes. But what about the long skirts and boxer shorts? Why do the Olim campers cross-dress for the Israeli dance? That is a question I put to both Abi and the twelve Olim campers she gathered.

The campers are aware that the boys' skirts go back to the 1990s and believe it came to camp from the rock group Phish. (More below.) They know the girls' boxer shorts began only last summer (2016), when a camper complained that while the boys had the tradition of the skirts, the girls had nothing. The campers came up with boxer shorts as a male item the Olim girls could wear. Once adopted, the boxer shorts have quickly become a camp tradition.

What most excites the campers about this camp tradition is handing down the skirts and shorts from one camper to the next. Toward the end of camp, a time is set aside when each Olim camper decides to whom in the next group he/she will be handing over his skirt or her shorts. The Olim camper puts his/her name on the garment and makes the presentation. It is an honor to receive the skirt/shorts, which has on it the names of all those who wore it before you. The campers feel this is an important tradition that places each of them in a line of reception at camp. The staff make sure there are enough skirts and shorts so every camper in the next group receives one.

When I ask Abi why they cross-dress, she insists the campers do not see this as cross-dressing. The skirts were "a thing" and now the shorts are "a thing." The point is not to cross-dress, but to keep the camp tradition alive and pass "the thing" down from person to person. Abi gathers three of her counselors, who all tell me they remember this from when they were campers and what matters is who has your garment now and who wore that garment before and after you.

I am fascinated by this invented camp tradition and want to know more. I was fortunate that Wendy Grinberg, the educational director, offered to turn to her alumni contacts and provide testimony from several Eisner alumni on how the practice of wearing long skirts began and developed. In their memory (and other alumni remember differently), this camp practice began in 1993 and was inspired by the rock group Phish. The immediate inspiration was Jon Fishman, the Phish drummer, who would wear dresses at their performances. Male counselors, who were Phish devotees, and their older campers began wearing long skirts to Shabbat services, dinner, and Israeli dancing. That Shabbat behavior was part of a broader pushing of gender boundaries, with guys wearing skirts and painting their nails. At some point the camp leadership pushed back and limited the skirts on Shabbat to Israeli dancing alone and that became the camp tradition. It was only later (someone thought in 2004) that the practice of handing down the skirts began, with the campers developing "rules" in relation to handing down the skirts. First, the skirts could not be washed, and second, they were—whenever possible—to be handed down from family member to family member (Grinberg 2018).

When I heard about camp's pushing back, I asked Louis about his role.

> We had a large group of staff who were really into Phish in the early 1990s. When I took over in 1999, I did not want kids to be confused about sexuality or gender. This was before where we are today. I am thinking this is not good for the younger kids. I said, "You cannot put them on until after the sixth graders have gone back to the bunks." I did it for a year or less. I was really rigid. But at some point I watched and thought, this is harmless fun. That is all anyone sees. So I said, go for it. (Bordman 2018)

Louis was at first concerned that it could be confusing for younger campers to see older campers cross-dressing and hence put a further limit on donning the skirts. But after a while, he had a change of heart and saw that the practice is "harmless fun." As I reconstruct these events, male staff and older campers in the 1990s began wearing the skirts as a conscious act of cross-dressing and a challenge to the prevailing dress norms of camp. When better to challenge those norms than on erev Shabbat, when the camp tradition is to dress up in gender-specific clothes? Camp leadership responded not by outlawing the practice, but by containing it and limiting the skirts to Israeli dancing. When, several years later, Louis pushed back harder, he realized he was overreacting. By 1999 this practice had become a camp tradition that campers viewed as what Olim does on Friday night. It was not as threatening or confusing as Louis initially had thought.

As time went on, the gender rules at this and other camps have changed. There are now more opportunities for campers to explore alternative gender behaviors, and at Eisner transgender campers are welcome (Grinberg 2020). The original countercultural gesture of cross-dressing seems to have lost its sting. Nevertheless, this camp tradition continued and was recently expanded when the girls decided to get in on the act with their boxer shorts. While the girls chose boxer shirts as a male item to match the boys' skirts, Abi is emphatically telling us that for today's campers Phish is ancient history and testing those boundaries is not relevant. What they want is the opportunity to pass their garments on to a next group of campers. They hope to come back in a couple of years and see their skirt or boxer shorts being worn by a younger peer.

To understand this change, let me draw a parallel to the history of playing Indian at American camps (see chapter 2). Camp is a natural place for staff and kids to dress up and assume alternative identities (Paris 2008). Often the staff members who originate a camp tradition are motivated by a deeper social cause, such as returning to nature or challenging rigid gender norms. But over time, the social practice persists as part of camp life even while the original motivation fades. Campers were still playing Indian in the 1950s, but few were in touch with the ideas that generated this tradition (Van Slyck 2006). So too, I believe, the cross-dressing at Eisner has lost its protest meaning. The social practice is still meaningful, but its significance has evolved.

Following Barbara Myerhoff in her book *Number Our Days* (1979), when looking at these invented camp traditions as expressive rituals, I ask: What needs and wishes might the campers be expressing through the ritual that they may not articulate in direct speech? In this case, the key ritual action takes place when the Olim campers are completing their last summer as campers and before their transition to becoming camp staff. At this transitional moment, when they are most concerned with their "legacy" and leaving their mark on the camp, they have created a rite de passage (Turner 1982). At the end of their Olim summer, they carefully consider the recipient for this garment. Their search for a younger camper to whom to give this garment expresses their need for a successor to carry their name forward after they are gone. By passing this garment on, they bestow on one younger camper the power to wear this "holy" garment with its attached names when he or she dances the special dances on Friday nights for celebrating Shabbat.

This reading of the ritual opens to another dimension of Shabbat at camp. Eisner does a great deal on Shabbat to build a sense of camp as one's extended family. At the erev Shabbat meal, campers are encouraged to sit with their family members. Then everyone at the table blesses one another as if they were all members of a single family. Given these associations of Shabbat and creating an extended camp family, it is not surprising that at the end of the Olim summer, these campers have found a powerful way to ritually express their wish to be remembered by bestowing this garment on a younger "sibling." Through this rite de passage, they can be assured that their "sibling" will wear the garment and keep alive the bond of names attached to the skirt/shorts. At the very moment when they are passing beyond their camper years, Olim is symbolically taking their place in the succession of generations at Eisner.

From this perspective, dance session takes on added meaning. Wearing these "holy" garments, Olim campers take center stage. They are surrounded by both younger campers and staff members who have come to dance. Olim campers are wearing the skirts/shorts that likely bear the staff's names. At this special moment, Olim represents the continuity between the staff and the younger campers who are dancing alongside. Olim, clad in these garments, becomes in the dance the symbolic fulcrum between past and future in the succession of generations. While each of the dancers may eventually leave camp, dancing with these garments represents the continuity of camp. Eisner on erev Shabbat assumes the role of a secondary family and assures these adolescents that in a rapidly changing world, the Shabbat traditions they have enacted will continue at camp for years to come.

LATE EREV SHABBAT AT YAVNEH

Song leaders, amplified music, and outfit changes—the crucial elements of erev Shabbat at Eisner—have no place at the more observant Camp Yavneh. Yet Yavneh lives on its Jewish spiritedness and has created a set of late Friday night rituals that parallel the celebration at Eisner. These are scenes from Yavneh during the summer of 2017.

As the traditional Friday evening meal draws to a close and camp is about to sing the Birkat (grace after meals), the oldest division, Kerem (Vineyard), comes to the front of the dining hall and stands with arms around one another. The forty-three Kerem participants are the oldest campers who also serve as counselors-in-training. They are entering eleventh grade and spend the whole summer at camp. They are given multiple leadership roles on Shabbat, the first of which is to lead the singing of Birkat on erev Shabbat. This they do with gusto, adding hand motions, extra words, and sounds to which the other campers respond with glee.

When Birkat concludes, everyone leaves the dining hall, and all but the youngest move to the adjoining Ben Zvi hall. Kerem lines up to provide the bridge between the hadar and Ben Zvi.

With staff and campers seated in concentric circles of benches, the singing of *zemirot* (traditional Shabbat songs) commences. The co-division heads of Kerem lead the singing of three zemirot in moderate tempo. Then comes a series of Hebrew Shabbat songs with intensifying tempo. With the last two songs, everything truly intensifies. Seated in place, campers and staff begin gesturing with a set of hand and body motions, pouring their hearts and souls into these songs. As earlier happened with "Minyan Man," the group builds toward a crescendo of sound and movement as they bring this segment of singing to a close.

The next act belongs to Kerem. These oldest campers arrange a rectangular formation of single benches, cordoning off about half the space. They stand on those benches facing inward. The younger campers have left and the remaining teen campers and their staff stand inside that rectangle in small same-sex circles. A few Kerem campers hand out a sheet that lists the twelve songs they will lead. On the sheet are directives: "Be loud!!" "Energy." "We love you."

Kerem begins the singing while standing on those benches. There is a diversity of songs, with each being led by a small group of Kerem campers.

Some are well-known Hebrew songs like "David Melekh Yisrael" and "Ana B'Koach." Some are Israeli songs like "Od Yavo Shalom" and "L'Shana Haba." One is an English song called "Who's That Man?" But the most elaborate ones are traditional Shabbat songs modified by Yavneh ritual. In one modification the traditional chorus is kept in place, but campers insert funny phrases having nothing to do with the original song. In the other, the traditional song is sung verse by verse in Hebrew and the Kerem leaders assign each verse to one of the small circles. That circle sings or shouts that verse in its own invented way. Then the next group competes to outdo the previous one. As the song progresses, each group grows more inventive and wilder in how they present their lines. On the final song, "L'Shana Haba," the Kerem campers jump down from their benches and rush toward the other campers for a frenzied finale. At that point, without gym shorts or accompanying guitars, the Yavneh kids look much like their peers at Eisner, with bodies bumping together in a mosh pit at the center of their created space.

This invented ritual is artfully designed. Standing on their benches, the Kerem campers tower over the younger campers. But they also face inward toward their peers and lead the singing, which relies on their peers' participation. They have twelve well-known songs that are mostly traditional but open to rearrangement. The campers strive to outdo one another and strut their stuff. But this strutting is contained and at the right moment the ritual ends. The younger teen campers leave for their bunks while the two oldest divisions, Maalot and Kerem, each moves to hold its *tish*.

The term "tish" comes from the Shabbat practices of the Hasidic community. Samuel Heilman describes visiting the tish at the Belz yeshiva in Jerusalem. "The tish was any formal meal at the rebbe's table. Commonly it was the first festive meal of his Sabbath" (1992, 83). There the male Hasidim gathered to witness the *rebbe* (grand rabbi) bless the wine and challah, pass the food around, give his Torah talk, and then join together singing the Shabbat songs. The practice of holding a tish at Yavneh derives from Hasidic practice, but actually has little in common with what Heilman describes.

Before tish begins, Kerem takes a five-minute break during which the custodian comes in to turn off the lights. The Kerem campers and staff return to the darkened room, sit on benches facing one another, and begin to sing softly. The tish is run by the campers themselves. The mood has dramatically shifted. The tish is soft, dark, revelatory. A camper announces, "If you wish to speak, come up and tell me and you can between songs." Campers use the tish to speak from their heart to the group. Some campers told me that they have learned more about one another from the tish than from any other occasion. Staff have told me this is the moment when a camper has come out as gay or told about a parental illness or spoken of a recently discovered life dream. What I hear this Shabbat are several campers expressing their wishes for Kerem to become even closer during the closing weeks of the summer. At the end of the tish, all quietly exit the hall.

Parallel to the changing outfits at Eisner are the changing configurations of the late evening at Yavneh. First there are the well-lit, orderly circles in which everyone sings zemirot together. Then the older campers build a contained space in which to explore a wilder Shabbat joy. Finally, in a darkened room, the oldest campers sing gently to one another and open their hearts to speak and hear. Following them through this sequence of moves, I wonder what the Kerem campers are expressing by enacting their late erev Shabbat rituals in this sequence.

From Mosh Pit to Zemirot at Yavneh

At each of these camps, Shabbat ritual practices evolve and change over time. At Yavneh, the change has been dramatic. It was one of the first things that Debbie Sussman told me about Shabbat at Yavneh.

> The way we do zemirot has totally changed. We used to do a real raucous zemirot in the hadar after Birkat. We did it for many years and changed just a few years ago. I finally said, "It is not how it should be." (Sussman 2016)

A year later, Debbie elaborated on the need for change.

> "Freilich" [joyous] it wasn't. I would say they were screaming and not singing. It was also exclusive. Half the older campers felt excluded and did not participate. It was very uncomfortable . . . Those who liked it called it "great ruach." From my perspective it went on and on and became increasingly negative. (Sussman 2017)

Debbie is describing an erev Shabbat practice that had been going on for many years, but had gotten out of hand and grown increasingly negative. It is never easy for a camp director to change Shabbat practices, yet Debbie clearly felt she needed to act even though many had deeply loved the Yavneh ritual.

Counselor Sara Schulwolf described an earlier version of these zemirot in glowing terms:

> I glanced around the hadar ochel and this is what I saw—people of all ages . . . singing zemirot together with unparalleled ruach. Jumping, clapping, energized by the palpable spirit of Shabbat, an entire group of people came together as one unit, one family. (Schulwolf 2014, 38)

In Sara's view what was wonderful was "the unparalleled ruach" that was expressed by people of all ages jumping and clapping together "as one unit, one family." There had been a richness to the ruach of erev Shabbat; however, over time that ruach, in Debbie's view, had grown excessive and problematic. The joy had turned sour.

It was my good fortune that a veteran Yavneh staff member, Herschel Singer, came to study at Brandeis University and took my course on Jewish summer camps. Herschel decided to write his course paper on a change process at Yavneh that he called "From Mosh-Pit to Z'mirot." In that paper he described in greater detail the changes that Debbie referenced in her interview. I will rely on Singer's account to put flesh on the bone of this change process. Here he describes what had grown excessive on erev Shabbat.

> One of the highlights of the Friday night program comes after dinner when historically the oldest aydah, Kerem, would create a circle of benches in the chadar ochel large enough for nearly the entire camp to fit. They would stand on the benches and lead a spirited song and dance session, a mosh pit of sorts. Campers of all ages as well as counselors would bring a huge amount of energy to these sessions, singing, dancing, playfully pushing, and sweating as one cohesive group. While this was fun, exciting, and enjoyable for many, there were a number of safety concerns. It was not infrequent that eyeglasses might get jumbled off of someone's face and be promptly (accidentally) stomped upon. Sometime the excitement would lead to people being overly squished, tripping, or falling. (Singer 2018, 3)

I asked Herschel what he meant by "mosh pit." He wrote back, "It used to be screaming, pushing. More like what you think of as a mosh pit." He left little doubt that some celebrants came to feel that screaming and pushing was the way to express their Shabbat joy. Little wonder Debbie felt a need for dramatic change.

When the change came in 2012, it was a complex move planned and imposed by the *hanhallah* (leadership) involving both erev Shabbat and the annual Zimriyah (song competition).

> Without question Zimriyah is the single most important program of the summer. The structure of the evening has been for decades that each aydah sings three songs: a *shir chassidi* [religious song], a *shir yisraeli* [an Israeli song], and a *shir aydah* [a Hebrew lyric about your age group]. It was announced that this summer Zimriyah would include a new category, *shir zemer*. (Ibid.)

Yavneh leaders were distinguishing between two types of religious songs that are sung on Shabbat, the *zemer* and the *shir*. The former is a special category of traditional religious songs that were composed specifically to be sung around the Shabbat dinner table. They are usually called *zemirot* (plural) and in many traditional homes are sung at the Shabbat meal. The term *shir* is the broader category of religious songs that put to music verses from the Bible or other traditional sources. At many intentional Jewish camps, these two types of songs are so intermixed that it is hard to tell them apart. But the Yavneh leadership felt that camp needed to be teaching the campers to sing the zemirot.

> Mosh pit is camp Shabbat and not Shabbat-Shabbat. We thought our kids will not know the songs that people sing at home. So at Zimriyah we took the shir chassidi and it became shir zemer, quiet singing for a peaceful Shabbat. (Rubins 2018)

Lisa Rubins looks back at the older practice—the mosh pit in the hadar ochel—and believes it had gotten to be so campy that it no longer had much overlap with traditional home practice. To bring camp practice more in line with home practice, the leadership decided to teach the campers to sing zemirot via the Zimriyah. They assigned each division a specific zemer to sing at the Zimriyah. They knew that the campers and staff would learn to sing that zemer well, for they would be competing against one another at the Zimriyah.

That same summer they introduced the big change of moving the song/dance circle out of the dining hall and into the newly built Ben Zvi hall. There the whole camp (except the youngest campers) would sit in concentric circles and sing the zemirot they had learned for the Zimriyah. Only after singing these zemirot and a few other *shirim* (songs) would Kerem be invited to push the benches together and assume their leadership of the mosh pit. But the key differences were that in Ben Zvi there is much more room to move and hence less tendency to push and shove, and the mosh pit is limited in duration to the twelve songs that Kerem leads.

Herschel is clear that originally he and other staff members resisted this change and experienced the leadership as imposing this unwanted change upon them. Yet in assessing this change process five year later, Herschel notes that "looking back at the life cycle of this change now, it seems it was the right decision to make." Just five years later, "there are very few who still lament the loss of the old way" (Singer 2017). I would have to agree. Had I not learned this history, I would never have known from observing that I was watching a dramatically altered Shabbat ritual from what had been before 2012. I noticed that current Kerem campers do not even use the term "mosh pit" but rather call this practice "Shabbat zemirot." When Lisa arranged for me to meet the Kerem group and ask them a few questions, they never mentioned the old practice and listed as their current favorite aspects of Shabbat zemirot and tish.

The Kerem Tish at Yavneh

The erev Shabbat celebration at Yavneh does not culminate with Shabbat zemirot, but with the tish. At Ramah, the oldest division also holds a tish as the final event on erev Shabbat, but it has little of the intensity of the Kerem tish. At Eisner there is no tish, but their oldest campers have the special cross-dressing role at the culminating dance session.

The Kerem tish, like cross-dressing at Eisner, is a Shabbat practice that was first initiated by staff for one purpose and then developed over time to serve different camper needs. Lisa recalls that in the year 2000 there was a Yavneh staff member who had become a *ba'al teshuva* (turning to Orthodox practice) and wanted to bring Hasidic practices to camp. He introduced a tish with singing and eating the stew called cholent. The cholent did not last, but the tish and the singing did. This tish began in the dining hall and later migrated to Ben Zvi. Lisa thinks of the tish as a *masoret* (tradition) that the staff initiated but that Kerem has taken over (Rubins 2018).

The tish stands out for its four prominent elements: (1) darkness, (2) camper leadership, (3) soft singing, and (4) personal sharing. Let's look at each.

Darkness: During the break between zemirot and tish, the custodian, who as a non-Jew is not bound by the rules of Shabbat observance, comes in to turn off the lights. This unusual step signals that the tish will be different from the earlier rituals. The darkness creates a special atmosphere that allows for greater intimacy for this coed group of teen campers.

Camper leadership: The Kerem tish is entirely led by Kerem campers. It is designed as an intimate conversation among peers. The staff are in the room but hover in the background.

Soft singing: To aid in the radical shift of mood from the zemirot to the tish, the music shifts. At tish, Kerem is singing the gentlest of Jewish songs. To my mind the singing sounds like lullabies that a parent might sing at bedtime.

Personal sharing: The key element of tish is sharing personal feelings. When a camper chooses to speak, he or she notifies the leader and the singing stops. The speaker begins with "Shabbat shalom, Kerem" and the group responds, "Shabbat shalom, so-and-so." The expectation is that the speaker will speak personally and share what he or she is feeling at that moment. When the speaking ends, there is silent affirmation. Then the singing continues until a next camper chooses to share.

The tish comes after Kerem has led the Birkat and then the zemirot. Those are moments when Kerem stands before the camp and leads spirited singing and movement. The tish is a turn inward: toward being alone as a peer group, softer singing, and personal sharing. For while Yavneh tends to whole-camp celebration, from ReLish at the beginning of Shabbat to Havdalah at the end, this is an occasion when Kerem chooses to be alone and explore together the softer and gentler dimensions of ruach Shabbat.

At the center of this invented ritual is the personal sharing. When I asked staff at Ramah, they said the personal sharing there takes places among the oldest campers back in their bunks after the communal activities have ended. But the Yavneh teens have created this ritual of sharing that takes place in a coed group of teens who have mostly known one another since they were young campers. Here in the closing hours of their time together as campers, they express their need to know one another on a deeper level and form a tighter interpersonal unit. Indeed, when Kerem alumni return as staff members, which many do, they are still identified by their Kerem cohort, such as "Kerem 16" or "Kerem 17." The Kerem group remains a foundation of their camp identity for all their years at Yavneh.

The salience of the tish is underscored during the last week of camp. Kerem gathers together with Levi'im (campers two years their junior) to teach them how to hold a tish. Levi'im has seen Kerem leading the zemirot, but has yet to be initiated into the secrets of the tish. At the moment when these oldest campers are ending their years as campers and feeling intensely the loss of their camper status (many will cry at the end of their last tish), they create a ritual bestowing this special gift on younger "siblings." At Yavneh this is not a gift to an individual, but a collective gift to a younger group. Yet the effect is the same. As they are giving up their camper status, Kerem can be assured that this precious Shabbat practice will be continued beyond their camper years. They may be leaving camp, but Yavneh will be there for them as a second family for years to come and their precious tish will be carried forward by successive groups of older campers.

LATE EREV SHABBAT AT RAMAH WISCONSIN

Zemirot and tish are also very much part of the late erev Shabbat celebration at Ramah Wisconsin. Yet, Ramah has designed these very differently than Yavneh. Communal joy is integral to Shabbat, but Ramah is unique in seeking on erev Shabbat to balance that joy with rigor and highlight the camp's informal Jewish learning agenda.

The oldest aidah at Ramah is Nivonim—those who are wise. Nivonim campers are entering eleventh grade, spend the whole summer at camp, live up on their own hill, and have a two-week internship at the start of camp. They have as many leadership roles at camp throughout the summer as their peers at Eisner and Yavneh. Yet, curiously, they have a lower leadership profile on Shabbat, as we will see in these scenes from Nivonim 2017 and 2018.

After the traditional Shabbat tefilla and dinner in July 2017, Nivonim joins with the next oldest aidot—Machon and Bogrim—for singing zemirot in the hadar. What I observe for the next half hour takes me by surprise. A few of the youngest counselors lead the singing while the more senior staff sit to the side. Some of the older campers—mostly males—get into the action singing four traditional Shabbat songs with loud voices and body movements. But then the event simply ends. Observing this shapeless session left me confused. Why are there no song leaders or teen leaders organizing and leading zemirot, as I saw at Eisner and Yavneh?

Leaving the dining hall, I unexpectedly run across a circle of girl campers standing on the dark lawn outside the hadar singing the songs I heard the night before at mishmar (see chapter 4). Then I notice a parallel circle of boy campers. Both circles sing for about ten minutes. When they finish, I ask a counselor who is standing there, "What have I just seen?" He tells me that this aidah, Machon, began this practice the year before. Each Shabbat after dinner and before the *peulat erev* (evening activity), they organize themselves into these circles of song. On their own, these campers have created a mini-mishmar for erev Shabbat.

I rush up the hill to attend the evening activity with Nivonim. Each older division has as its main late erev Shabbat activity an informal learning session based on the Shabbat theme that the division head developed and the counselors worked on with the mercaz staff (see chapter 4). The theme of this Shabbat for Nivonim is Jewish views on death and dying. The thirty-seven Nivonim campers and their staff are seated in their *maodon* (clubhouse) listening to a panel of three people talk on this topic. The first, a young male counselor, tells the story of when a few years ago his grandfather died in the middle of the summer. As a camper, he had to go home for the funeral and *shiva* (mourning period). He emphasizes how thoughtfully his counselors received him back into the bunk and responded to his pain and dislocation.

Didi, a camp social worker, contrasts her memories of when her mother died when she was a teen camper with her father's dying this past year. She wants them to understand that a teen can barely comprehend the immensity of death, while now she sits with that sadness every time she says the Mourner's Kaddish. But the speaker who most wins their avid attention is a young counselor who describes his decision a few years earlier to join his local *chevra kadisha* (holy society). He was by far the youngest member of this group that takes on the ritual responsibility of cleansing the bodies of the departed before they are buried. It is hard to believe that a teenager would volunteer for this responsibility. He describes this work as "life changing." The camper questions go mostly to him. They want to know, "What is it like to wash the body of the departed?" They are eager to learn from this near-peer what is involved in enacting these Jewish rituals for the newly departed.

The contrast between singing zemirot and this panel discussion is evident. The former lacked a clear design and unfolded haphazardly. The panel is carefully planned, well balanced, and highly engaging. The teens ask one question after another until the hour is up. The next day, when I talk with a few teens, they tell me the topic was compelling. This is what it sounds like when the educational planning works well and Nivonim campers are deeply engaged in discussing how Jews live their Jewish lives.

A few minutes after this session ends, the tish begins. The Nivonim tish is voluntary and I count about ten campers and a few staff in attendance. Maya, the rosh aidah, leads and the campers choose the traditional Shabbat songs to sing. The singing is gentle; everyone is tired. They sing for a half hour before ending. Maya tells me this is usually better attended, but even with more campers, this remains a pale version of the tish at Yavneh. I wonder why this same group of Nivonim campers who rushed to attend the mishmar at 10 p.m. the night before has little energy for their Shabbat tish. True, this is the seventh week of camp and they worked hard all week to stage the Nivonim musical. Yet I suspect there is more to this story and am left to wonder how these Nivonim campers balance between their wish to celebrate a joyous Shabbat and the educational demands of the Ramah program.

Ramah Staff Perspectives

Jon Adam Ross is a unique character at Ramah Wisconsin. He grew up a Ramah camper, went on to study theater and acting, and returned to camp as the head of dramatics. Since Jacob has become the camp director, he has asked JAR (as he is known at camp) to take on a number of different top leadership positions. JAR also works as a consultant to the Foundation for Jewish Camp (FJC) and has consulted at many different Jewish camps. He has been one of my main informants at Ramah Wisconsin (Reimer 2012). It felt natural to bring him my questions about Shabbat at Ramah.

The first thing I have to understand, JAR tells me, is that Rabbi Soloff built an aidah-centered camp and Jacob shares that commitment. The camp as a whole only comes together for a few occasions, such as the Thursday night musicals and the Kabbalat Shabbat services on Friday night. Otherwise, the primary community is the division.

The second thing is that Rabbi Soloff and Jacob are both "cerebral" and "not feelers." They favor "a culture of rigor" with "serious programs." While they want campers to have fun, it is not a primary goal. Lastly, I need to know that not all Ramah camps are like this one. Rabbi Soloff and Jacob share a vision of what Ramah *should be* and are not that interested in how other camps are run. This Ramah has always had serious educational programs on Shabbat and that is not about to change. Indeed, there has been a tremendous investment in making these programs of higher educational quality (Ross 2017).

The second staff member to whom I turn is Maya Zinkow, the division head of Nivonim. Maya grew up at this camp and has served on the staff for eight years. This is her third year as the rosh aidah for this group of campers and she is very attached to them. Maya is also a rabbinical student at JTS and wants me to know three things about Shabbat for Nivonim.

First, the two leadership roles the campers care deeply about are mishmar and the opening of Kabbalat Shabbat. They want to be at mishmar seated around that table as leaders. Likewise, they want to be the first to arrive on Fridays at Kabbalat Shabbat to greet everyone else and hand out the siddurim.

Second, the last week of camp all the Nivonim campers come to the erev Shabbat tefilla dressed in black. They stand throughout the service with their arms around one another and listen to their peers speak to the whole camp, reflecting on their years together as campers at Ramah. It is a very special culminating event for them in which they get to tell their story and leave their mark on the whole camp.

Third, while the staff does not do enough discussing with campers about the significance of Shabbat, last week they held a session on Conservative Judaism's approach to the use of electronics on Shabbat. She knows full well that few of these campers observe Shabbat consistently at home. Yet she is encouraged that they listened, were curious, and asked good questions about science and religion, God, and halakha (Zinkow 2017).

Maya is aware of how important camp rituals are to these teens and respects their need to lead at mishmar and greet others at the outset of Shabbat. What she is most passionate about is discussing a halakhic approach to Shabbat. She wants the teens to feel Shabbat joy, but she equally wants them to learn about Shabbat observance. Camp is her opportunity to develop their curiosity about science and religion, God, and halakha. This is an educational agenda I hear about only at Ramah Wisconsin. The Nivonim summer is a key opportunity to have these conversations, and Maya leads the way.

Ramah's Singing Campers—Nivonim 2018

I leave my visit to Ramah Wisconsin in 2017 in a quandary. I have learned from my observations at Eisner and Yavneh to appreciate the salience of communal joy in the celebration of Shabbat at those camps. Yet I am not seeing much evidence of that joy at Ramah. Yes, it was certainly present at mishmar on Thursday night and then again at the conclusion of the tefilla on erev Shabbat. But neither the singing of zemirot nor the Nivonim tish was particularly joyous. Indeed, only a minority of Nivonim campers actively participated in either one and the majority sat them out. How to make sense of that?

At the same time, there were the circles of singing campers that I discovered outside after the singing of zemirot. These Machon campers had found a creative way to import a mini-mishmar into their erev Shabbat schedule. This camper-generated ritual seemed to express a need for more soulful Shabbat singing. What, I wondered, would these campers be like in Nivonim? I was fortunate to find out during my next visit to Ramah in July 2018.

Nivonim 2018 is a larger group of fifty-three campers. Daniella Elyashar, a veteran staff member, is their rosh aidah and has her own ideas about how to run Nivonim. I would see several interesting changes from the year before. Let's begin with singing zemirot. This time, Nivonim stays in place in the dining hall and several of them come forward to lead the singing. For thirty-five minutes, they enthusiastically sing familiar Shabbat songs. They close with "MI-PI-EL," a favorite. Now they are up on their feet, standing in small groups, singing loudly, jumping up and down, and edging toward what I would call Yavneh territory. A whole aidah is up on its feet going mildly wild for Shabbat celebration. That is an encouraging sight at Ramah.

I leave and, sure enough, find the same circles engaged in the mishmar singing on the dark lawn. I stand and count ten female campers and one counselor. They sing for ten minutes, leave their circle, and walk arm in arm up the hill singing another mishmar song. Two minutes later, the guys come along arm in arm singing their mishmar song. Once inside the clubhouse, the boys and girls join together and sing a final song before the evening activity begins. They have kept alive and even expanded upon their innovative ritual.

The counselors announce they will reverse the usual order and hold the tish first. They bring out the refreshments and start leading the tish singing for the whole aidah. Now I realize the contrast between camper-led singing and the tish. There is little camper energy invested in the tish singing. The counselors transition to the educational activity, which focuses on understanding the meaning of the Hebrew words of the songs that they sing. The aidah is divided into smaller subgroups and the counselors lead discussions focused on the meaning of different traditional Hebrew songs. Here the counselors are fully in charge and have worthwhile textual knowledge to convey. Yet, there is none of the excitement that I witnessed the year before. It is the staff telling and the campers listening.

What happened to the camper joy that I witnessed earlier? Why are the counselors not building upon it? This is a real tension at Ramah Wisconsin. Of our three camps, Ramah has by far the most ambitious learning agenda and places it at the heart of erev Shabbat. This has great educational advantage and yet comes at a cost to ruach Shabbat. If I am correct to posit that communal joy is a primary ingredient that makes older campers love Shabbat at camp, then Ramah may be minimizing that love by limiting its free expression. Some Nivonim campers are dedicated to importing mishmar singing into erev Shabbat. They do so voluntarily with an innovative ritual that they invest with their youthful energy. One wonders why that amazing energy is not more central to how this Ramah celebrates erev Shabbat.

CONCLUSION: THE CHANGING NATURE OF CELEBRATING SHABBAT AT CAMP

While stressing how essential ritual celebration is to the dynamic life of Jewish communities, Barbara Myerhoff, in her book *Number Our Days*, notes how vulnerable rituals are to disruption. "All rituals are paradoxical and dangerous enterprises . . . Paradoxical because rituals are conspicuously artificial and theatrical . . . Dangerous because when we are not convinced by a ritual, we may become aware of ourselves as having made them up" (1979, 86).

The late Shabbat evening camp rituals are at once "conspicuously artificial and theatrical" and yet vital to the celebration of Shabbat at camp. For the older campers and their staff, these are the moments when they feel most alive to celebrating Shabbat. Yet, so much can go wrong with the ritual process and threaten the shared joy of Shabbat at camp.

Both Eisner and Yavneh reached a crisis moment when the ritual process was greatly threatened. At Eisner that happened in 2005, when Louis Bordman decided to move song session out of the dining hall and into the newly built social hall. That decision occasioned "an Olim uprising" in which 120 oldest campers and their staff protested that this move would ruin song session for them. Louis knew he had to take their protest seriously, for Shabbat at Eisner depends on their energy and participation. So Louis negotiated a settlement in which Olim would escort the way into the social hall and take the lead in song session. But this initial agreement could last only so long. The first arrangement was for the Olim campers to be seated in the front of the hall while the song leaders played from a low stage.

As the modes of music changed in the larger youth culture, older campers began to rise from their seats and bang on the stage. The song leaders no longer felt safe, and camp leaders decided to build a higher stage to protect them. But once the song leaders were higher up, campers could stand and create a mosh pit. Now they were jumping and bumping as they sang. The outside music world spilled into the Eisner song session and changed the way campers and staff celebrate Shabbat. This time Louis chose to work with the "wild song session" and do what he could to preserve the possibility that most campers could still participate even though song session had grown louder and wilder.

Mosh pit behavior spilled as well into the Shabbat celebration at Yavneh. Debbie Sussman found that increasingly more difficult to abide. As soon as the new Ben Zvi social hall was completed in 2012, she and her leadership team swiftly moved the late evening ritual out of the dining hall and into Ben Zvi where there was more room and they could put more limits on mosh pit behavior. Their move drew resistance from camp staff, who viewed this move as destroying all they loved about celebrating Shabbat at camp (Singer 2017). Yet, as happened in Eisner, Yavneh leadership was careful to position their oldest campers as leaders and encourage them to own a part of the ritual so they could still feel Shabbat joy. That balance worked. Five years later, few at Yavneh even remembered the wilder days of the mosh pit in the dining room.

These parallel crises illustrate much about celebrating Shabbat at these camps. First, camp leadership and the older campers are dependent upon one another in making Shabbat work. The campers cannot plan the rituals by themselves and need the camp leadership to set up the Shabbat framework. But the leadership needs the older campers and their staff to bring their energy and dedication to make the celebration joyous. The two sides must find ways to balance their needs: the safety and integrity of the Shabbat celebration with the wish to express youthful energies and enthusiasm.

Second, older campers today need a way to celebrate with greater intensity. Tefilla alone does not fulfill that need. In these times, when youth culture has grown more intense in its modes, that energy will find its way into camp.

Leadership has to design Shabbat rituals that can safely channel their youthful energy.

Third, when that balance is achieved, oldest campers are moved and wish to lead their younger peers in expressing Shabbat joy. Moreover, they experience their camp as a second family and actively seek ways to leave their mark and prepare their younger peers to learn to take their place as future camper leaders. I return to their wish to be leaders and leave their mark in a fuller analysis in chapters 8 and 9.

If this is the case at Eisner and Yavneh, does it apply as well to Ramah Wisconsin? Ramah leadership has designed a different framework for late erev Shabbat that highlights the informal educational evening activity. That results in a diminished tish in which the oldest campers invest little of their energies. Nevertheless, older campers have invented their own mini-mishmar for Friday nights in which they form a circle, choose songs to sing, and march up the hill singing with full hearts. That tells me that these campers feel the same need as their peers in the other camps to express their soulfulness and create a more intense musical celebration. While that is not true for everyone in Nivonim, the whole division dresses in black on the last Friday night of the summer and tells their story to the assembled camp. The whole aidah may not need the greater intensity, but they do need to leave their mark on camp and find their place in the generation of campers at Ramah Wisconsin.

7 / SKILL BUILDING AND CONCLUDING SHABBAT

WHILE FRIDAY NIGHT AT CAMP builds toward intensifying joy, Saturday morning has a very different energy. It is a morning to sleep late and often skip breakfast. The high emotional energy of erev Shabbat has peaked and by morning camp is trying to awaken their campers and staff to engage in a second Shabbat prayer session with Torah reading. After a full Friday night of celebration, there is a wish to spend the day relaxing. The challenge for camp is to ease people into tefilla, awaken them with song and prayer, and ready them to hear the Torah reading.

Shabbat lunch retains some of the mood of the morning but also opens on to the expansive summer afternoon. Shabbat afternoon at camp is the most leisurely time of the whole week. Few activities are planned; campers and staff have the opportunity to choose how to spend their time. That can be challenging for younger campers but also exhilarating for those ready to unwind. The afternoon has its own mood and affordances, very different than the morning. By late afternoon, camp calls its campers back for reflective sessions, *seudah shlishit* (the third meal), and the closing rituals of Havdalah (separating Shabbat from the week). Jewish camps understand that how Shabbat concludes is educationally significant. Last impressions matter, and staff want campers to part from Shabbat with a sweet taste and a wish for its return.

It will come as no surprise that our three camps follow this outline for Shabbat day while putting their own spin on how campers experience it. In this chapter, I describe each of the phases of Shabbat day and focus on how these camps structure the rituals to educate campers in how to celebrate Shabbat as well as take their place as leaders within these Jewish communities.

SHABBAT MORNING: BUILDING THE SKILL BASE

Each of our camps recognizes the need to actively involve campers in the Shabbat morning prayer sessions. The staff knows that passive participation leads to camper apathy. They search for how to make this morning tefilla as engaging as possible while offering campers opportunities to develop their skills by leading aspects of the communal prayer. While leadership opportunities also exist on Friday evening, the number of leadership roles grows on Shabbat morning, especially with reading and interpreting the weekly Torah portion.

What I had not realized before conducting this research is that while there is a consensus among these camps around developing skills in Hebrew usage, singing, and chanting Torah, there are marked differences in how they understand what other leadership skills to develop. By examining carefully *how* each camp structures these leadership opportunities, we can discover their implicit conceptions of how to prepare their older campers for future leadership roles in the larger Jewish community. For Shabbat morning, more than erev Shabbat, is when these camps look ahead to how what campers learn at camp can prepare them for leading active Jewish lives beyond camp.

SHABBAT MORNING AT RAMAH WISCONSIN

When visiting Ramah Wisconsin, I would often awake on Shabbat morning to a totally quiet campus. Most everyone would sleep until 8:30 a.m. Only around 9 a.m. would I see some staff and campers heading out of their bunks toward the dining hall for what Ramah calls "a light breakfast." The larger numbers emerge closer to 9:30, dressed in their Shabbat clothing and heading for the morning tefilla at the multiple sites where their divisions usually pray. Many campers appear sleepy and a bit disheveled, and I could see latecomers following in the rear. Fortunately, the staff appear more awake and ready to launch the tefilla.

Shabbat morning services are longer at Ramah. There is the full Shacharit (morning service) followed by Torah reading and Musaf (additional service). Visiting clergy and educators are recruited to give a short dvar Torah in English. Tefilla is highly participatory, and by the time of their bar or bat mitzvah, campers are asked to lead parts of the tefilla and to read Torah and Haftorah. All this is done in Hebrew. The reward after tefilla is the long and tasty kiddush (reception) to which campers, staff, and guests are all invited. At Ramah, you pray first and only then eat, relax, socialize, and (if you wish) freely run around.

Shabbat Morning with Ramah's Youngest Campers

I spent Shabbat morning in June 2015 with the youngest Ramah campers, the nine-year-olds in Kochavim. They gather in their Shabbat clothes in the library at 9:30 a.m. for their Shabbat morning prayer. Their counselors hand out the specially designed siddurim that has each of their names on the cover and the relevant prayers on photocopied sheets. The group makes its way through the Hebrew prayers of Shacharit (the morning prayer), singing a different tune for each prayer. The counselors lead and the campers participate with hand motions and even a brief dance step. The tefilla feels relaxed and engaging. At the end, a male counselor teaches a new song, "Thank You, God." This song calls for thanking God for two rhyming blessings like *rain* and *brain*. The campers are eager to offer their rhymes. Soon they have thanked God in rhyme for their many blessings.

Elana, the division head, announces they would next be joining an older group for Torah reading. This catches some campers by surprise. I hear one boy ask his counselor, "Didn't we just pray?" The counselor responds, "We are lucky. We have Torah reading just once a week. The older campers have it three times."

Off they go to the social hall where that service is in progress. They fit into the benches that have been left open. When it comes time for the Torah reading, Danny, the presiding staff member, explains that they will be receiving the Ramah *chumash* (printed Torah) with its English commentaries on the weekly portion. He invites campers to read along. A visiting rabbi then gives a short Torah talk before the staff members read the Torah portion in Hebrew from the scroll. Campers are called up for *aliyot* (reading an assigned passage from the Torah). I look around to see how the other campers are responding. A few are reading the English commentaries. Most are squirming in their seats while paying little to no attention to the Torah reading. When the Torah reading is complete, the staff put the Torah back in the ark and end the prayer with closing songs. I hear another counselor say in jest, "Just one more hour of prayer."

The campers leave for the gym next door. I watch the nine-year-old boys take off running around that gym. Round and round they go, letting off the accumulated steam from two hours of sitting through services. The counselors joke with the campers before blessing the wine and partaking of the refreshments. The campers have now earned Shabbat free time.

The contrast between the small, cozy morning service for Kochavim and the Torah service is jarring. I ask Danny about the Torah service. He explains that they do this part of the service as fast as they possibly can because they know that most campers are lost. Some months later I ask Jacob about this contrast. He explains that having a full Torah reading is halakhically mandated for the oldest two aidot. Reading Torah is the camp norm, but the younger divisions read a shorter (triennial) portion. He acknowledges that what I witnessed is far from ideal and needs more educational attention (Cytryn 2016).

The morning service for Kochavim exemplifies Ramah at its best. This tefilla introduces these first-time campers to the basic elements of the traditional liturgy that Ramah uses. By comfortably singing their way through these Hebrew prayers, they are learning to master the Hebrew words and recognize the order of the prayers. Using a personalized siddur allows each camper to feel special. Adding their rhymes to the last song reinforces that they can thank God in their own words. It is hard to imagine a better way to engage their interest, sponsor their active participation, and introduce these nine-year-olds to Ramah tefilla.

How to understand the transition to the joint Torah service that has none of these positive features? Clearly, someone missed an opportunity to prepare the campers to understand what a Torah service can be. Even the counselors, who normally serve as positive models for these campers, cannot contain their view that this Torah reading is excessive. While it is important to introduce young campers to the Ramah way of reading Torah, this introduction was more to be endured than enjoyed.

Nivonim Tefilla: Skill Building, Learning, and Relaxing at Ramah

Nivonim meets in its own building called Ohel Yitzchak. There they gather at 9:30 a.m. in July 2017 for Shabbat morning tefilla. These sixteen-year-olds are dressed in their Shabbat clothes with all the boys wearing *kippot* (skullcaps) and *tallitot* (prayer shawls). Some of the girls also don tallit and the seating is mixed. Everyone has a siddur and most have them open to the page. In Ramah style, the staff are there to help, but this is a camper-led service. All who lead have impressive Hebrew skills and know their way through the traditional liturgy. There is not much spiritedness, but Nivonim has achieved a comfort level with tefilla where most of the campers quietly participate while being guided by competent peer leaders.

Torah reading is more difficult. Reading from the Torah scroll—with no vowels and cantillation signs—demands a higher level of preparation. I count eight camper Torah readers for the whole parsha of D'varim (Deuteronomy 1–3). Each reads directly from the Hebrew scroll. Most read fluently; some struggle. After each reading, the other campers express their verbal appreciation. The girl who reads the Haftorah employs the two different tropes traditional for this Shabbat, exhibiting her high level of skill and preparation.

What most catches my attention is the dvar Torah. The speaker, Rabbi Eric Cytryn, is a congregational rabbi and also Jacob's father. Rabbi Cytryn speaks about that week's Shabbat theme of Jewish views on death and dying. In very personal terms, he shares with the campers how as a rabbi he helps families cope with the death of a loved one. He also shares how he dealt with his own parent's death. He speaks in clear and moving terms, conveying how as a rabbi he uses Jewish rituals to assist the bereaved. The teens are more attentive than I have seen before on Shabbat morning.

The tefilla ends with a camper-led Musaf service, which flies by. What the campers are waiting for is the refreshments at the kiddush (reception) that follows. This is their lucky week; there is a brief aidah kiddush, and then a "super kiddush" brought by visiting parents. This is like a catered affair. I meet the proud parents who have driven a long way to spend Shabbat at camp to celebrate their children's birthday with Nivonim.

Making Sense of Ramah's Morning Tefilla

Neil Gillman noted long ago that "there is a distinctive Ramah-style tefilla" (1989, 94). The liturgical structure is halakhic, the ritual is egalitarian, the leadership is democratic, and the mood is relaxed and informal. All these stylistic elements are still in evidence. What is missing is "an abundance of singing" (ibid.). This is not a singing group. A year later, in 2018, their successors will bring a livelier, more upbeat tone to this tefilla.

While spirited singing is lacking, there is an evident display of what Gillman calls "synagogue skills" (ibid., 87). Many of these campers know how to lead a tefilla and read Torah and volunteer with commitment. Ramah helps them develop these competencies and sends them off after camp ready to lead tefilla back home or on a future college campus. Not all the Nivonim campers are so invested; close to half do not choose to lead, and a few sit passively throughout tefilla. But those who are skilled in leading receive much encouragement to remain active in leading services. Ramah has long taken seriously its role in creating both lay and professional leaders for Jewish communities and has invested heavily in developing these particular skills.

Rabbi Cytryn's dvar stands out for capturing camper attention and effectively teaching about the role of the rabbi in the mourning process. It is illustrative of continuing the Shabbat theme that began to be explored on erev Shabbat (see chapter 6). That visiting rabbis are drawn into this role is purposeful. Ramah is invested in having its campers learn about how rabbis, cantors, and educators draw on their Jewish knowledge and skills to serve their communities.

Finally, the kiddush at Ramah plays an important role on Shabbat morning. Let's remember that most campers have skipped breakfast and are hungry by 11:30 a.m. Ramah uses the kiddush not simply to feed hungry campers but also to build links between the camp and home communities. This Nivonim kiddush is brought by parents, but multiple others are sponsored by visiting clergy and educators. Kiddush has become the time for a visiting rabbi or cantor to gather all the campers and staff from that home congregation to spend time together. It builds the connection between camp and congregation, campers and clergy. Kiddush provides a relaxed social time after the tefilla. That balance is essential. Tefilla at Ramah Wisconsin will always be serious and usually low-key. By the time campers reach Nivonim, they have learned to participate and lead. But once tefilla is over, everyone needs time to relax and enjoy one another's company with refreshments not commonly available during the week.

SHABBAT MORNING AT YAVNEH

To move from Ramah to Yavneh on Shabbat morning is to see a different version of traditional Jewish practice. While Ramah Wisconsin places its focus on developing campers' more traditional skills, Yavneh moves the focus toward the "lighter skills." While Ramah waits until kiddush to allow people to relax and enjoy, Yavneh brings that joy into the service itself.

Yavneh's Two Shabbat Morning Minyanim

By 8:30 a.m. on Shabbat morning in August 2018, Yavneh campers and staff are out of their bunks and on their way to choosing between two multiage services:

the mechitza or the egalitarian (egal) minyan. The mechitza minyan takes place indoors, is male-led, and follows the Orthodox practice of same-gender seating divided by a partition. This is a traditional Hebrew tefilla with a full Torah reading. The egal minyan takes place outdoors in Gilboa, features mixed seating, and has a shorter (triennial) Torah reading. On the surface, the egal tefilla looks and sounds like services at Ramah. It is a camper-led traditional Hebrew service in which the older campers (male and female) display their skills in tefilla leading. It has little spirited singing. But there the similarity ends. This does not have the intimate feel of an aidah-based tefilla, and since the egals read a third of the weekly parsha, the Torah readers (a mix of older campers and staff) read shorter Torah portions, which take less time. That results in their finishing Torah and Haftorah reading about a half hour before the mechitza minyan.

What to do with the extra time? Yavneh devotes the time to the weekly parsha quiz. Campers are divided into two quiz teams that compete for points. A staff member leads this quiz by asking factual questions about the Torah portion. (For example, "Which tribe has the largest number of males in the census?") The team that gets the most correct answers wins the quiz. After a sleepy tefilla, these campers come alive to display their knowledge of the biblical text in competing to win. As soon as the quiz ends, everyone rushes off to the dining hall for kiddush and breakfast. Yavneh relies on a halakhic decision that after one has heard Torah reading on Shabbat, one can hear the reciting of Kiddush and then eat a full breakfast. So, by 10:15 a.m. the whole camp is enjoying breakfast. Having a break between the early and later tefilla allows the whole camp to fill up on breakfast foods and caffeinated drinks and then move to the Ben Zvi hall for the Musaf (additional) tefilla.

Musaf is a whole-camp tefilla prayed Orthodox style with a mechitza. (This mechitza was specially built for Ben Zvi and is easily put in place and taken down.) First, the Torah is returned to the ark and a girl camper from Kerem offers a short dvar Torah. Then Musaf is led by a male staff member. For many years Debbie's husband, Joel Sussman, led Musaf with a distinctive style. Since Debbie retired, Meir—a veteran head counselor—has taken over. He follows Joel's style of leading Musaf with a musical flair that culminates with a highly participatory, ruach-rousing Kaddish at the end.

As soon as Meir concludes, down comes the mechitza. Younger girl campers come up to lead the singing of "Ein Keloheinu" while the Kerem campers move to a different stage at the back of the hall. The official tefilla ends with reciting Aleinu and the Mourner's Kaddish. Then, as if on signal, everyone turns his or her chair around to face the stage at the back of the hall. Standing there are the Kerem campers, divided into two same-gender half-circles, ready to lead the concluding hymn of "Adon Olam." First everyone sings together a face-paced, well-known version of "Adon Olam." Then the Kerem girls sing "Adon Olam" to a popular hit tune and the boys follow suit with their own tune. That is followed by a second round of girls versus boys singing. Then both Kerem groups join together and sing "Adon Olam" to two additional popular tunes before concluding.

As the Kerem campers come off the stage, out come a group of ten staff members for Parsha Players. Historically, Parsha Players is a widely practiced dramatization of scenes from the weekly Torah portion. But this version has little to do with the parsha and more to do with the life of Camp Yavneh. The counselors have prepared a number of short skits. Two stand out to me. The first is about a married couple on staff where the wife is portrayed as the dominant partner. The second skit consists of two male counselors expressing their insecurities about how they come across as males. They mask their feelings of insecurity by singing and dancing at camp. With that, Parsha Players ends and everyone leaves for free time before Shabbat lunch.

Making Sense of Musaf at Yavneh

Musaf is recited quickly at Ramah Wisconsin, skipped at Eisner, and made a focal point at Yavneh. This difference can be attributed to denominational stances, but at Yavneh denominational stance is only part of a fuller story.

Yavneh has always prayed a full Musaf, but not as they do today. Back in the 1980s, the whole camp did not come together, but the two minyanim—mechitza and egalitarian—each held its own service. The egals consistently finished a half hour earlier and that necessitated filling the time. Parsha Players was introduced to fill that gap as a dramatization of the weekly portion. It became so popular that campers in the mechitza minyan clamored to have it as well. The solution was to combine the two minyanim into a whole-camp Musaf service where everyone could enjoy Parsha Players after the prayer (Rubins 2020).

Debbie's husband Joel became the official leader of Musaf. Joel was known outside of camp as a vocal leader of the Jewish performing group Safam. He had a great voice, exuded lots of charisma, and brought a special status to this tefilla. For many years Joel led Musaf, campers led the concluding songs, and the staff led Parsha Players. After Ben Zvi hall was opened in 2012, Kerem moved their leading to the back stage. That required taking down the mechitza and turning the chairs around to face the stage (ibid.).

How did Parsha Players change? Herschel Singer, who performed for Parsha Players for five years, filled in the history.

> It used to be a humorous skit based on parsha materials. Then it started to have more camp-related jokes and content. Then it evolved to exclusively camp content with only a tie-in to the parsha. It is all counselors and rosh aydot. They prepare it just beforehand. It is just a chance to have a humorous look at the last week's events . . . There were times they cut us off. They never canceled Parsha Players, but at times they said, "You are done." (Singer 2016)

Listening to Herschel, I thought, "This could never happen at Ramah or Eisner." Humorous skits about the week at camp could be shared at other times, but never at services. I am not surprised that the Yavneh leaders at times cut off the skits and said, "You are done." I am only surprised that the younger staff has the freedom to be as direct as they are in Parsha Players.

Watching Parsha Players raised this question: How is it possible that Yavneh at the same time is devoted to a traditional Musaf and yet ends with Parsha Players? Yavneh is both the most Orthodox of our camps and the freest in terms of ritual expression. Yavneh expresses its Orthodoxy in making sure to meet its halakhic requirements for reciting Musaf. But once those requirements are met, the mechitza comes down and Yavneh seamlessly transitions to camper- and staff-generated humor and satire. It is as if the leadership is saying, "We meet multiple needs within the same Shabbat morning service."

Yavneh's comfort with allowing this satiric Parsha Players contrasts with Ramah Wisconsin. When the younger staff pulled Parsha Players away from its focus on Torah, Yavneh relaxed its boundaries and welcomed humor into Shabbat morning services. By contrast, Ramah carefully guards the boundaries of the tefilla and relaxes only for the kiddush that follows. This difference reflects how these camps balance pleasure and obligation on Shabbat. Ramah separates the two, while Yavneh mixes them by inserting a breakfast break between the two halves of tefilla and then allowing humor and satire to conclude the morning service. These are stylistic differences that convey varying conceptions of how Shabbat is to be celebrated.

Developing Leadership Skills at Yavneh

Let's compare how the two camps develop camper leadership skills on Shabbat morning. Clearly, Ramah Wisconsin does this more systematically. By sponsoring aidah-based tefilla, Ramah creates multiple morning tefillot, and at each tefilla, campers have the opportunity to develop their leadership skills. Yavneh sponsors only two minyanim and thereby limits the number of campers getting those opportunities. Yet, Yavneh offers its campers a variety of leadership opportunities that include: (1) the Kerem camper who gives the dvar Torah, (2) the younger girl campers who lead "Ein Keloheinu," and (3) the Kerem campers who lead "Adon Olam."

Let's look at the Kerem campers. On erev Shabbat, Kerem leads the camp in an over-the-top recital of Birkat in the dining hall (see chapter 6). This performance of "Adon Olam" is the Shabbat morning parallel. It allows the oldest campers to be in front of the camp and ham it up in ways that delight the younger campers. This is considered part of Kerem's leadership role. In fact, one Yavneh teacher pointed to this particular moment as the embodiment of Kerem's role of setting the tone for how younger campers experience Shabbat.

It is easy to understand how reading Torah or giving a dvar Torah at camp offers older campers leadership skills they can build upon in their later Jewish lives. But is the same true for Kerem's leading "Adon Olam"? A skeptic might claim that this is an antic role limited to camp and irrelevant to later life. But I would argue otherwise. The important skill they are developing is bringing the community together. It hardly matters how well they sing. This is a ritual performance that everyone anticipates and enjoys. The younger campers have seen Joel or Meir leading a traditional Musaf. Now they see a shift from one mode of celebration to the other. By stepping into their Kerem role, these oldest campers are learning that the serious mode can be blended with the humorous, and the combination can be more satisfying than either one alone. Yavneh prepares its campers to live in and lead a Jewish community that is traditional, but adds a vision of high-spiritedness that contrasts with Ramah Wisconsin.

SHABBAT MORNING AT EISNER

To move from Ramah and Yavneh to Eisner on Shabbat morning is to see a very different approach to engaging camper interest and developing their skill base. Eisner alone prays the whole tefilla as a camp, draws upon the power of amplified music, and prepares a full unit of campers to help lead the Shabbat morning tefilla.

Shabbat Morning Tefilla at Eisner

Arriving at the outdoor beit tefilla at 9:30 a.m. on Shabbat morning in July 2017, I find that the Chaverim campers, entering eighth graders, are already present. It is their unit's turn to help lead the service. They are divided into four subgroups: those who will speak, sing, dance, and display their art. Rabbi Liz, the tefilla coordinator, is with the speakers; DJ, the head song leader, is with the singing group; and an Israeli dance counselor is with the dancers. Each is reviewing their campers' part in the service and when they will come up to lead. I also see a small band of Torah readers who alone among the campers have donned colorful tallitot. The other campers are dressed in a variety of outfits—from summer dresses to shorts and T-shirts—but without tallitot or kippot. I hear Rabbi Liz assuring her group that she has their written statements waiting for them and not to worry. To my eye, they appear quite calm.

The rest of camp streams in around 10 a.m. They seat themselves around this large beit tefilla with its many rows of metal benches. Some are carrying the Reform siddurim, but most are not.

Standing up front are Rabbi Liz, DJ, and another song leader. They are playing the first musical piece as the staff and campers find their seats. Rabbi Liz welcomes. She says a few words about the theme for this Shabbat, which is sacrifices, contrasting the ancient use of animal sacrifices in the Torah portion with our ways of drawing close to God through *avodah sheba-lev* (worship of the heart) and *mitzvot* (good deeds). Rabbi Liz is setting the stage for what the campers will be presenting.

The tefilla itself is led by the song leaders. After preliminary songs, the tefilla moves through Shacharit, with the Borkhu, Sh'ma, and Amidah. Between singing these prayers, groups of three and four campers come up to read their individual themed statements. There are also pauses for the singing and dance groups to perform their theme-related pieces. The tefilla is more subdued this morning, with fewer moments of intense engagement than the evening before. Yet there are sporadic moments when the ruach-rousing staff stand, clap, and move to engage the campers. That helps keep the tefilla a bit more spirited.

The Torah scroll is then taken out of the ark and brought to a table, where it is read by Chaverim campers. I count six Torah readers who each read a couple of verses from the Hebrew scroll. There are three aliyot that are given out by Louis. The first is given to visiting members of the camp board and alumni, the second to the staff of the two units who helped lead the Shabbat tefilla, and the third to the faculty who helped prepare these units. No Haftorah is read. The Torah scroll is put away and the tefilla ends with Aleinu and the Mourner's Kaddish. It lasts about ninety minutes.

Making Sense of the Eisner Tefilla

This is a strikingly different morning service. To make sense of that difference, let us begin with denominational stance. In Reform synagogues, Shabbat morning tefilla often revolves around the celebration of bar or bat mitzvah. Since Eisner does not generally celebrate bar or bat mitzvah, camp has to find another focus, which is involving their older campers in leading the tefilla. That becomes the focal point.

Rabbi Liz pointed out that while Ramah and other "more traditional" camps sponsor daily morning tefilla, Eisner and most Reform camps have weekday Ma'ariv (evening) services. Their campers have less experience with the morning prayer service and know that liturgy less well (Hirsch 2018). That leads Eisner to have a shorter Shabbat morning tefilla where they can highlight prayers—like Borkhu and Sh'ma—that campers already know from Ma'ariv, though there are some prayers recited only on Shabbat morning.

All the elements of camper engagement are in place: the whole camp is together in the outdoor beit tefilla with its beautiful setting; the song leaders are leading with carefully selected tunes; the counselors are seated among the campers and modeling participation; the ruach rousers occasionally engage more active participation; and fellow campers are up on the bimah leading parts of the service. All this effort keeps the tefilla moving along with a modest degree of camper engagement.

The older units are selected to lead on Shabbat morning so that their bnei mitzvah campers can read Torah and present more mature perspectives on the Torah portion. Holding a camp-wide morning tefilla allows these older campers to address the whole camp and articulate the value structure of this camp community.

Developing Leadership Skills at Eisner

What stands out about the Eisner tefilla is the number of campers who are given active roles in leading parts of the service. It is essential to Eisner culture that all their campers have the opportunity to lead some aspect of the tefilla and express some connection to the Shabbat theme. All are publicly thanked and their staff and faculty are honored by receiving an aliyah on Shabbat morning.

Eisner consistently communicates the message that there are multiple ways of leading and each way is to be honored as a legitimate contribution to tefilla. At the same time, there is a substantive difference between campers who participate in a group performance and those who address the camp in their own voice. The former work in a group with a specialist to learn the song or dance they will perform. The latter work directly with faculty to fashion a personal statement that will offer their own take on the weekly theme. During the tefilla, the dancers and singers go up as a group and perform their pieces together. In contrast, the campers who speak are asked to articulate their thoughts and speak clearly to the assembled camp. A lot more campers want to speak than there is time for in the service (Grinberg 2020).

I was curious what the faculty hope these older campers will learn from this process. When I asked, faculty members seemed focused on helping the campers develop their own thoughts on the weekly theme. When I pushed a little harder, they referred me to Rabbi Liz, who thought the best way to answer my question would be to send me the written statements that the fourteen-year-old campers had composed one week earlier and had delivered at the camp tefilla. With those statements in hand, I could make my own judgment of what approaches to the text the campers take.

Rabbi Liz sent me thirteen different camper-composed statements. The theme of that Shabbat came from the well-known Haftorah taken from the prophet Micah, who calls on us "to do justice, love mercy, and walk humbly with your God" (Mic. 6:8). Of the thirteen camper statements, I will highlight one particular joint dvar Torah that Dee and Jay (pseudonyms) presented together.

> DEE: This week's Haftorah portion has the quote, "Do justice, love mercy, and walk humbly with G-d." This quote is said by the prophet Micah, which happens to be both of our middle names. We relate to this quote

not only because of our names, but also because it is very meaningful in our lives. To explain, we'll translate this into something easier to understand.

JAY: "To do justice" means to do the right thing even if no one is watching. One example is when you pick up trash around camp even when no one asks or is looking. At home, doing justice may refer to getting involved in the community and helping others.

DEE: In the quote, another main point is to love mercy. "To love mercy" is to appreciate what others do for you and the second chances they give you. Here at camp, we can love mercy by talking to and thanking kitchen staff as well as offering sincere apologies when needed. This overall lesson in loving mercy is to look at things from others' perspectives before you make a judgment.

JAY: The final point in the Haftorah is to walk humbly with God. This means to do God's work, not for attention but instead because you should be doing this. An example of this at camp is being respectful during prayers and tefilla. Along with this, "walking humbly" can include participating in your temple and finding a connection to God outside of camp.

DEE: All in all, the prophet Micah had ideas that can be implemented into our lives today.

JAY: Even if your middle name isn't Micah, you can still learn from his quote.

What I find impressive about their joint dvar is how fully they treat the weekly theme. They begin by announcing the theme and locating it in the Haftorah from Micah. Their sharing that Micah is their middle name makes this talk more personal. They translate the prophetic terms of "do justice, love mercy, and walk humbly" into action terms that are accessible to their peers, and locate those actionable practices in both a camp and a communal context. In these ways, this joint dvar Torah embodies the fullest treatment I saw of the weekly theme.

What is distinctively Eisner about this dvar Torah? I would locate the Eisner touch in how these campers translate the prophetic word into actions that campers can perform. For each of the three prophetic terms, Dee and Jay offer possible actions. Dee, for example, explains that "to love mercy," one can "appreciate what others do for you and the second chances they give you." These actions are performable at camp and beyond. They exemplify a primary educational goal of Eisner, which Louis describes as "the opportunity to take Jewish rituals and connect them to real life, and to real people, and to real experience" (Grinberg 2020, 109). Dee and Jay let their peers know that "the prophet Micah had ideas that can be implemented into our lives today."

I earlier cited an instance at Ramah where on Shabbat morning a visiting rabbi spoke to the oldest campers about how he applied Jewish mourning rituals to heal the wounds of his bereaved congregants. That is a Ramah version of implementing Jewish tradition in the real world. But that is a rabbi speaking about his professional application of Jewish rituals. By contrast, on Shabbat morning at Eisner, Louis wants campers to hear from fellow campers who translate Torah into the actions that they can enact in their world (Bordman 2018). Developing that skill, he believes, is the most effective way to make Torah come alive at Eisner.

WHAT IS AT STAKE ON SHABBAT MORNING AT THESE CAMPS?

When camp leaders make decisions about who will lead Shabbat services, they are implicitly communicating to their campers and staff important conceptions about the nature of communal prayer and leadership. The easiest way to see these implicit conceptions is to view the contrast between Ramah Wisconsin and Eisner on Shabbat morning.

Ramah positions their older campers on Shabbat morning to take leadership of the Hebrew-based tefilla and reading of Torah and Haftorah. With the exception of Nivonim on the last Shabbat at camp, Ramah does not invite those campers to offer divrei Torah—though surely some could—and assigns that role to clergy and educators. By contrast, Eisner does not invite its campers to lead Shabbat tefilla, reserving that role for the staff song leaders, but Eisner positions a good number of campers to offer divrei Torah to the whole camp. That contrast is not incidental, but essential to how each camp understands Jewish leadership and the camp's role in preparing those leaders.

The Ramah movement has long seen itself as preparing future leaders for the Jewish community and does so in multiple ways through varied modalities throughout the camp season (Fox 2000). But on Shabbat morning, Ramah Wisconsin has chosen to focus on one particular form of leadership: developing its campers' skills in leading Hebrew-based tefilla and Torah reading. The camp's investment in developing these skills is considerable. That investment makes sense given Ramah's commitment to building a Jewish world where values like halakhic commitment, textual knowledge, and Hebrew mastery are central (Gillman 1989).

Eisner is educating a different camper population for a different Jewish world. Most of their campers do not have the Hebraic and textual skills that one commonly finds at Ramah. Rather, Eisner is committed to making Judaism available to American Jews who will know Torah primarily in translation and will pray through a mixture of Hebrew and English in a song-based service. Their tefilla is led by the song leaders who mediate between the Hebrew tefilla and the campers whose Hebrew skills are weak. Yet, Eisner asks these campers to develop the skills to get up in front of the whole camp and participate in leading one aspect of the Shabbat service.

Why does Eisner invest heavily in getting its campers up to lead some aspect of Shabbat tefilla? The first reason is its non-elitist stance on leadership: every camper can be a Jewish leader by expressing him- or herself in whichever medium comes most naturally. A camper does not have to be Hebraically literate or textually knowledgeable to be up on the bimah. That stance is strikingly different from Ramah or Yavneh's stance, which views Hebrew literacy as a key to leadership.

The second reason applies to the campers who offer their thoughts on the weekly parsha. They are enacting the Eisner principle of "Hineini—Here I am" (see chapter 3). At Eisner, "Hineini" has taken on the meaning of being present and standing up for what you believe is right. In the Jewish world that Eisner is building, that calls for camper leaders to get up before camp and share what the Torah portion means to them and how they intend to apply that meaning to their own lives. That is what Eisner hopes campers and staff will take away from camp: a personal vision—based in Jewish values—of how to make this a better world.

That is a different message than one hears at Ramah Wisconsin. In their worldview, individuals should seek their ethical and spiritual fulfillment through a life of study and action in a communal context whose evolving norms define the parameters of right thinking and action. Ramah is directing their campers and staff on a decidedly different Jewish path than the one on which Eisner sends forth its campers and staff.

Yavneh delivers a livelier message than Ramah, but the ruach-rich leadership it sponsors is also tied in with a highly "traditional" conception of tefilla. Yavneh offers a different balance between ruach (spiritedness) and *keva* (structure), but their primary value is Klal Yisrael—the primacy of community over individual. On conceptions of leadership development, Yavneh and Ramah line up fairly close to one another, while Eisner is pursuing a different trajectory where "Hineini" is the guiding star and individuals are empowered to seek their own paths of service.

These differences are not so much spoken as enacted through the Shabbat morning ritual. It makes great sense to build these implicit conceptions into the fabric of the Shabbat morning ritual and allow campers to get the message by celebrating Shabbat each week. Camps educate not as much through telling as through showing. Shabbat morning proves an ideal time to show who can lead and what skills are needed to lead the community.

SHABBAT AFTERNOON: RESTING THROUGH FREE TIME

After an intense Shabbat morning, Shabbat lunch serves as a transition point between the seriousness of the morning and the lightness of the afternoon. At Ramah and Yavneh, the campers and staff still wear their Shabbat clothing through lunch, yet there is little of the formality of the erev Shabbat meal. There are the blessings before and after the meal, but not the same singing of zemirot. At Eisner, few are still wearing their Shabbat clothes and lunch becomes a time to celebrate birthdays. Those with birthdays that day are called up for their celebratory cakes with everyone singing "Happy Birthday" in Hebrew.

Younger campers have a rest hour after lunch followed by an afternoon of free time for all. A division head at Ramah explained that the weekly camp schedule for younger campers is highly structured, while Shabbat is relatively open. That openness can be hard for some campers to handle, but part of Shabbat education involves learning what to do with your free time.

A curious feature of Shabbat afternoon at Ramah Wisconsin is what people call "the Shabbat walk." There is a path that leads around the camp and one can see all varieties of camp people walking in pairs and talking. It turns out that the Shabbat walk goes all the way back to Cejwin, where one walked with "one's summer sweetheart" (Krasner 2011, 306). The walk dates from a time when Jewish camps served as an intended meeting place for heterosexual couples and sought to launch future marriages. When I asked JAR whether this is still the case, he acknowledged that some use the walk for romantic purposes but most, he insisted, just "want to talk to one another" (Ross 2015).

Division head Shira Forester (2020) offered a more nuanced view. Her female adolescent campers would receive invitations from male peers to walk and "worry over the potential of a romantic/sexual relationship." They would sometimes "feel pressured to determine their feelings before the end of that day." Shira would tell them that a "Shabbat walk is just a walk," but that is not how they experienced it. The fact that when you walk with someone you are in full public view only adds to the pressure. Everyone knows that a romantic relationship is in the offing. The walk is still implicitly pressuring these adolescent campers into relationships for which they may not be ready.

Romance is not the only agenda pursued on Shabbat afternoon. Formality is gone and the main activity seems to be enjoying one another's company. The lakefront and basketball courts are open for swim or play. At Eisner, the arts and crafts are also open. At all three camps there is no instruction or organized team games. Many campers and staff can be observed playing sports and freely hanging out with their peers.

At Ramah, the theme-based educational activities for each aidah begin around 4 p.m. and last for about an hour. At Yavneh, the *sichot* (discussions)—often led by guest speakers—run from 5:30 to 7:30 p.m. Sichot (bunk processing sessions) at Eisner are in the morning run by cabin counselors. Each camp offers some educational activities on Shabbat, but keeps them informal. The mood throughout Shabbat afternoon is leisurely and relaxed. It is easy to see why many campers especially love this time.

CONCLUDING SHABBAT THROUGH HAVDALAH

Starting back at Cejwin, camp leaders realized that if Shabbat at camp was to leave a lasting impression, they had better make Havdalah impressive and memorable. Havdalah is the traditional closing ritual of Shabbat though which celebrants part from the Sabbath and reenter the weekday world. At home, Havdalah can be recited in a brief time with wine, a braided candle, and spices. But because Havdalah is recited after Shabbat has halakhically ended, camp leaders are free to engage all the senses to amplify the elements of the ceremony.

The more removed camp Havdalah is from the practices of city life, the better for leaving a lasting impression (Krasner 2011).

The most spectacular conclusion to Shabbat I have ever seen was at Camp Alonim in California. Right after it grew dark on Saturday night, the whole camp made its way into a small building, completely darkened, where everyone squeezed tightly together in concentric circles. Suddenly in the midst of the darkness there were candles everywhere; Havdalah was sung and all of our senses were touched by the ceremony. Taken by the drama of the event, I recalled that Shlomo Bardin, the founder of Alonim and the Brandeis College Institute, had once joked, "My grandfather would have gotten out of his grave if he saw what I had done with his Havdalah" (Leventhal 2012, 19).

Something has changed in camp culture since the days of Bardin. Few camps are competing with Camp Alonim for the most spectacular Havdalah. Instead, they are following a path set out by composer Debbie Friedman. In the 1990s, Debbie recorded a new tune for Birkat Havdalah that has since swept the Jewish world across religious movements. Her music has turned Havdalah into a folk-singing ritual where everyone stands in a circle, holds one another, and brings Shabbat to a harmonious conclusion. Each of our three camps performs Debbie's Havdalah blessings in its own characteristic way.

CONCLUDING SHABBAT AT YAVNEH

Shabbat afternoon at Yavneh is leisurely. After the sichot end, the whole camp gathers at the Tzippori amphitheater for counselor-led activities. The third meal—seudah shlishit—begins at 8 p.m. The meal is brief and is followed by camp-wide singing. There is a set of five to seven songs before Birkat that ramp up in intensity to prepare the way for Havdalah. The ruach-rousing staff are on their feet, moving around the dining hall, inspiring campers to sing with feeling.

When it is fully dark, some staff and campers go off to pray Ma'ariv (evening tefilla). Kerem creates a path between the dining and social hall. The rest of camp walks down the path into the social hall, where the band is set up to play. This is the same band that played for ReLish. Campers and staff form circles by division and hold one another. The band plays a series of five Hebrew songs, starting off slow and building in intensity. While the singing is just beginning, a staff member holding a lit candle walks around to each circle and lights their candle. Then singing intensifies and everyone, arm in arm, is jumping up and down in their circles in a state of intense fervor. This is the buildup to Havdalah.

Havdalah is composed of an introductory paragraph, three blessings—on the wine, spices, and fire—and a final paragraph that separates Shabbat from the weekday world. Everyone sings two lines from the first paragraph before a male staff member (for halakhic reasons) holds the cup of wine and recites that whole paragraph. He is then joined by the whole camp as they begin singing Debbie's tune. Still holding one another and swaying together, they sing the three blessings. For the blessing over the spices each circle passes around some spices, and for the final blessing everyone holds their hands up to the candle. Reaching the closing verse of the third paragraph, they shout out the final words as a crescendo of sound. Candles are blown out and everyone begins hugging those in their circle and then beyond. With those hugs, Yavneh parts from Shabbat and welcomes a new week.

The band quickly leaves and Marcello, the director of dance, sets up with his prerecorded music. Yavneh shifts quickly to its first weekly activity—the Israeli dance hour. Everyone dances these dances. Between dances, the younger divisions are sent back to their bunks, and by the end, it is the oldest campers and staff dancing with intensity. At Yavneh it is totally cool to dance with full heart.

Making Sense of Yavneh's Concluding Shabbat

In one continuous flow, Yavneh moves from seudah shlishit to Havdalah to dance session. These are three phases of a single cycle that Yavneh has joined together to provide a weekly experience of concluding Shabbat that has no parallel at the other camps. Let's look at this cycle in greater detail.

The whole camp moves together through this cycle. They do so even though it is quite late and the younger campers will be up later than usual. But this camp community acts like a second family and includes all the children. Starting seudah shlishit at 8 p.m. allows Yavneh campers to move directly from the dining hall through the path set by Kerem into the social hall where the band is waiting. The mood set by the singing in the hadar carries people directly into Havdalah.

Upon entering the social hall, campers and staff form circles by aydah. Those circles hold each camper through the ritual. Campers and staff experience

Havdalah simultaneously as members of their division and of the whole camp. First hugs will be for aydah members and then hugs spread out to embrace the larger camp.

The band takes everyone through the building intensity of the five preliminary songs. Campers and staff are in each other's arms, jumping up and down, allowing themselves to really feel the shared joy and intensity of the moment. This is not a time to rush, but to steadily build to full engagement. When they reach the formal Havdalah, the opening two songs are slow. Then everyone switches to Debbie's tune, which carries them harmoniously through the blessings and into the final paragraph. At the end they explode with sound and begin the hugging, starting from within their circle and moving out to cover much of the hall. They are retracing their steps from ReLish, this time wishing "Shavua tov" (a good week) in place of "Shabbat shalom."

At most other Jewish camps, when the concluding ritual ends, everyone leaves. Not so at Yavneh, where they move directly into Israeli dance. No one seems ready to leave; they are happy to stay together and move to the dance steps that Marcello calls out.

CONCLUDING SHABBAT AT RAMAH WISCONSIN

Back in 2009, long before this study began, I spent a Shabbat at Ramah Wisconsin. That Shabbat fell on July 4th. I remember a Havdalah ceremony quite different from what I would later observe. The whole camp gathered on the *kikar* (lawn) near the lake, with someone leading the ritual using Debbie's tune. As soon as she concluded, everyone rushed to the road where there was a huge torch announcing the beginning of Yom Sport. Out on the dock there were the letters of R-M-H in Hebrew lit up in fire. This, Rabbi Soloff explained, was the Ramah way of celebrating July 4th and kicking off the daylong competitions of Yom Sport. But in this aidah-focused camp, that camp-wide Havdalah is gone and in its place are aidah rituals. I will describe that concluding ritual for the youngest and oldest aidot.

At 8 p.m. on their first Shabbat at camp in 2015, Kochavim (nine-year-olds) assembles on the basketball court after the seudah shlishit to enjoy active group activities before it gets dark. Forty minutes later their division head gathers them in a circle, tells them to go back to their bunks, change into pajamas, and come back for "PJ Havdalah," where they will be getting a surprise. That

FIGURE 15. Havdalah, Saturday night, Ramah Wisconsin

surprise will be a book from PJ Library. Ramah has arranged this week for these youngest campers to receive at the end of their first Shabbat a selected book from this national organization that sends free Jewish books to Jewish families across the world (pjlibrary.org).

A half hour later the nine-year-olds clad in pajamas are back on the court. They gather in a large circle that includes the thirty-two campers, the aidah staff, and a few senior staff. Everyone stands with arms around one another. The counselor with the strongest voice steps forward and sings by herself the first paragraph of Havdalah. Then everyone joins together for Debbie's tune for the three blessings. The campers seem to know her tune as well as what to do with the spices and how to hold their hands up to the candle. They continue singing Debbie's tune through the last paragraph. When the candle is blown out, Havdalah is complete. The campers sit down and up comes a member of the mercaz staff. She introduces herself and speaks briefly about the importance of reading Jewish books. Each child receives a book from PJ Library to read at camp. Off they go with book in hand back to their bunks. Jacob turns to me and whispers, "It will take a good while for them to fall asleep tonight."

Two years later, in July 2017, I am walking around camp as it is getting dark on Shabbat. Campers are still playing sports on the soccer field and basketball court as the sky is darkening. At 9 p.m. I walk over to Ohel Yitzchak, where

Nivonim has gathered and their division head is talking to the group. When she finishes, they pray Ma'ariv (the evening prayer) and then gather for a camper-generated event I had not seen before. The campers address one another by name and share an appreciation for one another. Each camper speaks of something specific that she appreciates about another camper. They do this until each camper has been appreciated. Then they rise and form with the staff a semicircle for Havdalah, arms around each other. Lights are turned out so it is dark in the room. Two girl campers step forward with a lit candle. They sing the first paragraph by themselves. Then everyone joins in for a joyous rendition of Debbie's tune, passing around the spices and holding fingers up to the flame. When they come to the end of the final paragraph, they shout out the last line. With candle blown out, the hugging begins until everyone has been hugged. That completes Havdalah and everyone goes off into the new week and their evening activity.

Making Sense of Ramah's Havdalah

Havdalah is an intimate ritual at Ramah, binding the aidah together at the close of Shabbat. Whether in or outdoors, campers and staff form a single circle, holding one another and feeling everyone's presence. In that formation, singing Debbie's tune for Birkat Havdalah only accentuates the harmony that their circle engenders.

Viewing the Kochavim Havdalah reminds us that even the youngest Ramah campers mostly enter camp with some familiarity with this Shabbat ritual. The staff leads so the campers can learn the specifics of the Ramah Havdalah, and the campers seem ready to learn. Having the campers in pajamas creates a family-like scene that allows a quick transition from Havdalah to bedtime rituals back in the bunk. These campers are lucky to have a new book to read as they go to bed.

It comes as no surprise that the Nivonim Havdalah would be camper-led and end with hugging. But what catches me by surprise is the camper-led appreciations before beginning Havdalah. That move reminds me of the tish at Yavneh. This Shabbat falls late in their summer, and these oldest campers may be feeling that their time together is coming to an end. They seize on this intimate moment to do interpersonal sharing that feels warm and genuine. When Shabbat rituals work well, they allow older campers to express their attachment to their peers with whom they have been celebrating Shabbat for all these years.

CONCLUDING SHABBAT AT EISNER

While at Yavneh and Ramah Shabbat concludes only after it is deeply dark on Saturday night, Eisner has a more flexible schedule. Dinner on Shabbat late afternoon in July 2016 is scheduled for 7 p.m., and after this meal, I accompany Chaverim up the hill to the social hall, where they will celebrate Havdalah. I enter the social hall and the thirteen-year-olds are seated on the floor. Up front is the song leader. The counselors ask for quiet and get the campers to form the unit circle. The song leader leads them in singing Debbie's Birkat Havdalah with the accompanying wine, spices, and lit candle. This is the shortest Havdalah I have seen at camp.

On the way down the hill, I meet Aaron Gurvis, the unit head of Olim that summer. Aaron invites me to the Tzofim Havdalah that will take place back up the hill at 9:30 p.m. He says it will be special and I should not miss it. Tzofim are the fourteen-year-olds who are one year younger than the oldest Olim campers. This special Havdalah is designed to prepare them for becoming Olim the following summer.

At the appointed hour I return to find that the counselors are letting the campers into the hall one at a time. Once inside the hall I see the room is dark and in the middle is a circle of candles. Seated around those candles is a circle of staff whom I do not recognize. The unit staff and campers form an outer circle. Two song leaders from the inner circle stand and lead Hebrew songs that the campers do not seem to know. Then they begin Debbie's Birkat Havdalah, but stop after the first blessing. Up from the inner circle stands a male staff member, who identifies himself as having been a counselor with this group from their early years at camp. He tells a brief, humorous story about them as young campers. After the second blessing, a woman staff member stands to recite a similar story about them from the past. Then after the third blessing a male counselor from last year stands and is widely cheered before his brief reminiscence. The song leaders lead them through the concluding paragraph using Debbie's tune.

Just then Aaron enters the hall. He is clearly well known to these campers, who cheer his presence. He repeats the purpose of this ritual. He describes Olim as being "at the top of the hill" and envisions that Tzofim will have to work with intention "to become Olim." The good news is that they can begin that transition right now. How? By "being their best selves" and becoming models for the young campers. If they work at that, they could "become the best Olim ever" and "Eisner will remember you for that." With that, Aaron ends and hands the microphone to the current unit head of Tzofim. After acknowledging that "you guys can drive me crazy," she echoes Aaron's message about becoming Olim, and ends with, "We love you."

The song leaders stand again and end this concluding ritual with an English song that campers clearly know. Now, with arms around one another, the campers sway and sing with full voice. They are fully vested as they close the evening with heartfelt song.

Making Sense of Eisner's Havdalah

Moving from Yavneh and Ramah to Eisner, I sense that Eisner campers are not as familiar with Havdalah as a concluding Shabbat ritual. They do not enter this ritual with as much readiness as their counterparts. They are not resistant, but neither are they eager.

Eisner has one special Shabbat where they do the whole-camp Havdalah by the lake. But that is the exception. The norm is to conclude Shabbat as a unit. When Aaron guides me to see the special Havdalah for Tzofim, I wonder: Why is Havdalah chosen as the right moment for preparing Tzofim campers to become Olim?

Aaron and the other staff want these fourteen-year-old campers to think of what lies ahead as different from past years at camp. Each year at camp, if they did not mess up terribly, these campers will be invited back for the next summer. Yet Aaron wants them to believe that this time the transition has a spiritual dimension different from the usual invitation to return to camp. He wants them to view moving from Tzofim to Olim as essentially a spiritual journey, one to be undertaken with purpose and intention. For as Olim, they will be the ones to whom the younger campers look up, the ones "at the top of the hill" who will set the spiritual tone for the rest of camp.

Eisner truly depends on its oldest campers to set that standard for celebrating Shabbat. Olim are expected to step up to that honored role, and as such, it makes sense that this preparatory ceremony be held at Havdalah. As Shabbat is separated out as the most holy day of the week, so Olim is separated out as the highest unit as camp. Eisner is using the symbolic language of Havdalah to separate out and elevate Olim as the ones who will make the difference on Shabbat.

HAVDALAH ACROSS THE THREE CAMPS

> Whereas we began Shabbat with individual candles, we end it with one candle whose wicks are intertwined, as if Shabbat has created a unity that was lacking before. —*Siddur Lev Shalem* 2016, 283

At camp, Shabbat is indeed a powerful unifier, a day that "creates a unity" that is lacking during the camp week. Jewish camps have long realized that to make Shabbat vital for their campers and staff, they have to use the full power of dramatic ritual to make it special. Hence, the elaborate preparations for and transition into Shabbat and the harmonious conclusion to Shabbat before transitioning back to the weekday camp schedule.

Yavneh stands out for the power of its concluding rituals. They alone regularly bring the whole camp together to conclude Shabbat. Yavneh lives by its ruach and brings that spiritedness to full expression as they bid farewell to Shabbat.

Ramah Wisconsin begins and ends Shabbat with its aidah-focused rituals of transition. Those rituals—as we saw with Nivonim—build an attachment to celebrating Shabbat together and allow the older campers to express their close ties to one another. They begin Shabbat by peers blessing one another and end by peers appreciating one another. Shabbat ritual becomes their vehicle for expressing that special closeness.

Eisner places more emphasis on beginning than concluding Shabbat. Their campers seem less familiar with Havdalah than do their peers in the other camps. Nevertheless, Eisner staff know how to use Havdalah to celebrate and highlight a key transition in camper life, that of becoming Olim. In that case, separating Shabbat from the weekday world proves to be the reigning metaphor for setting Olim "at the top of the hill," the unit that will lead the other campers in key aspects of celebrating Shabbat at Eisner.

As I watch the campers and staff at all three camps form the Havdalah circles, stand arm in arm and sway together as they sing, I realize I am seeing embodied in those circles the person-to-person closeness that makes Shabbat at camp matter for these Jewish youth.

Part Three

LEARNING FROM SHABBAT AT CAMP

THE ETHNOGRAPHY IN PART II presents how Shabbat is celebrated at three residential Jewish camps: Eisner, Ramah Wisconsin, and Yavneh. The ethnography provides a vivid picture of what is special about Shabbat at these camps and how each camp varies the rituals they celebrate to communicate their particular visions of Jewish life in North America.

One feature all these camps share is a high level of camper engagement with the Shabbat celebration. Campers of all ages are prepared for the coming of Shabbat and then transition into a camp-wide celebration that fills the community with a shared joy. Most impressively, most teens at these camps bring extra energy to celebrating Shabbat. This reversal of usual trends in non-Orthodox synagogue life deserves our attention. While camp draws more committed Jewish adolescents, their vital engagement with Shabbat still needs to be better explained.

Part III addresses this question in two different ways. First, chapter 8 takes a close look at how these camps engage the interest of their campers and support those campers' learning how to celebrate Shabbat at camp. This begins when children first arrive as new campers and continues through their last year as oldest campers. Three theories of learning will guide this inquiry and help explain how these camps keep the learning fresh so that even their oldest campers remain deeply engaged. Then, chapter 9 asks what these cases of Shabbat at camp have to offer other leaders and educators in the North American Jewish community who in their own contexts are seeking to create robust Shabbat celebrations that can engage and educate their constituents.

8 / LEARNING TO CELEBRATE SHABBAT

SALES AND SAXE (2004) observe that Jewish residential camps have uncommon success at engaging their campers with celebrating Jewish life and use their theory of Jewish socialization to explain that success. They argue that structurally, residential summer camps are set up to create alternative realities for youth and, in this unique environment, camp leaders can create the conditions that lead to this strikingly different camper response to Jewish practice. This can happen, though, only when camp staff have bought into this alternative reality and are prepared to act as agents of socialization who steer the campers in this direction.

While agreeing that residential camps have the power to create alternative realities, I differ on how they understand the roles that staff play. I wish to distinguish between staff's "acting upon" and "acting with" campers. While there is no denying that camp staff set up the Shabbat celebration and that their buy-in is crucial to its success, I present a different theoretical model that focuses on a partnership between counselors and campers. By acting *with* campers, counselors guide campers into active participation in Shabbat celebration. They open a door and then walk together with campers through that door and into Shabbat activities. Once guided, campers can learn through their active participation how to celebrate Shabbat at camp. Participation is the royal road to active learning.

Let me begin by explaining what I mean by "learning." In our culture, we tend to associate "learning" with what happens at school. A common perception is that children *learn* at school and *have fun* at summer camp. I propose a different formulation. Schools and summer camps are both intentional educational spaces that sponsor different predominant modes of learning. Schools tend to be more instructional in emphasis. They highlight certain types of cognitive learning with the goal of helping each student master the skills and content featured in that year's curriculum. Summer camps also have instructional spaces in which educational staff teach campers specific skills, like acquiring new swim strokes or dance steps. Those spaces operate much like a school. But outside those instructional spaces, residential camps tend to educate less by instruction and more by what learning theorist Barbara Rogoff calls "guided participation."

> To broaden our view of the collaborative nature of learning that occurs outside of explicit instructional situations, I proposed the concept of *guided participation* in cultural activities (Rogoff 1990). Guided participation helps us to focus on the *varied ways* that children learn as they participate in and are guided by the values and practices of their cultural communities. (Rogoff 2003, 283–84)

If one thinks of learning as beginning when children are born, it becomes evident that long before entering kindergarten or even preschool, young children are learning from their interactions with the caretakers who guide these interactions (Gopnik 2016). Learning at camp resembles less what happens in the classroom and more what happens with play, make-believe, and interacting with caretakers and older peers. Whether playing sports, swimming in the lake, or practicing for a play, campers are challenged to learn through participation. Yet campers rarely stop to think about the learning they are doing, and camps play down any mention of "learning" so that campers can feel less pressure and focus on participating in camp activities. Camps, I claim, are constantly promoting camper learning while emphasizing how much fun the campers are having making friends and hanging out with peers and counselors.

What is true during the week is also true for Shabbat. Camp staff use their power to create "Shabbat" as a regular part of the camp week. For many campers, celebrating Shabbat on a weekly basis is itself powerful learning. However, for the camps in this study, simply celebrating Shabbat is not enough. Their goal is to guide campers to become part of the celebration by participating in every aspect of Shabbat. They design Shabbat rituals to draw campers in, engage them as full participants, and help them learn how to celebrate Shabbat while never calling attention to that learning process. From children's first days at these camps, they are guided by the staff to actively participate in these Jewish rituals.

JEWISH LEARNING THROUGH GUIDED PARTICIPATION

Wendy Grinberg (2020) tells of the time she was contacted by the social media crew at Eisner who wanted to capture "Limud"—the Jewish education program at camp. She showed the crew all the different educational activities going on that day. But when the crew sent back the images they wanted to include in the camp video, they were all images of campers reading and writing. Nothing else in the crew's mind counted as "learning"—the learning they associate with being in school.

Sales and Saxe (2004) know from their research that there is much more to Jewish learning at camp than reading and writing, but they characterize the rest as "socialization"—that which the camp staff sets up to socialize the campers. By contrast, sociocultural learning theorists like Lev Vygotsky (1978), Lave and Wenger (1991), and Barbara Rogoff (2003) have been widening our understanding of how adults and children work together to promote sociocultural learning. It is their perspectives I bring to better grasp learning to celebrate Shabbat.

To understand "guided participation," think of a grandparent and child baking cookies together. This is not a cooking class. The grandparent may not even be following a recipe or giving clear instructions. The two may mostly be having fun while baking. Yet the grandparent is guiding the process and allowing the child to participate and begin to learn how to bake cookies. Camps often work like this, with the staff in the role of the adult who guides campers to participate in an activity for which the child has little previous preparation. Campers learn a step at a time while never considering that anyone is teaching them or they are "learning" how to bake cookies or make Shabbat. They are just having a good time.

To see guided participation at work in preparing campers to celebrate Shabbat, let's begin with kikar dancing at Ramah Wisconsin (see chapter 4). This is the weekly event that heralds the coming of Shabbat. At 1:30 p.m. on Friday afternoons, the dance staff set up an outdoor platform for leading Israeli dancing. When the music starts, people from all over camp make their way to the line dancing. Whoever wishes may join; there are older and younger campers, junior and senior staff. Bystanders on the side talk and watch until deciding to join the dancing. People come in and out of the dance throughout the forty-minute activity.

When younger campers stand at the side watching the dance, I imagine it might feel intimidating to join in. They may not know the dances or have bunkmates to dance with. What I have observed is that counselors will usually guide these campers' initial participation, dancing next to them and helping them follow the steps. They ease the campers into the dance, holding their hands while the young ones find their footing and gain a sense of how the dancing goes. In its free-flowing structure, dancing on the kikar embodies learning by guided participation. No one is offering instruction, though the dance counselors are modeling the steps. Counselors and older campers guide the younger campers, and over time these campers learn the steps and the order of dances and become full participants in kikar dancing. They also learn to anticipate that Shabbat is coming.

If skeptical observers were to ask, "But do the campers actually learn the correct dance steps?" I would remind them that this is not instructional dance and the goal is not to learn the correct steps. This is free dance and the goal is to get whoever wishes dancing. Learning how to enter the dance lines and dance alongside others is for many younger campers an important step in becoming participants in the pre-Shabbat celebration at Ramah. Camp learning is often about overcoming hesitancy and fear so as to be able to enter the stream of moving action.

A second example of guided participation comes from Kabbalat Shabbat for Eisner's youngest campers (see chapter 4). The eight-year-olds gather late Friday afternoon with their staff in a circle on a hill where all the other units are also gathered. Their song leader stands within their circle and begins to play the first of four songs that will introduce Shabbat. The first is a simple song that they have learned earlier in the week. Most sing along. As the songs progress, they become more complex and most campers do not yet know the words. So, the counselors sing the words while campers do the hand motions and clap along. How do these eight-year-olds learn what to do? They stand in the circle with their staff, attend to the song leader, sing when they can, and otherwise do the hand motions. They learn in a low-pressure way with no instruction on how to participate. Guided by their staff and the example of the older campers, these newcomers get the rhythm of the ritual and, step by step, enter the stream to celebrate Shabbat together.

In a more technical sense, these counselors provide their campers with what Vygotsky (1978) calls a "zone of proximal development"—a space in which campers who cannot on their own fully participate may comfortably rely on the counselors' guidance while gradually learning to master the steps by themselves. The counselors are doing more than modeling and encouraging. They are also providing a social structure that allows campers to move forward in their learning while feeling supported by their staff. In that way, campers can begin to learn what they need to know while already participating in the Shabbat ritual.

Learning by guided participation works best when the young campers are motivated to learn. I have seen some youngest campers overwhelmed by anxiety on their first Shabbat at camp. They are not yet able to learn through participation and require more particular staff attention. But I have also witnessed many youngest campers who are ready to participate and learn. An example I cited (see chapter 5) is of several youngest girl campers at Eisner learning from an older sibling how to do the hand motions that accompany reciting Birkat (grace) at the end of the Shabbat evening meal. At Ramah Wisconsin (see chapter 4), I observed several youngest boy campers sitting outdoors eating the pizza lunch that follows kikar dancing. I heard the boys asking each other these questions:

Which is the cleanest bunk in camp?
Which is your favorite drink?
Which is the oldest bunk in camp?
Which is the newest aidah in camp?

They offer their own answers to the first three questions and consult their counselor on the fourth. During their first week as campers, they are actively seeking to learn more about their camp. Their minds are active, their curiosity is aroused, and their counselor is ready to answer their question. These are signs of incipient engagement and learning.

Guided participation does not end when campers are older and more experienced, but comes not only from staff but also their peers. An example of peer guidance is from Ramah Wisconsin's transitional ritual of hachana l'Shabbat, where late on Friday afternoons the oldest campers form same-sex circles to bless one another (see chapter 4). Campers have learned this practice from their years at camp when once they were probably guided by staff. By their last year, however, the campers have taken over leading the activity. They guide one another into the circle and recite the blessing out loud. That shows that the learning process has worked well and the campers have learned not only to lead the ritual but also to use the ritual to bond together before they join the whole camp in celebrating Shabbat.

WHOLE GAME LEARNING

Learning through guided participation provides an entryway for new campers into the world of camp and the celebration of Shabbat. It continues to operate as campers mature and explore new aspects of celebrating Shabbat. But celebrating Shabbat also calls on campers to become more skilled in their participation. As they move through their camper years, they are asked to lead more aspects of the celebration. How do campers learn to become more skilled participants? How does that additional learning take place? To answer, I have found it helpful to identify related modes of sociocultural learning that are best exemplified by David Perkins's (2009) theory of whole game learning.

Perkins focuses less on how children learn to participate in specific practices like kikar dancing or Kabbalat Shabbat and more on how children develop an understanding of the whole game they are playing. To use the example of learning to play baseball, Perkins is less interested in how young players learn to hit or field the ball and more in how they come to understand how hitting or fielding fits into the way baseball is played. He is intrigued that even though it is rare for adults or older peers to sit newcomers down and explain how the game is played, those newcomers usually manage to figure out what makes baseball as a game hold together. They piece it together as they play and observe others playing.

By analogy, I find it helpful to think of Shabbat as a whole game with its own rules, rhythms, and norms. As young campers are guided to participate, they are learning not only specific moves and practices but also what Perkins calls "an integrative framework" that helps them make sense of Shabbat as a whole. No one fully explains that framework to them; they piece it together by their own participation, watching what older campers do, and holding conversations with their elders. Figuring out what makes Shabbat hold together is an important aspect of Jewish learning at camp.

On a bright Shabbat morning at Eisner, I am watching young male campers playing with their peers outside their cabin when their counselor announces it is time for Shabbat morning services. One boy responds, "Wasn't it Shabbat last night?" The counselor smiles and responds, "No it is still Shabbat this morning." At Ramah Wisconsin, I am attending a kiddush after Shabbat morning prayers sponsored by a visiting cantor. A young male camper walks up to the cantor and asks, "Did you know we do not turn on lights in our bunk?" The cantor responds, "Yes, because it is Shabbat." These young campers are actively figuring out how Shabbat at camp works and turning to an adult for guidance. The adult responses affirm that this is how Shabbat works here.

From Perkins's perspective, a great advantage of learning while playing a whole game is that what these campers hear from their elders can be confirmed in short order. The conversation around morning services is followed by walking down to that service and seeing that all the campers and staff are still celebrating Shabbat. The rule about not using lights in the bunk on Shabbat is enacted in all Ramah bunks and is even known by the visiting cantor. What younger campers learn about Shabbat is corroborated by what they are observing all around. The knowledge gained is concrete, immediate, and helps the campers understand the rules for playing the whole game called Shabbat at camp.

Furthermore, much of what campers learn fits right into playing the whole game. When campers learn a new song before Shabbat, they sing that as part of a Kabbalat Shabbat service. When older campers learn a Torah portion, they will read that for a Shabbat morning service where other campers are also reading. What campers learn, they quickly perform, and that performance helps make Shabbat celebration happen. There is a close connection between learning and performing so that campers experience in real time that learning about Shabbat helps one gain entry into celebrating Shabbat. Learning and participation reinforce one another.

Another great advantage of learning while playing a whole game is that once children get invested, they are often more motivated to become skilled players by "working on the hard parts." Perkins (2009) offers the example of batting practice in Little League Baseball. It is not fun for players to attend a batting practice where the coach is watching how you swing the bat and making suggestions for how to hit better. But that is how players can learn to become better batters. At Shabbat at these camps, the hard part is gaining the skills needed to lead parts of the prayer services. At both Ramah and Eisner, the staff have developed structured ways for coaching campers to become more skilled participants in tefilla. The staff understand that participation alone will not necessarily lead to campers' becoming more skilled players. That requires more structured "coaching"—like batting practice—where campers get to practice their skills with the staff watching and offering feedback that can improve their Shabbat performance.

Adina Allen (2021), who served as assistant director at Ramah Wisconsin, described three ways that Ramah counselors coach their campers to become more skilled participants in tefilla. First, with the youngest campers, counselors organize tefilla groups that meet once or twice during weekday mornings to provide a small group of campers the opportunity to learn to recite specific Hebrew prayers that make up the morning service. In those smaller contexts, campers can try out their Hebrew and get feedback and support for reading the Hebrew out loud. With the counselor's help, they can also learn what those prayers mean and how they are sung in the prayer service. These campers are not yet ready to lead services, but are gaining skills that will one day allow them to lead.

Second, campers entering fifth grade take first steps toward leading morning service. Entering the space where their division prays on weekday mornings, campers see on the front wall a paper tree with Velcro leaves. On those leaves are the names of specific prayers from the morning service. Campers are encouraged to pick a leaf and lead that particular part of the morning service. They may do so alone or with a friend. In this way, campers gain practice in leading a single prayer in Hebrew. Over time they can try their hand at leading a variety of prayers without yet having to lead a whole service.

Third, when Ramah campers reach the summer before their upcoming bar or bat mitzvah, the preparations intensify. Campers are connected with an in-camp tutor who works (in an instructional mode) with campers on practicing the requisite skills. Campers in their bunks regularly practice out loud their Torah and Haftorah portions during the daily rest hour. On Shabbat the whole division at their morning service sings out loud the Sh'ma prayer (with its cantillation notes) and the blessings for the Haftorah. In these ways, campers practice together for their bar or bat mitzvah and develop the skills they can later use in leading Shabbat services at camp. What Perkins would appreciate about these coaching modalities is that the counselors encourage the campers to practice the hard parts—reciting the Hebrew and leading peers in prayer—without creating high-pressure situations. Campers have room to choose how to participate and with whom to participate. Much of the practice happens along with peers in a supportive environment. Further, what campers are practicing, they can perform as part of the service and experience as contributing to the whole game.

Eisner staff take a different approach to coaching their campers to become more skilled participants. The focus is not on mastering the Hebrew prayers but leading select parts of the camp-wide Shabbat service (see chapter 4). Camp staff and faculty have set up particular modalities for preparing campers for leading these parts. Let's look at two examples from a week when the units of Chalutzim and Tzofim were leading the Friday evening and Shabbat morning services. Within each unit, campers have been pre-divided into four groups that will lead different parts of the camp-wide Shabbat services.

Cantor Doob is working with the eleven-year-old Chalutzim campers who have volunteered to sing for the Friday evening service. The usual practice would be for the cantor to choose a familiar song and teach the campers to perform that song. Instead, she has taken the unusual step of composing a song for this Shabbat based on the theme for Chalutzim, emet and chesed (truth and kindness). The campers participated earlier in the week in a limud session where the faculty led a discussion of these Jewish values. The cantor has two sessions to prepare this group to sing her composition. At the Friday morning session, she hands out the words and rehearses the music. As the campers sing the words of the refrain, their counselors stand nearby and sing the chorus: "We are emet. We are chesed. Together we are one. Be the one." The counselors add energy to the rehearsal and support the campers in learning this new composition.

That Shabbat evening during the tefilla when Cantor Doob and the singing group ascend the bimah (stage) to sing this song, I discover that the counselors have taught the chorus to many other campers in Chalutzim. As the singing group is performing on stage, the counselors and campers stand by their seats, join in singing the chorus, and even add hand motions to go along with the chorus. At the end of the Shabbat service, Louis Bordman publicly thanks Cantor Doob for her composition and having added much to this Shabbat service.

Cantor Doob, by building her composition around the weekly theme, gives musical life to that theme. Her efforts are amplified by the counselors who teach the chorus to many more Chalutzim campers and enable their active participation in the Shabbat service. The cantor and counselors are building upon skills that these campers have already developed while directing their energies to learning the theme and becoming more comfortable leading a part of the camp-wide tefilla.

That same week, the fourteen-year-old campers from Tzofim are learning their parts for leading the Shabbat morning service. Their theme is taking responsibility. They too participate in a large group discussion with the faculty on their theme. On Wednesday morning the campers who have volunteered to speak individually at the service work together on writing their thoughts on the theme. They work in small groups, consult one another, and ask questions of the faculty. On Friday morning they rehearse speaking their statements, receive feedback from Wendy Grinberg, and prepare to address the camp.

At the Shabbat morning service several groups of Tzofim camper ascend the bimah to share their thoughts. One group catches my attention with their presentational strategy. Here is what they (pseudonyms) said.

> ANN: At camp we have a responsibility to be aware of our own actions and their consequences. All of us make mistakes, but what we learn is that we have to take responsibility and use the lessons to help us grow and move on.
>
> BETH: Raise your hand if you've made a mistake you've regretted. Keep your hands up and look around. Mostly everyone's hand is up. Now raise your hand if you've learned from a mistake you made.
>
> CARLY: The fact that you were all willing to raise your hands shows that you are taking ownership of your actions, which is the responsible thing to do. To be a good leader you have to be responsible. As we get older in camp, we assume new leadership positions. We learn from our mistakes and use those lessons to become better people.

Ann opens by announcing the theme and tying taking responsibility to learning from one's mistakes. When Beth asks the assembled camp, "Raise your hand if you've made a mistake," I look around and see very many hands in the air. When she continues, "Keep your hands up and look around," that is what most campers are doing. I am surprised by how many are listening and responding. These girls take a risk by assuming they can involve their peers, and they prove to be correct. They actively engage their peers in learning the Shabbat theme.

Perkins would appreciate how Eisner staff and faculty create different learning supports for the younger and older campers. With the younger campers, Cantor Doob and the counselors structure the learning for the eleven-year-olds who respond enthusiastically to learning the new song. But something else happens with the older campers. These campers work together in small groups and guide one another in composing their statements. It is their decision to take this risk of actively involving their peers. Their presentational moves take a maturity and skill that differentiate them from the younger campers.

Staff at Ramah and Eisner structure different learning opportunities for campers to work on the hard parts. What they have in common is a layered approach to learning. Staff provide younger campers with more structured modalities for working on basic skills while providing older campers with more open-ended learning opportunities to exercise their more developed skills and learn to assume new leadership positions. In both camps the guiding principle is that older campers will be prepared to take on more complex roles in leading Shabbat tefilla. In both camps a variety of staff are involved in coaching and providing feedback so that campers can learn to take on the hard parts.

ON BECOMING OLDEST CAMPERS

These Tzofim campers are one summer away from becoming Olim, the oldest unit at Eisner. There is a special Havdalah service to initiate Tzofim into becoming Olim (see chapter 7). That service reflects a practice common to all three camps: the oldest group of campers is accorded a special status and they are expected to set an example for their younger peers. That special status is highlighted on Shabbat when the oldest campers enact special leadership roles that model for younger campers what it looks like to be all-in on celebrating Shabbat at camp.

In the ethnography (see part II), the late Shabbat evening camp rituals were presented. This chapter asks a different question: What kinds of learning do the oldest campers as a group undertake in assuming their roles as leaders? Exploring this question entails revisiting a key Shabbat ritual at each camp. First, mishmar at Ramah Wisconsin, then song session at Eisner, and concluding with leading zemirot at Yavneh. Mihalyi Csikszentmihalyi's (1988, 1990) theory of flow and optimal experience will serve as a guide to understanding how these camps structure these learning opportunities and what challenges the oldest camper must meet to carry out their collective leadership roles.

MISHMAR AT RAMAH WISCONSIN

In beginning my research, I did not even know that the older Ramah campers hold a mishmar on late Thursday nights to anticipate the coming of Shabbat (see chapter 4). The staff who told me about mishmar were unsure whether to take it seriously or view it as a teen fad that might disappear by the next year. What drew my interest was how mishmar was powered by camper interest.

Mishmar at Ramah Wisconsin is restricted to teen campers from the three oldest divisions. Attendance is voluntary. It takes place in a crowded space in the library. It is led by Jeremy, a senior staff member. The seating is particular. The youngest group, Bogrim (age fourteen), sits on the outer rim of benches. Machon (age fifteen) sits in the middle space. Only Nivonim (age sixteen) sits around the inner table. Mishmar honors Nivonim by placing them at the center. Each year a younger aidah moves toward the center as it progresses toward becoming the oldest division.

Jeremy leads the singing but the Nivonim campers set the tone. They (with Jeremy) get to bang on the table and regulate the intensity of the singing. That intensity is what matters most. Mishmar contains both singing and study of Torah, but the singing dominates. It is through the singing that the campers express themselves. Ramah campers get many opportunities to sing these religious verses, but only at mishmar have I seen them close their eyes, open their hearts, and sing with an intensity that moves me. Nivonim campers could sing with that same intensity on late Friday nights at their tish, but most choose not to do so. They reserve this intensity for mishmar and, in the case of one group, for singing after dinner on Friday nights. That extension of mishmar is an innovation of two small groups of campers who choose to sing in the mishmar style before attending their division's main evening activity (see chapter 6).

Singing at mishmar calls upon a set of complex skills. First there is familiarity with the many Hebrew songs on the song sheet that Jeremy distributes. Second is the capacity to sing those with eyes shut. Third is knowing how to sing those songs in the intense style of mishmar. Fourth, for Nivonim campers, is knowing how to regulate the intensity through banging on the table. Mishmar is structured so that the Bogrim campers can practice these skills while seated in the back rows watching how Nivonim campers set the tone. The implicit expectation is that by the time these campers are in Nivonim they will have developed this set of skills so as to set the tone and model for their younger peers. Mishmar is a camper-powered activity where campers learn mostly by watching one another and gaining guidance from Jeremy.

Why do these older campers invest their energies in mishmar? There may be multiple motivations, but I will highlight an adolescent quest for intensity. They seek what psychologist Mihalyi Csikszentmihalyi (1990) calls "flow." When teens freely undertake a challenging task and work hard to accomplish a clear goal, they are likely to have what Csikszentmihalyi (1988) calls "an optimal experience." He has found that optimal experiences—which are characterized by flow—are most likely to occur when:

> we undertake tasks that we can complete,
> we can concentrate on what we are doing,
> the task has clear goals and provides clear feedback,
> we can act with a deep involvement,
> we can exercise a sense of control over our actions,
> our concern for self can disappear, and
> hours pass like minutes and minutes stretch out like hours.
> (Reimer 2012, 120)

Entering into flow "causes a sense of deep enjoyment that is so rewarding people feel that expending a great deal of energy is worthwhile simply to be able to feel it" (ibid.). That is what I believe these teens experience at mishmar and why I believe they return each week and even extend mishmar to Friday evenings. What flow theory adds to our understanding is an appreciation of how mishmar is designed to elicit flow. Mishmar is a tightly structured activity with clear goals well matched to the skill sets that these campers bring to the event. Mishmar also takes place in an isolated space cut off from the rest of camp. For this short period, time stops and the participants can give themselves to the singing with rare intensity. Over the three years, campers grow more skilled in this type of singing and the oldest campers learn to modulate the action and provide feedback to the younger campers. These are conditions most conductive to fostering an experience of flow.

I would not readily apply flow to the mishmar experience if Csikszentmihalyi had not expressed an active interest in the relationship of flow to religious rituals.

> Many of the optimal experiences of mankind have taken place in the context of religious rituals . . . This connection is not surprising, for what we call "religion" is actually the oldest and most ambitious attempt to create order in consciousness. It therefore makes sense those religious rituals would be a profound source of enjoyment. (1990, 76)

In his view, religious rituals are rich in potential for providing flow. I am building on that view by suggesting that Shabbat at camp is generally rich in flow potential and that there are specific moments, like mishmar, that are designed to particularly promote flow for older campers. While much of the empirical research on flow has focused on the experience of individuals, Csikszentmihalyi's student Keith Sawyer (2007) has developed the concept of "group flow" by studying how flow operates in improvisational theater groups and jazz ensembles. I am building on Sawyer's work in viewing flow here as a shared group experience.

What does flow theory teach us about what these older campers learn from enacting mishmar together? Let me cite Csikszentmihalyi.

> We found that every flow activity has this in common: it provided a sense of discovery, a creative feeling of transporting the person into a new reality. It pushed the person to higher levels of performance and led to previously undreamed-of states of consciousness. (1990, 74)

Ramah campers have many opportunities to sing these Hebrew songs together. Their staff has provided modalities where they could develop the needed skills. But mishmar provides a special opportunity: to sing by their own choice with rare focus and intensity. Under these conditions, older campers push one another to higher levels of performance. In the process, they can learn what it feels like to share that special state of consciousness that we call flow. Experiencing these moments of intensity may help these campers discover a new level of depth where they can join together to create communion and spiritual bondedness.

Mishmar is not for everyone. Csikszentmihalyi and his colleagues (1997) have consistently found in their studies of adolescents that there is great variation in the extent to which individual high school students seek flow in their free-time activities. Ramah may be wise to allow their older campers room to regulate how intensely they wish to be involved in Shabbat rituals. By supporting more intense Shabbat experiences like mishmar, Ramah allows these older campers who seek this intensity to grow more skilled in exploring their own spiritual resources and helping one another find a deeper expression for their Judaism.

SONG SESSION AT EISNER

Eisner structures its Friday night Shabbat celebration so that all campers move from the camp-wide Shabbat tefilla to the more intense song session. Intensity looks very different at Eisner than at Ramah. At Eisner there is no yeshiva influence, no reliance on all-Hebrew songs, and no gathering around a library table. Instead, there is a reliance on song leaders and the Reform song book, upbeat music and mosh pit moves, and an inclusive view of who will lead the ritual action. Song session and mishmar on the surface have little in common. Yet for all their clear differences, I hope to show that song session and mishmar are both carefully designed to provide flow-like experiences for the oldest campers.

After Shabbat tefilla concludes, most campers enjoy brownies before song session begins. During that break, the Olim campers go up to the gym to change from Shabbat into gym clothes. They then gather for a pep rally, which the staff lead to prepare these oldest campers to take on their leadership role. The campers then leave the gym and go outside to form the "tent" where they greet the younger campers and high-five with them. After the rest of camp has entered the social hall for song session, Olim makes its entry and situates itself immediately before the platform on which the song leaders play the music (see chapter 6).

This elaborate preparation for song session shows how carefully structured the experience is for Olim campers. They separate themselves from the younger campers and don special clothes. They are prepared by the staff to "become Olim" and step up to their leadership role. They channel that energy into a lively welcome for their younger peers and then locate themselves in mosh pit formation. Once the loud music begins, Olim campers and staff throw themselves into the music and movement. Song after song, well over 120 bodies jump up and down and bump into one another. They are by far the dominant force at song session. After a while, the campers break up and seek out their young buddies to dance with them. They then return to the center for the final songs, where they again dominate the action. Moving through these choreographed steps, Olim campers enact their role as leaders and model for the younger campers what it looks like to give your all to Shabbat celebration.

When I compare how these oldest campers act at the camp-wide tefilla and at song session, I can see why Abi, their unit head, describes them as taking on at song session "the obligation to enjoy Shabbat" and "embody that joy." At the tefilla, Olim campers are no more likely to be actively involved in the ritual action than their younger peers. Yet once they arrive at song session, Olim is dedicated to their role in a way that has no parallel at tefilla. They change their mind-set in preparing for song session so as to be fully available to fulfill their role as Olim.

Flow theory helps us understand that change in mind-set. At tefilla, their attention is split in many directions. They partially attend to the ritual, but also are busy talking with their friends and drifting off into their personal thoughts. But in preparing for song session, the campers rely on the staff to focus their attention on what is ahead, reminding them of their goals at song session, building their confidence, and creating a united group spirit. This focusing of attention, will, and spirit is what Csikszentmihalyi calls "creating order in consciousness" (1990, 76)—an essential step to prepare for a flow experience.

The staff could not prep these campers if the campers were not already on a learning journey to becoming Olim. The staff can remind them they have been learning how to undertake this leadership role and that their learning involves three interrelated steps. First, in the years leading up to Olim, these campers attended song sessions and learned how to move to this Shabbat music. As Olim, their new challenge is to commit themselves to being fully present and embody the joy of Shabbat. That entails a dedication and focus that may be new for them. Second, the campers have already developed a relationship with their younger buddies. Now, at song session, they have to remember to break away from their group and find those buddies to dance with them. They have to shift their attention and focus on the needs of their young charges. Third, they have been working all summer on overcoming the cliques in their group. Now, at song session, they have to work as a united group and present a unified presence for the younger campers. These are challenges that Olim can work on as they go out and lead the younger campers in song session.

While Ramah Wisconsin has an elitist view of leadership, Eisner has a more inclusive view (see chapter 7). Eisner does not ask an elite group of Olim campers to lead song session, but expects that of all the oldest campers. As a result, Olim campers are not asked to bring much Hebrew literacy or skill in song or movement to song session. What they need to learn is how to join together to enact the choreographed steps of leadership. That calls for focus, coordination, and transcending self-absorption so as to be available to the younger campers. Csikszentmihalyi and Larson (1984) have shown in their studies of American high school students that for many adolescents these capacities do not come easily. What is impressive is the degree to which these oldest campers learn to give themselves to this highly focused effort. That focus allows for a group flow experience.

At song session these teens are not thinking about flow, but are focused on acting together so that the younger campers can look up to them. This is the moment when Olim campers self-consciously choose to be Jewish role models for their younger peers. From a learning perspective, song session provides this large group of fifteen-year-olds the opportunity to practice these skills of focus, coordination, and transcending self-absorption so as to be able to lead song session. Their staff play a highly active role in focusing their minds and building their confidence so that these many teens can become Olim.

LEADING ZEMIROT AT YAVNEH

Yavneh structures its Friday night Shabbat celebration so that all campers—except the youngest—move from the Shabbat meal in the dining hall to the singing of *zemirot* (traditional Shabbat songs) in the Ben Zvi social hall (see chapter 6). The first half of the singing is led by the staff and the second by Kerem, the oldest division at camp. Of great interest is the second half when Kerem steps forward to lead their younger peers in intensified song and movement.

The group of forty-plus sixteen-year-olds takes control of the ritual action. Their first step is to cordon off a confined space in the social hall by setting up a rectangular formation of benches. All the younger teen campers and their staff gather within this confined space and arrange themselves in same-sex circles. Two Kerem campers hand out a sheet of twelve songs. The Kerem campers stand on the benches and tower over everyone else. They face inward so they can communicate with the younger campers. The Kerem leaders signal the ritual action is about to begin. Then in choreographed fashion, Kerem leads the whole group in a joyous, raucous singing with movement that the Kerem leaders have prepared for the erev Shabbat celebration.

Leading zemirot at Yavneh has elements similar to both Ramah's mishmar and Eisner's song session. Like song session, this event takes place in a large hall, but like mishmar, Kerem arranges their space so all the participants are in a confined smaller area. Like song session, all of Kerem is involved, but like mishmar, a few have volunteered to lead the ritual action. The singing is mostly in Hebrew without instrumental accompaniment, but the Kerem leaders are in constant motion interacting with and leading their younger peers. Leading zemirot grows out of a mosh pit culture, but one that has been redesigned to promote camper joy without camper excess (see chapter 6).

Leading zemirot allows for more active camper leadership than was evident at either mishmar or song session. The Kerem staff play no visible role in organizing or leading the event. A couple of Kerem campers plan the event and put together the twelve songs. They take inventive liberties with the text of these songs and insert their own humorous phrases within the traditional wording. Two or three Kerem campers are assigned to lead each of the twelve songs. They interact with the younger campers and direct their participation. The most intense moment comes toward the end with singing a traditional Hebrew song composed of many verses. This song is sung so that each circle of campers gets its turn to sing a verse and put their spin on the singing. As the action moves from circle to circle, the campers and their staff get more competitive trying to outdo one another with a louder and wilder performance. As the competition grows more intense, the Kerem leaders conduct this wild orchestra and move the action around the circles with a timing that is just right.

What do the Kerem campers need to learn to pull this off? All of Kerem needs to learn to join together to enact the choreographed steps of leadership, which call for focus, coordination, and transcending self-absorption so as to be available to the younger campers. As with mishmar, they need to know how to sing these Hebrew songs by heart. But perhaps the greatest challenge is for those who lead the twelve songs. They need to involve the younger campers in singing while coordinating the ritual action.

As at Ramah and Eisner, Yavneh structures this ritual so that younger teen campers get to participate in the singing and movement for several years before they reach Kerem. Besides learning the moves and timing of the ritual action and the words of the Hebrew songs, these younger campers have the opportunity to observe how the oldest campers lead the ritual. They have time to anticipate how they as a group would like to assume leadership and put their stamp on running the event. That allows for gradual learning of skills over time so that once a group arrives at their final year, they can smoothly take control and put into action what they have been planning. They are also learning how to build toward the intensity that is the hallmark of late Friday night celebrations at Yavneh. The joy of accomplishing all this has the hallmarks of a shared flow experience.

THREE MODES OF LEARNING THROUGH SOCIAL PARTICIPATION

In exploring how staff and campers work together to engage in the Shabbat celebration, I have relied on three theories of learning to illuminate three modes of learning through social participation. These modes of learning can be thought of as forming a sequence for how over time campers come to engage with Shabbat and learn the skills they will need to both actively participate in and lead the Shabbat rituals.

When novice campers first arrive, they rely on their counselors to guide their path into Shabbat participation. Rogoff's (2003) concept of guided participation illuminates how this happens. Novices at camp would not on their own know what to do on Shabbat. Their counselors guide participation by creating a space in which it is safe to take on new behaviors. In that zone, novices can still feel safe to participate because the counselors provide a structure of action into which they can enter while learning the words of the songs and the steps of the dances.

At some point later—often during their second summer—campers come to realize that there is more to participating in Shabbat celebration that involves learning the hard parts. This next dimension is best illuminated by Perkins' (2009) theory of whole group learning. The staff works skillfully to coach these young campers. Many campers are motivated to take on the hard parts because they can see that developing these new skills fits well into the whole game of Shabbat at camp.

By their last year, campers are asked to assume a next level of leading Shabbat rituals and to model for their younger peers how to be all-in embodying the joy of Shabbat. Their learning how to embody that joy is best illuminated by

Csikszentmihalyi's (1990) theory of flow. In their new role, the oldest are singularly focused on building an intensity of ritual action for themselves and for engaging the energies of their younger peers. This is a challenging demand, but one that the oldest campers usually embrace with joy. Setting and meeting these ambitious goals sets the stage for their experiencing a shared sense of flow.

In some ritual contexts—such as mishmar—this sequence of learning modes can be condensed into a shorter time period. Let's see how that works. The youngest participants are the Bogrim campers who are new to mishmar. They sit in the back benches so they can observe how this ritual is enacted. They are guided by their older peers to get to know the steps of mishmar singing. The middle group of participants, Machon, already know the mishmar steps. What they need to learn are the hard parts. So, each week they are provided with one song to lead. By leading that song, they are able to practice the hard parts. The Nivonim campers, as the oldest, face the challenge of setting the tempo for everyone's singing. They work on that as they lead, learning to focus on ensuring that the whole experience comes together in a spiritually satisfying way. They do so in partnership with Jeremy, who guides them in their leading role. So, at mishmar—as in other intense camp contexts—all three modes of learning operate simultaneously. At the same time, novices are being guided, middle campers are learning the hard parts, and the oldest are learning to lead.

THE INTERPLAY OF LEARNING AND ENJOYMENT

Let me conclude this chapter by connecting the modes of learning to the joy of celebrating Shabbat. Camp leaders seem to agree with Csikszentmihalyi that religious rituals should provide "a profound source of enjoyment" (1990, 76). Camps have few other ways to motivate their campers to engage with Shabbat rituals other than to ensure that shared enjoyment. Even at Ramah Wisconsin, where strong halakhic and educational norms shape the Shabbat celebration, the staff know that without experiencing joy, campers have little motivation to sit through long services in Hebrew.

What has not previously been noted in the camp literature is how joy and learning deeply interconnect. A common perception is that campers go along with the discipline of observing Shabbat because there are also many pleasures associated with Shabbat at camp (Sales, Samuel, and Boxer 2011). There are the pleasures of sleeping late, eating good food, and getting free time to hang out and celebrate with friends. These pleasures surely facilitate the Shabbat experience. Csikszentmihalyi (1990) would note; however, there is a fundamental difference between pleasure and enjoyment, and we often miss how they motivate people differently.

Pleasure is what humans feel when a basic biological or cultural need is met. It is pleasurable to eat well, sleep late, and enjoy the company of friends. While pleasure involves immediate gratification, enjoyment is earned. Enjoyment results from setting achievable goals in an interesting activity and challenging oneself (as an individual or a group) to meet those goals. To play together a complex piece of music brings enjoyment. And, I believe, leading mishmar, song session, or zemirot brings enjoyment to the oldest campers who set that as their shared goal. Enjoyment feels more deeply satisfying in the sense that we have accomplished something that we consider to be worthwhile.

Shabbat at camp still needs its pleasures to motivate camper engagement. Campers look forward to the Shabbat treats they receive and funny performances like singing "Adon Olam" or watching Parsha Players at Yavneh. These bring immediate gratification. But to understand why older teen campers remain deeply invested in the Shabbat celebration, the focus has to be on their enjoyment and what it means to them as a unit or an aidah to lead the Shabbat celebration. It matters deeply to many of them to live up to being Olim, Nivonim, or Kerem and leave their mark on camp. Many view that as a genuine challenge, and when they feel they have met the challenge of becoming leaders, they experience a shared sense of joy.

Although they rarely focus on this, these oldest campers could not have met that challenge unless they had devoted themselves to learning all the skills needed to lead mishmar, song session, or zemirot. They could not have reached this point without the guidance and coaching of the staff. For the Shabbat rituals they are leading are highly structured events where the players need to learn all the moves and focus on ensuring that the disparate pieces come together in the right way. In leading these rituals, the oldest campers are demonstrating all that they have learned, and thus experience the enjoyment of having successfully met their shared goals.

9 / LEARNING FROM CELEBRATING SHABBAT AT CAMP

I BEGAN THIS BOOK with two broad claims. The first is that Jewish residential camps have become—particularly through their celebration of Shabbat—creators of positive spiritual experiences for Jewish youth. The second is that these camps offer a model to other Jewish educators for how to provide their participants with powerful Jewish experiences. In this last chapter I revisit these claims by addressing the following questions: How do young people at camp learn to celebrate Shabbat more fully and joyfully? And how can Jewish educators and leaders in other contexts provide their participants with the tools needed to learn to celebrate Shabbat more fully and joyfully?

Let me begin by revisiting what it means to celebrate Shabbat at camp. I will start with a concrete instance and build out to what I have learned about celebrating Shabbat at camp. From there, I will turn to what other educators can learn from the model these camps have developed for celebrating Shabbat.

THE TISH AT YAVNEH

The tish at Yavneh is the culminating event on Friday nights for the oldest campers. It follows the singing of zemirot (see chapter 8), but contrasts sharply in mood. The tish is darker, gentler, and more revelatory. It serves to bring the older campers closer together. It is run by campers for campers.

The tish is loosely based on a Hasidic gathering around the rebbe's table on erev Shabbat. But the Yavneh tish bears little resemblance to Hasidic practice. The campers have fashioned the tish to meet their needs. When I met with the oldest campers to explain my research, their most pressing question was whether the two other camps in my study have anything like their tish. They were pleased to hear that while Ramah Wisconsin also holds a tish, it does not much resemble theirs.

What makes their tish special? The campers immediately pointed to the personal sharing. The tish is their opportunity to hear from peers who will share with the group their personal feelings and stories. That is one of several ways that the Yavneh tish is distinctive. This tish is attended by all the oldest campers, who sing soft Shabbat songs in a darkened room. Between songs, campers share their stories. Before sharing, a camper greets the group and is greeted in return. None of these features characterizes the tish at Ramah.

What to make of this special camp ritual? I could point to the ways that Yavneh differs from Ramah and why this ritual reflects the special features of the Yavneh community. But what I wish to highlight is how much the tish matters to these Yavneh campers. The tish engages the whole Kerem group, who bring to it their rapt attention and interest. It is hard to imagine their skipping tish or allowing it to fade away. Quite the opposite. The oldest campers at the end of the summer initiate the group two years younger into the ways of the tish to ensure its continuing after they have left camp for their summer in Israel.

Looking at the tish from the perspective of Csikszentmihalyi (1990), I see it is structured as an optimal experience. It has clear achievable goals that stretch the capacities of these adolescents. It has a definite structure that guides the campers to meet its goals. They can give themselves to the action and trust that the (ritual) process will bring them to their desired end goal, which makes the experience enjoyable for them. Their sharing also builds connection and belonging. The tish helps create a trusting community in which campers are safe to reveal personal stories that might be dismissed or even ridiculed in other adolescent contexts. Doing so ensures that this Kerem group will feel attached to one another even after their camp years are over.

Yet, were Ramah or Eisner campers transported to Yavneh, they would likely find this tish strange. They might wonder why it matters so much to the Yavneh campers. That is because each of these camps has a distinctive way of celebrating Shabbat. That distinctive way allows their campers and staff to know what to expect and supports their emotionally attaching to their camp's particular way of celebrating Shabbat. At each camp, what matters most is what is distinctive to their camp.

Jacob Cytryn (2011) once told me that the emotional dynamics of camp operate like a Texan town on the night when the local high school football team is playing a noted rival. The game takes on cosmic significance and every detail is emotionally magnified. Jacob may be overstating the case, but for older campers at these three camps, how the Shabbat ritual unfolds matters greatly, having both personal and collective meaning. At stake is their place in the group, the group's place in the camp's history, and the capacity of the camp tradition to be passed on to a next generation of campers. Shabbat celebration takes on special significance by being located at the vector of personal, group, and collective concerns.

Noting that nexus of concerns will help us clarify what it means to celebrate Shabbat at camp. By this point, it is not surprising to claim that celebrating Shabbat has personal significance for most campers at these camps. Most campers show up and seem eager to participate in greeting the Shabbat. Most jump at the opportunity to hug and be hugged. They enjoy the relaxing pace of Shabbat day and join together to bid Shabbat farewell at the Havdalah ceremony. Shabbat for most campers is a time to join with others and make visible all that they find positive about Judaism. As Rabbi Todd Markley remarked, Shabbat at camp is "a Jewish battery charger" (see chapter 5).

What I had not realized and learned from this study is that for the oldest campers their reputation as the oldest division at camp is also at play on Shabbat. Many of them want to step up and lead on Shabbat and be seen as a model for younger campers. At camp this perception of their group matters and creates a positive peer pressure for being all-in with the Shabbat celebration. The positive peer pressure is strong enough to overcome adolescent tendencies to distance from one's Judaism and results in teens eagerly participating in and leading Shabbat rituals. These camps need that adolescent energy to charge up the younger campers and get them excited to celebrate Shabbat more fully.

I had also not realized how powerful the feelings of attachment are to the particular rituals that characterize Shabbat celebration at their camp. At Yavneh, the tish has to be celebrated in the Yavneh way or a sacred order will be violated. While older campers and staff are happy enough to join together with their peers from similar camps, they often insist that their songs or rituals be performed in their distinctive way. That insistence testifies to how much celebrating "our way" matters and needs to persist over time.

Celebrating Shabbat at camp matters precisely because the celebration speaks deeply to who they are as campers, members of their group, and participants in a distinctive camp culture. The act of celebrating is their way of declaring, "This is who I am as an individual, as a proud member of my group, and as a loyal participant in this camp culture."

WHAT CAN OTHER EDUCATORS LEARN FROM CAMP?

Camp people often talk about camp as magical and Shabbat at camp as miraculous. But our ethnographic study reveals that while Shabbat may be experienced as magical or miraculous, its celebration is actually a carefully planned program that staff prepare for much of the preceding week. Bunk, divisional, and educational staff play a variety of roles in promoting camper participation and learning. The oldest campers lead aspects of the Shabbat ritual where they model for their younger peers how to be all-in with the Shabbat spirit.

Even while acknowledging that residential camps provide a unique setting that cannot easily be replicated elsewhere, I still believe there are lessons from Shabbat at camp that have relevance to other Jewish settings. The staffs of these camps are following an implicit model for how to create a vital Shabbat celebration that engages camper interest and promotes their learning. I am not imagining that Jewish schools, synagogues, or young adult gatherings will become more like camp. Rather, I believe there are educational perspectives and practices that have been developed at these camps that could be adapted to enhance how Jewish leaders work with their people to create more robust Shabbat celebrations that will matter to their participants.

There are three elements of the camp model that I will highlight for other Jewish educators and leaders. These stand out as essential to the camp model and yet are adaptable to other Jewish contexts. They are (1) building community, (2) maximizing participation and learning, and (3) developing a distinctive culture of celebration.

Building Community

One way to think about the relationship between learning and community is to envision a school or an informal educational forum as focused on a learning agenda. It is through learning together that participants form a community of learners. Learning has many social aspects and as the learners help one another, they also develop a connection to one another and a feeling of belonging to the group. This model should be familiar to many educators because it is employed in most Jewish educational settings.

Camps invert this familiar model by making building community the primary goal of Jewish education. The camp model begins with the assumption that in today's world children do not know how to form community. They need first and foremost to learn how to be part of a living Jewish community and then how to celebrate together as a community. Community will no longer form as a by-product of living and working together. It has to be actively tended so that young people can experience for themselves how different it is to live in community than to live as an individual in a busy and often lonely world.

Building community among campers is different because staff and campers are living together and have to learn how to get along and function together as a unit. That crucial piece is missing among adolescents or young adults in an urban or suburban context. Nevertheless, camp people would argue that the principle is the same. People of varied ages are seeking to overcome their individual loneliness and find ways to share their lives with others. What Judaism offers contemporary Jews is not so much textual knowledge and religious commandments, but rituals to perform that hold people together in community. The primary task of Jewish educators and leaders is to show people the way into a Jewish communal life.

Once they actively experience the power of a living Jewish community, participants can develop the language of Jewish practice through guided participation and learning.

Maximizing Participation and Learning

A familiar way to think about participation in Jewish ritual is that there are ritual experts who lead the ritual and everyone else is asked to participate by reciting verses, singing along, and enacting appropriate movements. In that way, the ritual is properly led and people may participate to the extent they wish.

Summer camps offer a different model of participation. At camp the purpose of the ritual is to get campers and staff to actively participate. The ritual is built and led to maximize participation. While camps also have ritual experts who lead at times, the experts view their roles as drawing in as many campers in whatever ways those campers are ready to participate.

These camps have come to realize that participation in ritual life does not happen by itself. It has to be prepared, modeled, and guided. From their first Shabbat at camp, novices learn how to participate. They learn the words to new songs and the accompanying hand motions. At Ramah Wisconsin, the youngest are taught a prayer in which they make up the rhyme scheme for thanking God. At Eisner, a counselor teaches the steps to a favorite Israeli dance. All these ways—singing words, enacting the accompanying hand motions, rhyming, performing dance steps, and even clapping along to the music—are legitimate modes for novices to participate in celebrating Shabbat. If the purpose of ritual is to maximize participation, then camp staff have to encourage campers to engage in varied ways. Reciting the Birkat with hand motions is to be encouraged alongside singing the Hebrew words.

There is a notable difference between *inviting* and *guiding* participation. I have been in Jewish settings where some participants get up to dance during a Friday evening service and invite others to join them. Their friends and acquaintances will do so, but many others will not. What works well for the in-crowd does little for newcomers. What camp people have come to understand is that you need to both invite and guide newcomers' participation. At Kabbalat Shabbat at Eisner, there is a song leader for the new campers and counselors who spread themselves out among the campers and create a space in which the campers' halting participation can be supported. Camps use their staff to guide new campers to venture into unfamiliar territory without worrying they will mess up. Guiding is that extra support that makes a crucial difference. If the goal is universal participation, then there must be more experienced practitioners ready to guide and support the newcomers.

A religious service will look and feel different when universal participation is the goal. All these camps are dedicated to using a Hebrew liturgy, and yet they know that some campers do not have facility with the Hebrew. While they never abandon the Hebrew, they find ways around it. Eisner adds song, dance, and art components to the service. Yavneh adds parsha quizzes and singing "Adon Olam" to hit tunes. These are ways to give a variety of campers entry into the action. From a purist perspective, universal participation might threaten the integrity of the ritual. Who needs campers singing "Adon Olam" to hit tunes? But if the goal is universal participation, then the service needs to accommodate a greater variety of expressive modes.

Yet while participation is essential, it is not sufficient. Participation allows campers to attend to and engage with Shabbat rituals. Participation builds group spirit and allows campers to feel that they have a stake in the celebration. But participation alone does not build the leadership skills needed to be able to lead aspects of the Shabbat ritual.

These camps have insisted that all campers not only participate in but also learn to lead aspects of the rituals. This is a bold move that can only work because the staff invest time in preparing campers to learn to lead. Leading can be much more challenging than participating. Thus, staff allow campers to choose what and how to lead. Some campers feel comfort leading in Hebrew while others prefer roles like dancing or creating art. Some take on brief roles like reciting the blessings of an aliyah while others volunteer to read a longer Torah portion. Staff normalize leading by finding many ways for campers to lead and then coaching and supporting campers to find the option that best fits their skill set. The expectation that many will lead creates a rich field for learning and skill building. When participants see that other peers are leading, they often wish to do so as well. That creates a strong motivation to develop the skills needed to lead. The ability to lead offers young people a strong sense of making the ritual their own.

In addition, camp asks Jewish leaders—rabbis, cantors, and educators—to envision their roles differently. While most often they are the ones up front expertly leading the congregation, at camp they are asked to prepare the campers to do that leading. Facilitating takes a lot of work and often the campers lead in ways that are not fully proficient. Yet, there is no better model for building their skills and investing them in the quality of the service. Once they have experienced leading, they can gain a different sense of what it takes to make a tefilla work.

But all this could not happen without the relationship between staff and campers. Camp staff are not experts but experienced older peers who work differently with campers than do most clergy and professional educators. While clergy and educators often employ an instructional mode of teaching, camp staff guide and coach (see chapter 8). When Cantor Doob at Eisner taught the campers to sing her composition, she also invited the counselors to prepare other campers to join in the singing. The counselors made that leading joyful by adding the elements of surprise and hand motions to the words. These young staff felt empowered to coach their campers, who responded eagerly to their lead.

While other Jewish contexts are not likely to employ staff like a camp, their leaders can learn the importance of distributing the educational work among the experienced peers in that setting. Experienced peers are an enormous educational resource that few organizations employ as fully as camps do. They become guides who inspire newcomers to see themselves becoming fuller participants and eventually leaders of the ritual. They help newcomers overcome barriers and enter the circle of participants. They offer to coach participants who feel ready to lead aspects of the ritual. This is not a usual teacher-student relationship, but a model of peers working together to facilitate universal participation. This model relies on a different social organization, a different way of understanding Jewish learning and teaching. The experienced peer is not so much passing on knowledge and skill as guiding newcomers to realize their potential, first as a participant and then as a leader.

In chapter 8 I highlighted the theories of learning put forward by Barbara Rogoff and David Perkins. These theories teach us that while there is value in having experts who can teach through instruction and modeling, there are also significant roles that nonexperts can play in promoting sociocultural learning. Camps make the most of their nonexperts, whom they hire as camp staff. What other Jewish leaders can learn from camps is how to activate their experienced lay members to step forward to coach those who are less experienced but open to being guided to participate more fully.

Developing a Distinctive Culture of Celebration

Throughout the ethnography I have shown how each camp puts its own stamp on the Shabbat celebration. That is not incidental to how they celebrate, but essential to what makes Shabbat special. There is at each camp a rich culture of celebration to which campers and staff become accustomed and attach their affections.

Herschel Singer at Yavneh is deeply attached to a specific aspect of celebrating Shabbat (see chapter 6). Five years after the Yavneh leadership had changed how the Shabbat singing was conducted on late Friday nights, Herschel was still upset with that change. Herschel was by then a graduate student and understood why the leadership had made the change and saw how the change had worked out well for subsequent groups of campers. Yet the change still rankled. The leaders had taken away the mosh pit that he loved. The mosh pit may have grown wild, but it still represented for him a high point of Shabbat celebration and its loss remained painful for him.

Youth who attend a Jewish camp for a stretch of years may come to experience their camp as a kind of extended family and become attached to some of the key people and practices. Even within a camp movement like Ramah or the URJ camps, each individual camp develops a distinctive culture of celebration. That culture is what campers know and come to care about. Campers and staff become attached to particular ritual practices that have a claim on their hearts. Herschel might not have cared whether the leadership changed Torah reading or Musaf. His heart was with the mosh pit. When at Ramah Wisconsin I heard that a group of fourteen-year-old campers insisted that their staff bring along the song sheets for mishmar on a canoe trip, I thought, "That is an attachment worth noting."

These camps provide their campers with many such particulars as part of a rich culture of celebration. Campers can attach to varied practices. At Ramah, some care about mishmar, others about dress-up, and yet others about the ice cream treat on late Shabbat afternoon. These are regular Shabbat practices they can anticipate and count on. I would argue that this attachment goes to the heart of what makes camp an effective Jewish educational environment. When young people care deeply, they also commit to camp and its particular practices. That caring can at times be excessive, and yet that excess goes a long way toward making camp Judaism emotionally significant for these American teens.

How does a camp develop a rich culture of celebration? We have the examples of mishmar at Ramah Wisconsin and ReLish at Yavneh. Mishmar was introduced by senior staff who came to camp to start a beit midrash for Torah study (see chapter 4). They initiated mishmar as an extension of the beit midrash, a practice they had seen in Israeli yeshivot. They had no idea whether mishmar would catch on. Indeed, it took a number of years before mishmar did catch on. Mishmar is a case of new staff bringing a practice to camp and its eventually catching on with older campers who would then invest their energy in keeping that practice alive and growing.

ReLish was born at Yavneh from a felt need for a ritual to transition campers into celebrating Shabbat (see chapter 4). The camp leadership approached their veteran musicians who were part of a band that played each Saturday night at Havdalah. They asked them to come up with a new transition ritual. The musicians worked on that before camp and launched ReLish at the start of a new camp season. No one knew whether ReLish would work. Yet it almost immediately caught on as campers and staff loved to sing and shout the verses of the ballad "Minyan Man."

These examples may be instructive for other Jewish leaders and educators. A rich culture of celebration is developed one step at a time by senior leaders who have a vision of what Shabbat might look like, which staff (or potential staff) can help build that culture, and which next steps might catch the attention and enthusiasm of their campers. Mishmar, while being new to camp, still fit the profile of how Ramah Wisconsin celebrates its Judaism. ReLish was an innovation at Yavneh, but it resembled Havdalah enough to fit well within the culture of that camp. The combination of innovation and fit is important for developing a culture of celebration.

Finding the right staff is crucial for developing a culture of celebration. When Louis Bordman hired senior staff like Liz Hirsch and Wendy Grinberg, he knew they would fit the needs of Eisner and build its culture. Louis spent a great deal of time developing song leaders and hiring a head song leader. These are such significant players in making Shabbat at Eisner. Developing and keeping staff talent is essential to developing a culture of celebration. At Ramah Wisconsin, Jacob and JAR tapped Josh Warshawsky when he was still a counselor and invested in his becoming a skilled song leader (see chapter 5). That was a long-term investment that paid off handsomely in terms of building the singing culture of the camp.

Celebrating a robust Shabbat at camp or elsewhere cannot happen without the contributions of many staff members from a variety of domains. Music and singing lead the way in ensuring a lively celebration, but dance and the arts contribute as well. Not to mention the contributions of the kitchen and dining staff. Shabbat is when the full resources of a Jewish educational space are on call and leadership needs the entire staff to make their contributions. Yet even when all is working well, leadership should be asking, "How can we continue to develop the culture of celebration?" For celebrating Shabbat is always evolving and leaders need to continuously search for the next generation of talented staff who will keep that celebration fresh, authentic, and engaging.

CAMP WITHIN THE CONTEXT OF THE LARGER COMMUNITY

I have highlighted what other Jewish leaders and educators can learn from how these camps celebrate Shabbat. I have done so in the belief that these camps have developed a model for celebrating Shabbat that has positive lessons from which other educators can learn. Yet it is also important to acknowledge that these camps are not islands unto themselves, but live in partnership with the larger Jewish community. Camps depend on the support of that community so they can provide their youth with the rare experience of living and celebrating in a fully immersive Jewish community.

Educating for Shabbat is also a partnership between the community and the camps. Families, synagogues, and schools all have their roles to play in preparing young people to engage with Shabbat. Camps rely on these partners to play their role so that cam p can educate in its unique ways. Most often

this partnership is more implicit than explicit. Yet it seems important to ask: Within this partnership, what are the special contributions that camps make to this larger project of educating youth to become engaged with Shabbat?

Jewish camps make their special contribution in three primary ways. First, they provide youth with the experience of celebrating a whole Shabbat in a peer community where everyone is doing Shabbat. Second, they fill that Shabbat with engaging rituals, lively music, and a shared sense of joy. Finally, camps turn Shabbat into a day of sociocultural learning where, with much support from the staff, campers can learn to participate in and eventually lead aspects of the Shabbat celebration. At camp, campers collectively own Shabbat to a degree that is unparalleled in most other Jewish contexts.

All three of these special contributions make the study of Shabbat at camp a fascinating area of inquiry that I hope will continue beyond this effort. If I have placed the greatest emphasis on how camps turn Shabbat into a day of learning, it is in the hope that other educators will see that learning and celebrating are closely linked and that the way to build a robust Shabbat celebration is through guiding participants toward a fuller and richer level of participation. These camps model how to get youth engaged with Shabbat so they feel deeply invested in the spirit and energy of its celebration.

I have written this book as a lover of Shabbat. That love drew me to research the practice of celebrating Shabbat at Jewish summer camps. It is a dynamic story that continues to change each summer. What I hope the larger North American Jewish community comes to appreciate is that these camps make Shabbat vitally available to thousands of youth and that this model of education holds promise for initiating many others into what Heschel (1951) calls this "palace in time."

ACKNOWLEDGMENTS

BOOKS ARE BORN FROM CONVERSATIONS. My conversations with Brandeis colleagues in the Jewish Education Working Group have given shape to this work. Without the back and forth with Sharon Feiman-Nemser, Ziva Hassenfeld, Danielle Igra, Jonathan Krasner, and Jon Levisohn, this book could never have been launched. I thank as well my many Brandeis colleagues and students who over the years have talked camp with me and helped to refine my ideas about celebrating and learning at Jewish camps.

I had wonderful partners at the summer camps I studied. At each camp, head staff opened the doors, connected me to the units I needed to observe, and answered my many questions. At Eisner Camp, I want to thank Louis Bordman, Laura Gurvis, James Gelsey, Rabbi Liz Hirsch, Wendy Grinberg, DJ Fortine, Aaron Gurvis, and Abi Oshins. At Ramah Wisconsin, my thanks to Rabbi David Soloff, Jacob Cytryn, Adina Allen, Jon Adam Ross, Jeremy Fineberg, Benjy Forester, Shira Forester, Natalie Blitt, Aryeh Bernstein, and Maya Zinkow. At Yavneh, Debbie Sussman, Bil Zarch, Lisa Rubins, and Herschel Singer were most helpful. Thanks to Bradley Solmsen for hosting me for a Shabbat at Surprise Lake Camp and expanding my understanding of Shabbat at various camps.

As my ideas about Shabbat at camp were developing, I had opportunities to present papers at The Network for Research in Jewish Education and publish an initial article in *The Journal for Jewish Education*. I thank my colleagues in the Network and at the journal for their support and feedback over many years.

Much of what I learned about American Jewish camps came from my contacts with The Foundation for Jewish Camp (FJC). I thank Jerry Silverman, Skip Vichness, Jeremy Fingerman, and Rabbi Avi Orlow for supporting my work and sharing their knowledge of and passion for Jewish camps.

While working at FJC, I came to know Joel Einleger from The AVI CHAI Foundation. Joel brought to our conversations his experience in funding Jewish educational initiatives and his understanding of how to make a difference in working with camp staff. I learned much from those conversations.

I wish to express my gratitude to AVI CHAI for financially supporting the publishing of this book and its distribution to Jewish camp leaders. AVI CHAI has since closed its doors, but the impact of its support for American Jewish camps will be felt for years to come.

As my research progressed, I began conversations with Sylvia Fuks Fried about preparing a book proposal for Brandeis University Press. Sylvia immediately got the idea, helped me think about the shape and content of the book, and guided my writing from start to finish. Without her help, this book could not have taken the shape it has.

Gail Twersky Reimer was my first reader who commented extensively on each chapter and helped me achieve greater clarity. Hannah Baker-Lerner helped with composing the bibliography.

I was delighted that as the writing progressed this book was chosen to be published in the newly created Mandel-Brandeis Series in Jewish Education. I thank the editors, Sharon Feiman-Nemser, Jonathan Krasner, and Jon Levisohn. Sharon and Jonathan provided detailed feedback on my chapters that improved every aspect of this work. Sharon guided my thinking about the connection between celebrating and learning. Jonathan added depth and accuracy to my thinking about the history of Jewish camps. I thank them and the anonymous reviewers whose comments were helpful for revising earlier drafts.

I wrote much of this book through the terrible months of COVID. The pandemic closed these camps for the summer of 2020 and forced them to modify their programs during 2021. None of us knows the long-term effects of this pandemic, but I acknowledge that all this research was conducted pre-pandemic. Shabbat at camp may change in ways that are as yet unforeseen.

When writing about a subject as intimate as Shabbat, I wish to acknowledge those who shaped my celebration of Shabbat. I began celebrating Shabbat before I can remember with my grandparents, parents, and sister. My adult celebration of Shabbat owes much to my years at Havurat Shalom and my Havurah friends. For fifty years Gail Twersky Reimer has made Shabbat with me in our home, where we brought our daughters Tamara and Ziva into the celebration. In recent years, we have enjoyed making Shabbat with Jonah, Yoni, Amal, Tehila, Moshe, and Rina.

I have tender memories of my Shabbat celebrations at camp and thank all the camp people who helped make the joy of Shabbat a constant in my life.

GLOSSARY OF JEWISH CAMP TERMS

"Adon Olam" The hymn sung at the end of the Shabbat morning service.

Aidah An age division at Ramah and Yavneh (also spelled aydah).

Aleinu A concluding prayer recited at Shabbat prayer services.

Aliyah Going up to bless the Torah or going up to live in Israel.

Amidah The standing prayer recited during all the Shabbat prayer services.

Beit am A social hall at camp.

Beit tefilla A house of prayer where Eisner Camp holds its outdoor camp-wide prayer services.

Bimah Where the service leaders stand to lead the prayer service.

Birkat Hamazon Grace after meals. A prayer sung communally after meals.

Blessing the children An erev Shabbat tradition of parents blessing children that has been transformed at camp to peers blessing peers.

Borkhu The call to worship in the evening and morning prayer services.

Bracha A blessing.

Chadar ochel Dinning hall where the camp meals are communally eaten.

Challah The sweet braided bread eaten at Shabbat meals.

Chalutzim Pioneers. Often refers to founders of the pre-state Yishuv in what would become Israel.

Chevra kadisha A local Jewish organization responsible for caring for a recently deceased body and preparing it for burial.

Dvar Torah A Torah teaching.

Eicha The biblical book of Lamentations read on the fast of Tisha B'Av.

"Ein Keiloheinu" One of the concluding hymns sung at Shabbat morning service.

Erev Shabbat Shabbat eve on Friday evening.

Eruv An enclosure that delineates an area where observant Jews may carry on certain activities that would otherwise be forbidden on Shabbat.

Hachana Preparing for Shabbat on Friday late afternoon.

Haftorah A reading from Prophets usually read after the Torah reading on Shabbat.

Halakhic Pertaining to the corpus of Jewish law (halakha) that governs the religious behavior of observant Jews.

Hamotzi The blessing over bread recited before most meals.

"Hatikva" The Israeli national anthem sung at times in camp.

Havdalah The ritual marking of the end of Shabbat on Saturday night.

Hineini Here I am. A term central to the mission of Eisner Camp.

Hora dancing Circle dancing in Israeli folk dance.

Kabbalat Shabbat Greeting the Sabbath. The Shabbat Friday evening prayer service.

Kaddish A prayer at services associated with mourning the dead.

Kiddush A prayer recited over the wine to sanctify the Sabbath.

Kikar The lawn. A central meeting place at Camp Ramah in Wisconsin.

Kippah The skullcap often worn by traditional Jews especially when praying.

Klal Yisrael The whole of Israel. The way that Camp Yavneh describes its Judaism.

Limud Study. The term Eisner Camp uses for its daily hour of Jewish study.

Ma'ariv The evening prayer recited after Kabbalat Shabbat on Shabbat.

Mashgiach ruchani A spiritual guide. The term Camp Yavneh uses for its rabbinic advisor.

Mechitza The partition that separates the men and women's section in an Orthodox prayer space and used at Camp Yavneh.

Menucha Rest. Used at camps for a period of rest and to describe the calm of Shabbat.

Mercaz A center. Camp Ramah's center for staff development.

Middot Jewish ethical practices.

Mifkad The lineup at the flag pole before Shabbat begins at Camp Yavneh.

Mincha The afternoon prayer.

Minyan The quorum of ten needed to conduct a communal prayer service.

"*Minyan Man*" A ballad sung each week at Camp Yavneh's ReLish ritual.

Mishmar A late Thursday night singing and study session held at Camp Ramah.

Mo'adon A clubhouse or place for informal social gatherings.

Musaf The additional prayer recited on Shabbat morning at Ramah and Yavneh.

Nikayon The cleanup of bunks preparing for Shabbat on Friday afternoons.

Parsha The weekly Torah portion read on each Shabbat.

Peulat erev An evening activity.

Pirke Avot The Ethic of the Fathers. A rabbinic collection of ethical sayings.

ReLish Camp Yavneh's transition ritual before Shabbat.

Ruach Spirit. Used at camp for the spiritedness of celebrating Shabbat.

Ruach rousers Camp staff who take an active role in creating greater ruach on Shabbat.

Sabbath Queen A metaphorical image of the Shabbat spirit that the community greets.

Seder The family ritual held to celebrate Passover.

Seudah shlishit The third meal held on Saturday evening toward the end of Shabbat.

Shabbat The Jewish Sabbath that begins Friday evening and ends Saturday night.

Shabbat shalom Sabbath peace. A common greeting between people on Shabbat.

Shabbat Shirah The erev Shabbat song session held at OSRUI camp.

Shavua tov Have a good week. A greeting for after Havdalah.

Shir HaShirim The biblical Song of Songs. One chapter is recited each Shabbat at Ramah.

Shira Song or a song session.

Shiva Mourning practice at home during the week after a funeral.

Shlichim Israeli staff sent to camp to be emissaries and fulfill regular staff roles.

Shomer Shabbat One who halakhically observes the Sabbath. The term used at Camp Yavneh to describe their policy of a stricter level of Shabbat observance.

Sh'ma The prayer of "Hear, O Israel" recited Shabbat evening and morning.

Sichot Sessions. Used to describe informal learning sessions on Shabbat.

Siddur Jewish prayer book.

Tallit Prayer shawl used during tefilla.

Tefilla Prayer. Used at camp for any communal prayer session.

Tish A singing session on late Friday evenings.

V'Shamru A prayer within the Ma'ariv service.

Yeshiva A place of intensive Torah study where some staff go for a year or more.

Zemirot Traditional Shabbat songs sung at the conclusion of the Friday night meal.

Zimriyah A festival of Hebrew song held yearly at Yavneh and Ramah.

BIBLIOGRAPHY

Ackerman, W. I. 1999. "Becoming Ramah." In S. A. Dorph, ed., *Ramah Reflections at 50: Visions for a New Century*, 3–24. New York: National Ramah Commission.

Allen, A. 2021. Personal interview.

Ammerman, N. T. 2014. *Sacred Stories, Spiritual Tribes: Finding Religion in Everyday Life*. New York: Oxford University Press.

Benor, S. B., J. Krasner, and S. Avni. 2020. *Hebrew Infusion: Language and Community at American Jewish Summer Camps*. New Brunswick, NJ: Rutgers University Press.

Bernstein, A. 2020. Personal interview.

Blas, H. I. 2010. "Campers with Developmental Disabilities: The Tikvah Program." In M. Cohen and J. S. Kress, eds., *Ramah at 60: Impact and Innovation*, 209–227. New York: National Ramah Commission.

Blitt, N. 2018. Personal interview.

Bordman, L. 2008. Personal interview.

Bordman, L. 2016. Personal interview.

Bordman, L. 2018. Personal interview.

Brown, M. 1999. "The Most Important Venture Undertaken by the Seminary: Ramah in Its First Four Decades." In S. A. Dorph, ed., *Ramah Reflections at 50: Visions for a New Century*, 25–88. New York: National Ramah Commission.

Cahan, J. 2010. "Reclaiming Piety." In M. Cohen and J. S. Kress, eds., *Ramah at 60: Impact and Innovation*, 228–236. New York: National Ramah Commission.

Camp Ramah in Wisconsin. 2018. Welcome to Visitors Days.

Cohen, J. M. 2006. "Singing Out for Judaism: A History of Song Leaders and Song Leading at Olin-Sang-Ruby Union Institute." In M. M. Lorge and G. P. Zola, eds., *A Place of Our Own: The Rise of Reform Jewish Camping*, 173–208. Tuscaloosa, AL: University of Alabama Press.

Cohen, J. M. 2008. "Musical Tradition and the Crisis of Place: Reform Jewish Song-leading, Shabbat Shirah and the Dining Hall." *Western Folklore* 67, no. 4: 321–349.

Cohen, M., and J. S. Kress, eds. 2010. *Ramah at 60: Impact and Innovation*. New York: National Ramah Commission.

Cohen, S. 2010. "Reflections." In M. Cohen and J. S. Kress, eds., *Ramah at 60: Impact and Innovation*, 332. New York: National Ramah Commission.

Cohen, S. M., and L. Kotler-Berkowitz. 2004. *The Impact of Childhood Jewish Educa-*

tion on Adults' Jewish Identity: Schooling, Israel Travel, Camping and Youth Groups. United Jewish Communities Report Series on NJPS 2000-01. Report 3.

Cohen, S. M., and J. Veinstein. 2011. "Jewish Identity: Who You Know Affects How You Jew: The Impact of Jewish Networks on Adult Jewish Identity." In H. Miller, L. D. Grant, and A. Pomson, eds., *International Handbook of Jewish Education.* Heidelberg: Springer Doddrecht.

Cohen, S. M., and A. M. Eisen. 2000. *The Jew Within: Self, Family and Community.* Bloomington, IN: Indiana University Press.

Conyer, B. 2011. "Pluralism in Jewish Education." In H. Miller, L. D. Grant, and A. Pomson, eds., *International Handbook of Jewish Education*, 267–284. Heidelberg: Springer Doddrecht.

Csikszentmihalyi, M. 1990. *Flow: The Psychology of Optimal Experience.* New York: Harper Perennial.

Csikszentmihalyi, M. 1997. *Finding Flow: The Psychology of Engagement with Everyday Life.* New York: Basic Books.

Csikszentmihalyi, M., and I. S. Csikszentmihalyi, eds. 1988. *Optimal Experience: Psychological Studies of Flow in Consciousness.* New York: Cambridge University Press.

Csikszentmihalyi, M., and R. Larson. 1984. *Being Adolescent.* New York: Basic Books.

Cytryn, J. 2011. Personal interview.

Cytryn, J. 2016. Personal interview.

Cytryn, J. 2017. Personal interview.

Cytryn, J. 2020. Personal Interview.

Dorff, E. 2010. "Reflections." In M. Cohen and J. S. Kress, eds., *Ramah at 60: Impact and Innovation*, 335–36. New York: National Ramah Commission.

Dorph, S., ed. 1999. *Ramah Reflections at 50: Visions for a New Century.* New York: National Ramah Commission.

Eisner Camp. n.d. www.eisnercamp.org.

Eisner, M. D. 2005. *Camp.* New York: Warner Books.

Erikson, E. H. 1964. *Insight and Responsibility.* New York: Norton.

Feiman-Nemser, S. 2019. Personal interview.

FJC Overnight Camp Census 2018. https://jewishcamp.org/wp-content/uploads/2018/09/FJC-Overnight-Camp-Census-2018.pdf. Accessed December 20, 2019.

Forester, S. 2020. Personal interview.

Fortine, D. J. 2017. Personal interview.

Fox, S. F. 2019. "Laboratories of Yiddishkeit: Postwar American Jewish Summer Camps and the Transformation of Yiddishism." *American Jewish History* 103, no. 3: 279–302.

Fox, S., and W. Novak. 2000. *Vision at the Heart: Lessons from Camp Ramah on the Power of Ideas in Shaping Educational Institutions.* New York: Council for Initiatives in Jewish Education.

Freidenreich, F. 2010. *Passionate Pioneers: The Story of Yiddish Secular Education in North America, 1910–1960*. Teaneck, NJ: Holmes and Meier Publishers.

Futterman, M. 2010. "Reflections." In M. Cohen and J. S. Kress, eds., *Ramah at 60: Impact and Innovation*, 339. New York: National Ramah Commission.

Gamoran, H. 2006. "The Road to Chalutzim: Reform Judaism's Hebrew-Speaking Program." In M. M. Lorge and G. P. Zola, eds., *A Place of Our Own: The Rise of Reform Jewish Camping*, 124–150. Tuscaloosa, AL: University of Alabama Press.

Garfinkel, E. 1999. "Mikraot Ramah: The Ramah Summer Chumash." In S.A. Dorph, ed., *Ramah Reflections at 50: Visions for a New Century*, 271–278. New York: National Ramah Commission.

Gillman, N. 1989. "Tefillah as a Religious Obligation." In S. C. Ettenberg and G. Rosenfeld, eds., *The Ramah Experience: Community and Commitment*. New York: Jewish Theological Seminary and National Ramah Commission.

Gillman, N. 2010. "Reflections." In M. Cohen and J. S. Kress, eds., *Ramah at 60: Impact and Innovation*, 347. New York: National Ramah Commission.

Gopnik, A. 2016. *The Gardner and the Carpenter*. New York: Picador.

Green, A. 2020. *Judaism for the World: Reflections on God, Life, and Love*. New Haven, CT: Yale University Press.

Grinberg, W. 2018. Personal interview.

Grinberg, W. 2020. "Jewish Education at Eisner Camp: 1993–2018." Unpublished dissertation. New York: Jewish Theological Seminary.

Heilman, S. 1992. *Defenders of the Faith: Inside Ultra-Orthodox Jewry*. New York: Schocken Books.

Heschel, A. J. 1951. *The Sabbath: Its Meaning for Modern Man*. New York: Farrar, Straus, and Giroux.

Hirsch, L. 2017. Personal interview.

Hirsch, L. 2018. Personal interview.

Hurwich, L. 1999. *Memoirs of a Jewish Educator*. Boston: The Bureau of Jewish Education of Greater Boston.

Isaacman, D. 1970. *Jewish Summer Camps in the United States and Canada: 1900–1969*. Philadelphia: Dropsie University.

Jacobson, J. 2019. "The Role of Music in Jewish Summer Camps: A Case Study of Camp Yavneh in the Early 1960s." Unpublished manuscript. Waltham, MA: Brandeis University.

Joselit, J. W. 1993. *A Worthy Use of the Summer: Jewish Summer Camps in America*. Philadelphia: National Museum of American Jewish History.

Koffman, D. S. 2018. "Playing Indian at Jewish Summer Camp: Lessons in Tribalism, Assimilation and Spirituality." *Journal of Jewish Education* 84, no. 4: 413–440.

Komisar, Y. 2018. "Klal Yisrael at Camp Yavneh." Unpublished document. Northwoods, NH: Camp Yavneh.

Krasner, J. B. 2011. *The Benderly Boys and American Jewish Education*. Waltham, MA: Brandeis University Press.

Lave, J., and E. Wenger. 1991. *Situated Learning: Legitimate Peripheral Participation*. New York: Cambridge University Press.

Leibovich, S. 2009. Personal interview.

Lev, J. 2008. "Case Study of URJ Eisner Camp." Unpublished manuscript. New York: New York University.

Leventhal, J. 2012. *The Brandeis-Bardin Institute: A Living History*. Los Angeles: American Jewish University.

Levine, R. 2010. "Reflections." In M. Cohen and J. S. Kress, eds., *Ramah at 60: Impact and Innovation*, 365–366. New York: National Ramah Commission.

Lipstadt, D. E. 2014. "And It Not Be Stilled: The Legacy of Debbie Friedman." In M. A. Meyer and D. N. Myers, eds., *Between Jewish Tradition and Modernity: Rethinking an Old Opposition*, 110–122. Detroit: Wayne State University.

Lorge, M. M., and G. P. Zola. 2006a. "The Beginnings of Union Institute in Oconomowoc, Wisconsin, 1952–1970: Creation and Coalescence of the First UAHC Camp." In M. M. Lorge and G. P. Zola, eds., *A Place of Our Own: The Rise of Reform Jewish Camping*, 52–84. Tuscaloosa, AL: University of Alabama Press.

Lorge, M. M., and G. P. Zola, eds. 2006b. *A Place of Our Own: The Rise of Reform Jewish Camping*. Tuscaloosa, AL: University of Alabama Press.

Luhrmann, T. M. 2012. *When God Talks Back*. New York: Vintage Books.

Markley, M. 2015. Personal interview.

Markley, T. 2015. Personal interview.

Moss, D. 1999. "Ramah Is My Palette." In S. A. Dorph, ed., *Ramah Reflections at 50: Visions for a New Century*, 215–224. New York: National Ramah Commission.

Myerhoff, B. 1979. *Number Our Days*. New York: E. P. Dutton.

Myerhoff, B. 1992. *Remembered Lives: The Work of Ritual, Storytelling and Growing Older*. Ann Arbor, MI: University of Michigan Press.

Offit, D. 2016. Personal interview.

Olin-Sang-Ruby Union Institute. n.d. www.osrui.org.

Oshins, A. 2017. Personal interview.

Paris, L. 2008. *Children's Nature: The Rise of the American Summer Camp*. New York: New York University Press.

Perkins, D. 2009. *Making Learning Whole: How Seven Principles of Teaching Can Transform Education*. San Francisco: Jossey-Bass.

Pew Research Center's Religion & Public Life. October 1, 2013. "A Portrait of Jewish Americans." Pew Research Center. www.pewforum.org/2013/10/01/jewish-american-beliefs-attitudes-culture-survey. Accessed March 1, 2020.

PJ Library. n.d. www.pjlibrary.org.

Prell, R.-E. 1989. *Prayer and Community: The Havurah in American Judaism*. Detroit: Wayne State University Press.

Prell, R.-E. 2006. *Jewish Summer Camping and Civil Rights: How Summer Camps Launched a Transformation in American Jewish Culture*. Ann Arbor, MI: University of Michigan.

Prell, R.-E. 2007. *Women Remaking American Judaism*. Detroit: Wayne State University Press.

Prell, R.-E. 2011. "'How Do You Know That I Am a Jew?': Authority, Cultural Identity, and the Shaping of Postwar American Judaism." In R. S. Boustan, O. Kosansky, and M. Rostow, eds., *Jewish Studies at the Crossroads of Anthropology and History: Authority, Diaspora and Tradition*, 31–57. Philadelphia: University of Pennsylvania Press.

Reimer, J. 2007. "Beyond More Jews Doing Jewish: Clarifying the Goals of Informal Jewish Education." *Journal of Jewish Education* 73, no. 1: 5–23.

Reimer, J. 2010. "Vision, Leadership and Change: The Case of Ramah Summer Camps." *Journal of Jewish Education* 76, no. 3: 246–271.

Reimer, J. 2011. "Informal Jewish Education: The Decisive Decade." In H. Miller, L. D. Grant, and A. Pomson, eds., *International Handbook of Jewish Education*. Heidelberg: Springer Doddrecht.

Reimer, J. 2012. "Providing Optimal Jewish Experiences: The Case of Camp Ramah in Wisconsin." *Journal of Jewish Education* 78, no. 2: 114–134.

Reimer, J., and D. Bryfman. 2008. "Experiential Jewish Education." In R. L. Goodman, P. A. Flexner, and L. D. Bloomberg, eds., *What We Now Know About Jewish Education*. Los Angeles: Torah Aura Productions.

Reisman, B. 1990. *Informal Jewish Education in North America*. Cleveland, OH: The Commission on Jewish Education in North America.

Rogoff, B. 1990. *Apprenticeship in Thinking: Cognitive Development in Social Context*. New York: Oxford University Press.

Rogoff, B. 2003. *The Cultural Nature of Human Development*. New York: Oxford University Press.

Ross, J. A. 2015. Personal interview.

Ross, J. A. 2017. Personal interview.

Roth, P. 2010. *Nemesis*. New York: Houghton Mifflin Harcourt.

Rothenberg, C. E. 2016. *Serious Fun at a Jewish Community Summer Camp: Family, Judaism and Israel*. New York: Lexington Books.

Rubins, L. 2018. Personal interview.

Rubins, L. 2020. Personal interview.

Sales, A. L., and L. Saxe. 2004. *"How Goodly Are Thy Tents:" Summer Camps as Jewish Socializing Experiences*. Hanover, NH: Brandeis University Press.

Sales, A. L., N. Samuel, and M. Boxer. 2011. *Limud by the Lake Revisited: Growth and Change at Jewish Summer Camp*. New York: AVI CHAI Foundation, Cohen Center for Modern Jewish Studies.

Sarna, J. 2004. *American Judaism: A History*. New Haven, CT: Yale University Press.

Sarna, J. 2006. "The Crucial Decade in Jewish Camping." In M. M. Lorge and G. P.

Zola, eds., *A Place of Our Own: The Rise of Reform Jewish Camping*, 27–51. Tuscaloosa, AL: University of Alabama Press.

Sarna, L. 2014. "Paradise." In J. Sussman, ed., *A Ray of Light in Yavneh*, 38. Northwood, NH: Camp Yavneh.

Sawyer, K. 2007. *Group Genius: The Creative Power of Collaboration*. New York: Basic Books.

Schulwolf, S. 2014. "Discovering Family." In J. Sussman, ed., *A Ray of Light in Yavneh*, 38. Northwood, NH: Camp Yavneh.

Schwartz, S. 1987. "Camp Ramah: The Early Years, 1947–1952." *Conservative Judaism* 40: 12–42.

Shulevitz, J. 2010. *The Sabbath World: Glimpses of a Different Order of Time*. New York: Random House.

Siddur Lev Shalem. 2016. New York: The Rabbinical Assembly.

Singer, H. 2016. Personal interview.

Singer, H. 2017. "From Mosh-Pit to Z'mirot: Programming Change at Camp Yavneh." Unpublished manuscript. Waltham, MA: Brandeis University.

Soloff, D. 1999. "The Artist-in-Residence Program." In S. A. Dorph, ed., *Ramah Reflections at 50: Visions for a New Century*, 225–229. New York: National Ramah Commission.

Soloff, D. 2016. Personal interview.

Soloff, D. 2018. Personal interview.

Soloff, D. 2020. Personal interview.

Sperber, S. Y. 1996. "Springboard for a Musical Career in Israel." In R. Shulsinger-Shear Yashuv, ed., *Massad Reminiscences*, 49–60. Jerusalem: Massad Hebrew Summer Camps Alumni Organization.

Splansky, D. M. 2006. "Creating a Prayer Experience in Reform Movement Camps and Beyond." In M. M. Lorge and G. P. Zola, eds., *A Place of Our Own: The Rise of Reform Jewish Camping*, 151–172. Tuscaloosa, AL: University of Alabama Press.

Sussman, D. 2016. Personal interview.

Sussman, D. 2017. Personal interview.

Switkin, S. 2010. "Reflections." In M. Cohen and J. S. Kress, eds., *Ramah at 60: Impact and Innovation*, 390–391. New York: National Ramah Commission.

Tecotsky, J. August 8, 2017. "Hineini: The Continuing Power of Eisner Camp." eJewish Philanthropy. https://ejewishphilanthropy.com/hineini-the-continuing-power-of-eisner-camp. Accessed March 11, 2020.

Turner, V. 1974. *Dramas, Fields and Metaphors: Symbolic Actions in Human Society*. Ithaca, NY: Cornell University Press.

Turner, V. 1982. *From Ritual to Theater*. New York: Performing Arts Journal Publication.

Van Slyck, A. A. 2006. *A Manufactured Wilderness: Summer Camps and the Shaping of American Youth*. Minneapolis: University of Minnesota Press.

Vygotsky, L. S. 1978. *Mind in Society: The Development of Higher Psychological Processes.* Cambridge, MA: Harvard University Press.

Warshawsky, J. 2017. Personal interview.

Warshawsky, J. 2018. Personal interview.

Wertheimer, J. 2018. *The New American Judaism: How Jews Practice Their Religion Today.* Princeton, NJ: Princeton University Press.

Woocher, J. S. 1986. *Sacred Survival: The Civil Religion of American Jews*. Bloomington, IN: Indiana University Press.

Zarch, B. 2020. Personal interview.

Zeldin, M. 2006. "Making the Magic in Reform Jewish Summer Camps." In M. M. Lorge and G. P. Zola, eds., *A Place of Our Own: The Rise of Reform Jewish Camping,* 85–123. Tuscaloosa, AL: University of Alabama Press.

Zinkow, M. 2017. Personal interview.

INDEX